Ephesians

THE WONDER AND WALK OF BEING ALIVE IN CHRIST

DARRELL JOHNSON

"Darrell Johnson has done it again! This commentary is theologically deep, easily accessible and pastorally practical. I love his heart for the scriptures to come alive and for us to encounter Jesus himself. As with his commentary on Revelation, I highly recommend this for study, devotions and for genuine encounter."
— **JON THOMPSON,** Senior Pastor of Sanctus Church and the author of "Convergence" and "Deliverance"

"Few master builders share their trade secrets. Few world-class chefs reveal their recipes. But Darrell Johnson – in my opinion, the best living expository preacher on the planet – does more than merely hand us the key to his treasure house: he throws wide the door, beckons us in, gives us a personal tour, and urges us to take anything we want. Yet for all this, his commentary on Ephesians is more still: an experience of worship as much as an exercise in scholarship. Reading it is like being caught up and seated in the heavenly realms Darrell so brilliantly describes. Ah, this is good news at its goodest."
— **MARK BUCHANAN,** Author of "God Walk: Moving at the Speed of Your Soul"; Associate Professor of Pastoral Theology at Ambrose University

"Like his other books, Darrell Johnson's Ephesians: The wonder and walk of being alive 'IN Christ' is valuable to both pastors who are preparing to preach and teach as well as congregants wanting to understand God and His Word more; readers will soon find themselves moving from merely 'understanding' Ephesians to being drawn into the wonder of God and of a life spent pursuing Him."
— **REV. MILISSA EWING,** Lead Pastor of Redwood Park Church

"Darrell Johnson is a master preacher. One of the reasons is because he is a master student of the Bible. My wife Becky and I will never forget the day Darrell showed us his personal study of the Ephesians manuscript. Darrell's meticulous form of diagramming the original Greek sentences is 'gospel grammar' at the highest level! This book is a gift as it combines all of Darrell's study, prayer, and ministry experience that we might also live in the text. As you 'walk in the wonder of Christ' be prepared to 'fall on your knees in worship of Christ!'"

— **JOHN TETER,** Senior Pastor of Fountain of Life Covenant Church, Long Beach; Author of "Get The Word Out" and "The Power of 72"

"Some commentaries on biblical books inform, some educate, some inspire, and very rarely some do it all while transforming the reader. Darrell Johnson's work on Ephesians is that rare kind. The power of these words is the way they fade as they facilitate a fresh encounter with the Living God. These aren't just words on a page, they're windows into 'heavenly places' and solid footholds for life with Jesus. Whatever stage or place of life you find yourself in, if you're longing for the 'fullness of God,' let Darrell walk you through Paul's letter to the Ephesians."

— **MATT MENZEL,** Lead Pastor of Westside Church

"Darrell's work on Ephesians is illuminating. His words bring to life the power and continued relevance of Paul's epistle. Whether one is a scholar, a pastor, or a curious lay person there is something in these pages for everyone."

— **CHRIS PRICE,** Lead Pastor of The Way Church; Co-Author of "Everyday Apologetics" and "The Whole Church"

"Put your phone down, let the emails pile up, and find yourself a kneeling pad. This book will stir up a renewed passion for prayer and strike you with a new appreciation for the Word."
— **DORIELIS FRIESEN,** National Director of 24/7 Prayer Canada

"Darrell teaches us with the precision of a gifted expositor, and the tenderness of a loving father. A clear, thoughtful and accessible book that will inspire you to walk closer with Jesus."
— **HO-MING TSUI,** Lead Pastor of Richmond Hill Christian Community Church

"A reality of life is that our perceptions influence everything we do. Oh, how we need the proper perspective for our perceptions today, to put on a new set of glasses. I know of no better book than Ephesians and no better author to provide you with this new lens, for as Darrell states, 'things are not what they appear'. Be prepared to see things differently as you read this book, which I believe will become a classic to help us navigate to have the proper perspective. It will be my "go to resource", my new set of glasses."
— **DR. BRUCE GORDON,** Pastor at Peace Portal Alliance Church; Former President of Tyndale College & Seminary; Author of "As Long As I Have Breath"

"Darrell Johnson brilliantly invites us to see in Paul's letter to the Ephesians a world that is truly alive 'in Christ'."
— **BRYAN DUNAGAN,** Senior Pastor of Highland Park Presbyterian Church, Dallas

Ephesians: The Wonder and Walk of Being Alive "In Christ"
Copyright © 2022 Darrell W. Johnson
All rights reserved.

No part of this publication may be reproduced, stored in a retrieval system, or transmitted, in any form or by any means, electronic, mechanical, photocopying, recording or otherwise, without the prior written permission of the author, except in the case of brief quotations embodied in critical articles and reviews.

Published in 2022 by Canadian Church Leaders Network
512-1529 W 6th Ave, Vancouver, BC V6J1R1 Canada
www.ccln.ca

Design by Arielle Ratzlaff

Unless otherwise noted, Scripture quotations are taken from the NEW AMERICAN STANDARD BIBLE®, Copyright © 1960,1962,1963,1968,1971,1972,1973,1975,1977,1995 by The Lockman Foundation. Used by permission.

Library and Archives Canada Cataloguing in Publication

Title: Ephesians : the wonder and walk of being alive "IN Christ" / Darrell W. Johnson.
Names: Johnson, Darrell W., 1947- author. | Canadian Church Leaders Network, publisher.
Description: Includes bibliographical references.
Identifiers: Canadiana 20220171858 | ISBN 9781990331022 (softcover)
Subjects: LCSH: Bible. Ephesians—Commentaries.
Classification: LCC BS2695.53 .J64 2022 | DDC 227/.507—dc23

Contents

Introduction   1

1   Navigating an Alternative Reading of Reality   11

The Wonder of Being Alive "In Christ"
Ephesians 1:3–3:21

2   Location, Location, Location!   29
3   You're (Much) Richer than You Think   47
4   Gospel-Shaped Praying   73
5   Look Who is on the Throne Now   91
6   Rescued Out of a Deep Pit   107
7   Look Who Else is on the Throne Now!   123
8   Poetry in Motion   137
9   Look What is Being Built in the City   155
10   When Grace Grabs Hold   173
11   Praying the Gospel into Our Hearts   189

The Walk of Being Alive "In Christ"
Ephesians 4:1–6:24

12   Walking in Unity   215
13   Walking into Maturity   233
14   Walking as New Humans   249

15	Walking in Step with the Spirit	265
16	Walk as Imitators of God… Really?	281
17	When Christ Shines on You	299
18	Walk Filled with the Very Life of God	317
19	Spirit-Filled Relationships	335
20	First Example of Spirit-Filled Relationships	351
21	Further Examples of Spirit-Filled Relationships	369
22	Stand Firm Against the Powers	385
23	The Full Armour of God	405

Afterword	429
Acknowledgements	433
For Further Reading	437

Introduction

A while ago now, I was coming out of the Regent College Bookstore, one of my favourite places in the world!

A young Chinese woman, who was having tea with friends at the College, approached me. Someone had pointed me out as the author of the book she and her friends back home in Beijing were reading—*Discipleship on the Edge: An Expository Journey Through the Book of Revelation.*

"I am here in Vancouver for a brief visit," she said. "I have to catch a plane shortly, and only have a few minutes right now. But could I ask you a question I and my friends are asking?"

"Sure," I responded, saying, "I too only have a few minutes to visit."

We sat down at one of the tables in the College Atrium. She was probably in her late 20s or early 30s. Clearly alive in Jesus! Clearly very bright. And clearly competent in her vocation. With all seriousness she posed her, their, question.

"What would you say to busy, young disciples of Jesus, who

want to live in such a way that brings transformation to China?"

Great question!

One every disciple in every nation of the world needs to be asking right now about their own countries.

"In the few minutes we have together, what would you say to busy young disciples of Jesus living in China eager to bring transformation to China?"

I prayed under my breath. And said, "I would say three things.

First, stay close to Jesus. Do whatever it takes, however apparently costly, to stay close to Jesus. She nodded knowingly and approvingly.

Second, soak in His Word. Jesus tells us: "Humans do not live by bread alone, but by every word that proceeds from the mouth of God." Do whatever it takes to soak in His Word. She nodded, but not as intensely as she had regarding the first word to busy disciples.

Third, learn to pray. It is the only thing the first disciples of Jesus are recorded to have asked Him to teach them to do: "Lord, teach us to pray." So let Him teach you. Let Him show you how to pray.

She sat quietly, a sweet peace falling on her.

I have been asked the same question in other parts of the world since. And have given the same answer I gave the same answer I gave in the Regent Atrium: stay close to Jesus, soak in His Word, learn to pray.

"I only have a few minutes left," my new friend said. "So let me ask: in what part of His Word should we especially soak? In a few minutes please!

Yikes!

INTRODUCTION

So again I prayed under my breath. And here is what came to mind.

"He will meet you in any part of the Bible to which you turn. As He helped two disciples understand on the road to Emmaus on the afternoon of the first Easter Sunday. Read Luke 24 on the plane. Jesus says that all of Scripture points to Him. Or, better said, He chooses to manifest Himself in all of Scripture.

But in terms of your question—"How to live in a way that influences China?"—I suggest you soak in five critical sections. Not all at once, as young, eager disciples are wont to do! But over the next two to three years, soak in five critical sections of His Word.

One, Matthew 5-7. Jesus' great Sermon on the Mount. Wherein He describes the kind of people we become when He gets hold of us, and draws us into His Kingdom.

Two, Romans 5-8. Wherein the Apostle Paul develops essential dynamics of discipleship. People alive in grace, people dying to sin, people walking in the Holy Spirit, people groaning for God's new day, people confident God is really for them.

Three, John 13-17. The so-called Upper Room Discourse. Wherein Jesus prepares the first band of disciples to go on living in the absence of His physical presence. Not in the absence of His presence. For in the Upper Room Jesus promises that He will be present in the Person of the Paraclete, the Holy Spirit. Soak in His promises regarding the Spirit. And soak in Jesus' prayer for us, wherein He opens up His heart's desire for us.

Four, Revelation 1-3. Where we hear the risen, ascended Jesus speak to His church. Soak in the messages He speaks to the seven churches of Asia Minor, until you become keenly attuned and attentive to His Voice. So that His Voice drowns out the voices of Empire, and consumerism and fleshly-ness that clamour for our attention and allegiance.

And five, Ephesians. Soak in the letter to the Ephesians. Where Paul, the great interpreter of the mind of Jesus, opens up the world wide, cosmic dimensions of Jesus' Person and Work and Call.

The young Chinese woman thanked me. And headed for the airport.

I am writing this Introduction later summer of 2021. When many people are feeling that the world they have known for years is coming apart. So, "What would you say to disciples of Jesus living in a world rocked by a pandemic, and aware as never before of the sin of racism, and experiencing the harsh facts of climate change, who want to live in such a way that the world is transformed?"

I say, soak in Ephesians! Soak in the letter the apostle Paul wrote from a prison cell in Rome, from a place of forced self-isolation, to a young congregation in the first century city of Ephesus, located on the land mass we now call Turkey.

As one quickly realizes when reading the letter, Paul has composed it in two parts, of almost equal length. Chapters 1-3 and chapters 4-6. The first part begins with the foundational affirmation of the letter: "Blessed be the God and Father of our Lord Jesus Christ, who has blessed us with every spiritual blessing in the heavenly places in Christ" (1:3). The second part begins with the foundational exhortation of the letter: "I, therefore, the prisoner of the Lord, entreat you to walk in a manner worthy of the calling to which you have been called" (4:1).

We could entitle the first half "good news," the second half, "good advice." This is typical of the apostle Paul, and typical of

INTRODUCTION

the whole of Scripture. Any "good advice" is grounded in "good news," and any "good news" issues in "good advice."

I like to entitle the first half "the wonder of grace," the second half, "the walk of grace." Or, since as we will discover, grace brings us into intimate relationship with Jesus Christ—"in Christ," as Paul will say again and again—we could call the first half of the letter, "the wonder of being alive 'IN Christ'," the second half, "the walk of being alive 'IN Christ'."

What you have in the book you are holding right now is the written form of the series of sermons I preached for the congregation of the historic First Baptist Church of Vancouver, British Columbia, in 2014. Which will explain some of the ways I put things in each chapter: I wrote more for the ear than for the eye. I have tried to make the switch from the ear back to the eye, but may not have accomplished the move as well as you might like. Bear with me![1] I had taught the book in a number of contexts before preaching the full series of expositions: for a Woman's Bible Study Class of the Union Church of Manila, the Philippines in 1986: for the Tuesday Night Live class for Fremont Presbyterian Church, Sacramento, California in 1991; for the Wednesday Night Live class for Glendale Presbyterian Church, Glendale, California in 1995. I then taught the whole letter for Regent College in the summer of 2020 during the Covid-19 pandemic, doing so via Zoom!—no small challenge! In each case I witnessed the same effect—disciples, old and new, freshly caught up in the wonder and walk of being alive "IN Christ." I pray that the same thing will happen to you as you "soak" in Ephesians.

---

1 You could go to the website darrelljohnson.ca to listen to me preach to get a sense for how I speak; you would then "hear" what you "see" better.

So, come with me into this first century letter that brings about profound transformation in the lives of its readers in any century.

This will, by necessity, require a new set of glasses.

EPHESIANS 1:1-2

¹ Paul, an apostle of Christ Jesus by the will of God,

To the saints who are at Ephesus and who are faithful in Christ Jesus: ² Grace to you and peace from God our Father and the Lord Jesus Christ.

CHAPTER 1

Navigating an Alternative Reading of Reality

EPHESIANS 1:1-2

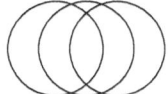

I have needed to get new glasses a number of times over the past years; part of the process of aging. On the most recent occasion, the young woman who helped me select the new frames said they made me look younger. Smile! She also said that the new colour of the rims matched my skin tone better. Smile again! She had been well trained! I had needed new glasses for some time, struggling to see clearly, in particular taking too long for things to come into focus as I turned my head side to side. The new glasses helped me see clearly, without having to strain!

This is what the New Testament document Ephesians does for us: it enables us to see clearly. This is what all of Holy Scripture does, or at least, is designed to do. But it does it nowhere more effectively, for me, than in the letter the apostle Paul writes to the disciples of Jesus living in the first century city of Ephesus.

It is, after all, what Paul tells the Ephesians, and us, he is praying for: "I pray that the eyes of your heart may be enlightened, so that you will know what is the hope of His calling, what are the riches of the glory of His inheritance in the saints, and what is the surpassing greatness of His power toward us who believe" (Ephesians 1:18-19a). Paul, and the Spirit of God who is inspiring Paul, wants us to see clearly, without having to strain. Thank you, Lord!

In the letter to the Ephesians, written in about 62 AD, we are given a new set of glasses, an "alternative reading of reality."[1] The alternative reading of reality that we discover in Ephesians is shaped by "the gospel of your salvation" as Paul calls it (Ephesians 1:13). The alternative reading is shaped by the events that constitute the Christian faith: Christmas, Good Friday, Easter, the Ascension, and Pentecost.

More than an alternative reading, through the letter to the Ephesians, we are slowly, but surely, drawn into the alternative reality itself. Slowly, but surely, we realize that we are not only seeing things differently; things really are different. "Things are not as they seem," Paul is saying to us. Or, more precisely, "Things are not only as they seem." There is more to reality than meets our unaided senses and emotions and intellect—a whole lot more! And no other book of the Bible, except the last book, the Revelation of Jesus Christ, opens up that more as expansively and concretely as does the letter from a prison cell we call Ephesians.

So, let us start reading. Beginning with Paul's opening greeting.

Paul, an apostle of Christ Jesus by the will of God, to the saints

---

[1] I owe this phrase to Walter Brueggemann. See, for example, Walter Brueggemann, *Interpretation and Obedience: From Faithful Reading to Faithful Living* (Minneapolis: Augsburg Fortress, 1991).

NAVIGATING AN ALTERNATIVE READING OF REALITY

> who are at Ephesus and who are faithful in Christ Jesus: Grace to you and peace from God our Father and the Lord Jesus Christ.
>
> Ephesians 1:1-2

Focus with me in turn on Paul, on Ephesus, on Paul and Ephesus, and then on the content of the opening greeting.

Who is this man Paul?

What was life like in Ephesus?

What is the connection between Paul and Ephesus?

And how does Paul set the stage for his alternative reading of reality?

But first, a word about the little phrase "at Ephesus." You may know that many manuscripts of the letter do not contain that little phrase. Scholars have different opinions as to why. Here is what I think: Paul's original letter, the first manuscript if you will, had the address "at Ephesus"; he sent the letter to his friends in the city of Ephesus. But people quickly realized that although Paul was writing to the specific people of that specific church in that specific city, he was also speaking more widely, to all the churches in the areas around Ephesus. This explains why, unlike Paul's other letters, he does not greet people by name and is not addressing any particular problem.

People soon realized that the letter to the Ephesians is really Paul's letter to churches anywhere and everywhere. The letter is a kind of encyclical to the whole church of Jesus Christ in the world. So, I think those who copied these manuscripts to pass them onto other churches realized that the letter also belonged to the other churches and just left out "at Ephesus." This means that in the "at Ephesus" slot, we can insert "to the saints at Laodicea," "to the saints at Athens," "to the saints at Rome," "to the saints at Hong Kong," and Seoul, Rio de Janeiro, Brisbane, Tucson, and Vancouver. The letter is also addressed to you in your city!

An Introduction to Paul

Now, what do we need to know about Paul as we make our own way through Ephesians?

At his birth he was given the name Saul, in honour of Israel's first king. He was born early in the first century, a few years after the birth of Jesus of Nazareth, to Jewish parents who happened to also be Roman citizens.

Paul was born in the city of Tarsus, in an area that is now modern-day Turkey. Tarsus was "a university town" known as a centre of learning.[2] Pythagoras spent time there, as did Parmenides, Zeno, and Democritus. Tarsus was a multicultural, multi-racial, multi-religion city. Jews, Greeks and Romans all lived, worked and worshiped there. In the early years of the first century, Tarsus had a population of nearly 500,000, which means that from the beginning of his life, Saul lived and worked in an urban world. Paul understands an urban world!

At some point in his late childhood, Paul's family moved to Jerusalem, or at least, they made many long-term visits to the Holy City. In Jerusalem, Saul became a student of the Rabbi Gamaliel (Acts 5:33-42, 22:3), grandson and successor of Rabbi Hillel (60 BC-20 AD), one of Judaism's greatest thinkers and teachers. Saul was an excellent student, rising in the ranks of the scholarly Pharisees. He was in such a high position that when the first Christians were brought to trial, Saul was in a position

---

2 John Drane, *Introducing the New Testament* (Oxford: Lion, 1999), 266.

to be able to cast votes for their punishment (Acts 26:10).

It is important to realize that Saul's first response to the gospel of Jesus Christ was horror, not belief or joy. The Messiah, crucified? No way! Heresy! Blasphemy! And then risen from the dead? No way! Nonsense! So problematic did he find the gospel that he decided it must be stamped out. Those who preached such "blasphemy" and "nonsense" must be destroyed.

He was on his way to the city of Damascus to arrest disciples of "The Way" and bring them back to Jerusalem for trial and then punishment. Luke, the medical doctor, tells the story in his Acts of the Apostles: Around noon one day, "suddenly a light from heaven flashed around him" (Acts 9:3). Saul fell to the ground. So would I! So would you! And he heard a voice saying to him, "Saul, Saul, why are you persecuting me?" (Acts 9:4). "Who are you, Lord?" Saul cried out. And the voice says, "I am Jesus, whom you are persecuting" (Acts 9:5). And Saul became Paul, the greatest of all Christian thinkers and missionaries.

In that Damascus encounter, Paul discovered grace. He hated the name Jesus. He hated all who named the name of Jesus. He was trying to erase the name from the pages of history. And yet, Jesus chose to love Paul; Jesus chose to love this man, to make Paul one of His chosen ambassadors (Ephesians 6:20). Grace! Sheer grace!

In that Damascus encounter, Paul discovered that Jesus is alive; the crucified One really is alive. The news from Jerusalem's cemetery was not nonsense: Jesus is risen! Paul discovered that Jesus is, therefore, Lord. Paul's first word to Jesus is "Lord." Paul knew the meaning of the word he used: *Kurios*. The word was used to refer to Israel's God, Yahweh. The word was used to refer to Rome's Emperor, Caesar. *Kurios*, Lord: Jesus is Lord.

And in that encounter, Paul discovered the wonder of being the church. "Why are you persecuting me?" Jesus asks me. Was Paul persecuting Jesus? He was threatening and harming disciples of Jesus. But, Jesus? Yes! For what we do to Jesus' disciples, we somehow do to Jesus. Jesus' disciples make up Jesus' body in the world. What we do to Jesus' body, we do to Jesus.

From that day on the Damascus road, Paul was a Jesus-captured man, a Jesus-apprehended man, a Jesus-enthralled man (Philippians 3:7-14). And from that day, Paul was a Jesus-sent man.

Thus the word "apostle": "Paul, an apostle of Messiah Jesus." That is how he introduced himself the rest of his life. "Apostle," sent one, one authorized by the sender to speak on his behalf. To be an "apostle of Messiah Jesus" is one of the greatest privileges any human being can ever have. Paul the persecutor, the terrorist, becomes one sent by the *Kurios*, to speak the Messiah's message to the world.[3]

An Introduction to Ephesus

Ephesus is located almost four kilometers inland from the Aegean Sea, on the west coast of modern Turkey. Years before, it had been a seaport, but over the decades, silt from the Cayster river slowly forced people to move inland. At the time when the gospel arrived in Ephesus, it had a population of between 225,000-250,000. From the beginning of the Christian era, believers have lived the gospel in urban centers.

---

[3] If you want to dive deeper into Paul's conversion and subsequent ministry you can read the masterful book, *Paul: A Biography*, by N.T. Wright (Harper Collins: New York, 2018). Also see the classic work *Paul: The Apostle of the Heart Set Free*, by F.F. Bruce (Eerdmans: Grand Rapids, 1977).

Ephesus was called "the first and grandest metropolis of Asia," ranking in importance in the Empire only behind Athens and Rome. It was the largest trading centre in Asia Minor, largely due to the fact that it was situated along major shipping routes. The so-called "Royal Road", linking East and West, went through the city bringing people from all over the world—people with all kinds of differing philosophical and religious perspectives, all kinds of alternative readings of reality.

The city had a fabulous theatre, with a seating capacity of 24,000. It was so acoustically engineered that a speaker standing at a particular spot on the stage need only whisper to be heard by all 24,000. I have experienced the phenomenon myself, at a similar theater in Baalbek in the Bekka Valley in Lebanon.

The city also had a massive temple, built for the worship of the goddess Artemis, as the Greeks called her, or Diana, as the Romans called her. She was the goddess of sexual fertility, represented by a statue with many breasts. Her temple was larger than any modern-day football field, and was four times larger than the Parthenon in Athens. It was the "largest building known in antiquity and was considered one of the seven wonders of the world."[4]

Understandably, life in Ephesus "revolved around" the temple of Artemis, who was spoken of as the "wife of Ephesus, the protectress and nourisher of the city."[5] Is this why Paul speaks so much of "temple" in his letter to the Ephesians? Is this part of the reason why he speaks of the relationship between Jesus

---

[4] Harold W. Hoehner, *Ephesians: An Exegetical Commentary* (Grand Rapids: Baker Academic, 2002), 83.
[5] Ibid., 85.

and His church in terms of a husband and a wife?

Ephesus was especially known as a center for magical practices. The city was "obsessed with demons and magic."[6] People, therefore, spoke a lot about spiritual power. Indeed, the goddess Artemis was thought to be one of the most powerful of all deities and was sought out for defense against other opposing "powers" and "spirits." Is this why Paul speaks so often of "principalities and powers" in his letter to the Ephesians?

> I pray that the eyes of your heart may be enlightened, so that you will know... what is the surpassing greatness of His [God's] power toward us who believe... in accordance with the working of the strength of His might which He brought about in Christ, when He raised Him from the dead and seated Him at His right hand in the heavenly places, far above all rule and authority and power and dominion.
>
> Ephesians 1:18, 19-21a

"Our struggle," he reminds the Ephesians, "is not against flesh and blood," not against other human beings, "but against the rulers, against the powers, against the world forces of this darkness, against the special forces of wickedness in the heavenly places" (Ephesians 6:12).

One more thing to know about Ephesus: It was proudly a center of the so-called "Imperial Cult," the worship of the Roman Emperor. Worship of Caesar as a god was the glue that held

---

6 Frank Thielman, *Ephesians* [Baker Exegetical Commentary on the New Testament] (Grand Rapids: Baker Academic, 2010), 20.

society together; it permeated all levels of society.[7] So the city constructed another temple (between 11-13 AD) and dedicated it to "Emperor Caesar Augustus, son of god," who was worshiped as the warrior god who had imposed unity and order on the world.

The rule of Augustus was thought to be so significant that the calendar needed to be changed. In 9 BC, the Ephesian City Council voted to change the calendar to begin on Augustus' birthday. It was claimed that Augustus had ended the time of suffering, and a city proconsul announced that Augustus had "restored the form of all things to usefulness."[8] The decree spoke of Augustus as a "saviour," *soter*, and as a "god," *theos*.

And his birthday was "the beginning of good tidings to the world." The word "good tidings" is *euangelion*, or *evangel*, which we refer to in English as "gospel." The birth and reign of Caesar Augustus was the beginning of the gospel for the cosmos. What had come to the world in Augustus was an eternal reign of peace.

Do you see why I use the phrase "alternative reading of reality"? The people in Ephesus who came to faith in Jesus Christ will have a new understanding of "gospel," a different "glad tidings." They will have a new understanding of power, and authority, and unity, and relationship, and time.[9]

Paul and Ephesus

Paul lived and served in Ephesus on two different occasions. The first time in 52 AD was quite brief (Acts 18:19-21); the second time

---

[7] Ibid., 21.
[8] Ibid., page?.
[9] For more on this, see Ibid., 22-23.

in 53-56 AD lasted about two and a half years (Acts 19:1-22; 20:31). At first, Paul taught and dialogued in the synagogue (Acts 19:8). But when he began to come up against "hardened hearts," Paul worked out of "the school of Tyrannus" (Acts 19:9). Apparently one of the Ephesian philosophers did not need his meeting room part of the day, and made it available to Paul. Luke tells us that Paul met with people in the Hall of Tyrannus, teaching every day for over two years.

During his two-and-a-half year stay in the city, many people were won to Jesus and His gospel. As a sign of their genuine conversion and intent to be Jesus' disciples, people broke with the Ephesian obsession with magic and the occult. Many brought their magic and occult books and burned them in a public square. Luke says that they counted up the price of the books: 50,000 pieces of silver, the equivalent of 50,000 days' wages![10] The gospel broke through and freed people from oppressive lies.

Paul's preaching of the gospel also spoke into the obsession with Artemis. The silversmiths of the city made much of their living crafting dolls with many breasts used in the worship of the goddess of sexual fertility. As people were won to Jesus and His gospel, sales of the dolls fell dramatically. One of the silversmiths, a certain Demetrius, was so incensed that he stirred up a riot. Luke says the city was thrown into confusion (Acts 19:29) and people rushed to the theatre, dragging some of Paul's companions with them. Cooler heads prevailed, and no one was killed, but the city was never the same. The gospel always starts fiddling

---

[10] According to Stats Canada, 2021, the average Canadian earns approximately $1,000 a week, or $200 a day. $200 times 500,000 is $10,000,000! That is quite a bonfire!

with the idols around which a city revolves! As my friend Jason Ballard says, "The gospel is always fighting bad ideas."

Paul then left Ephesus. Two years later, he ended up in jail and lived as a prisoner for five years, first in Caesarea on the coast of Syria, and then, after a harrowing trip by sea, in Rome. From Rome, in 62 AD, Paul writes in his letter to the Ephesians: "I, Paul, the prisoner of Christ Jesus for the sake of you Gentiles" (Ephesians 3:1). "Therefore I, the prisoner of the Lord, implore you to walk in a manner worthy of the calling to which you have been called" (Ephesians 4:1). Note that Paul does not call himself a "prisoner of Caesar," but a "prisoner of the Lord, of Messiah Jesus." An alternative reading of one's own reality!

The Opening Greeting

Paul begins the letter by reminding the Ephesians who they are. He calls them "saints," holy ones. And he calls them "believers." "Saints" does not mean "perfect ones"—at least not yet! "Saints" simply means "set-apart ones." Something is made holy by the Holy God simply by God claiming it for His own and setting it apart for His own purpose. Paul reminds the Ephesians right from the start of the letter that the Holy God has grabbed hold of them and set them apart for His redemptive purposes in the world. Put on Ephesian glasses and we discover that you and I are "holy ones"!

Paul reminds the Ephesians where they live. Yes, in Ephesus, but more essentially "in Christ." "Believers in Christ," he says. Paul will use the phrase "in Christ" or its equivalent 36 times in this letter: it is the essence of his practical theology.[11] In Christ we live and move and have our being. Put Ephesians glasses on and you and I discover we have a new address: In Christ!

Paul reminds the Ephesians what has been given to them: "Grace to you and peace." In Christ, set-apart saints have been given grace and peace. Grace is unmerited favour, something we could never earn, something we do not need to earn. Grace is God's free choice to be wholly disposed toward us for good. Peace is well-being, soundness, wholeness.

The word "grace" would especially ring chords in the souls of Gentiles since the greeting "grace to you" was a common Greek and Roman greeting. The word "peace" would ring chords in the world of Jews because "peace" [*Shalom*] was the normal greeting for Hebrews. "Grace and peace" to you is a multicultural greeting for a multicultural people. Put on Ephesian glasses and discover that you and I are recipients of God's unmerited favour and holiness.

And Paul reminds them who the God of the gospel is: "From God our Father and the Lord Jesus Christ." In and because of Jesus, His Father has now become our Father. We have become sons and daughters of the Father that Jesus knows and loves.

These are amazing words from a man who grew up as a faithful Jew. Everyday Paul would have spoken the Shema: "Hear O Israel! The Lord is our God, the Lord is one!" (Deuteronomy 6:4). It is *the* Jewish prayer. And look what Paul has done with it! In light of who he has learned Jesus to be, he has expanded the Shema. "Hear, O Israel! The Lord is our God, the Lord is one!" Yes, one. But not solitary, not alone. "Grace and peace from God

---

[11] See James S. Stewart, *A Man In Christ*.

our Father and the Lord Jesus Christ." Put on Ephesian glasses and you and I see the Living God in a whole new way!

And, in his opening, Paul points the Ephesians to the heart of the gospel: "Lord Jesus Christ." Things have changed, and there is a new *Kurios* in town, a new Lord. He is building a new temple. God has installed Him as the new Sovereign on the throne of the cosmos. God is building a very different kind of Empire with a very different kind of Emperor: "Lord Jesus Messiah."

And the letter the apostle and prisoner of the Lord Jesus Christ writes to the "holy ones" in the city of Ephesus is all about living this alternative reading of reality. It is all about making sense of, and then walking in (chapter 4, verse 1 and following), the alternative reality centered in "the Lord Jesus Messiah."

With these new glasses on, we are in for quite an adventure!

The Wonder of Being Alive "In Christ"

EPHESIANS 1:3–3:21

EPHESIANS 1:3

[3] Blessed be the God and Father of our Lord Jesus Christ, who has blessed us with every spiritual blessing in the heavenly places in Christ,

CHAPTER 2

Location, Location, Location!

EPHESIANS 1:3

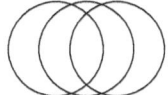

"Location, location, location." Realtors tell us it is the number one rule in buying property. And most realtors tell us that the key to the location is the view. What most people want in a location is a view: a view of the city, or the mountains, or the water. In Vancouver, if there is even a small glimpse of the bay or river or ocean from just one window where I live, it is enough to make the location very desirable.

The view from where we are located affects us more than we know. The view from where we are located shapes our sense of the city and our sense of the world—it can even shape our sense of well-being.

Something along these lines is what the apostle Paul is opening up for us in the letter he wrote to disciples of Jesus living in the first century city of Ephesus. Where we are located, or, more to the point, where we think or feel we are located, affects our sense of the world and our sense of well-being. What Paul wants us to realize is that where we think or feel we are located is not always the whole story.

Paul is located in Rome, with all that being in Rome entails. And Paul is located in jail. The recipients of the letter are located in Ephesus, with all that being in Ephesus entails. And they are located in all kinds of different circumstances. Some in nice homes and some in not so nice homes; some in great jobs, some in crummy jobs, and some are in oppressive jobs. Some are in thriving relationships, and some are in strained relationships. Some are in robust health, and some are in great pain.

In Rome, in jail. In Ephesus. In various states of being, mentally, emotionally, and physically.

But none of those locations is the whole story. Neither are any of the views from those locations. Paul writes from Rome to his friends in Ephesus to help them realize that they, and he, also live in another location. And the view from this other location is truly spectacular!

The view from where they are *truly located* gives them a very different sense of the city, a very different sense of the world, indeed a very different sense of well-being. The view from where *we are truly located* will give us the same.

The apostle opens all this up for us in his first major declaration. Right after his opening greeting, Paul lays out what turns out to be the theme of the whole letter. He gets right to the point: location, location, location. Where we are truly located brings us into a radically alternative alternative reading of reality.

> Blessed be the God and Father of our Lord Jesus Christ, who has blessed us with every spiritual blessing in the heavenly places in Christ.
>
> Ephesians 1:3

Yes, in Rome, in jail. And, yes, in Ephesus, in all kinds of circumstances. And, yes, where you are physically located, in the situation you are in. But also, and more fundamentally, "in the heavenly places in Christ."

Blessed Be

"Blessed be..." Let us focus on this phrase for just a moment.

This is not adequately rendered as "Praise be..." Yes, praise is involved in blessing God. But "Praise be..." does not adequately capture what is fundamentally involved in "Blessed be..." I know of no single English phrase that does or can.

Every word in the worship vocabulary of the Bible has a particular nuance involving particular actions of the human body. This makes sense, given that we are embodied creatures. And it makes sense given that the greatest commandment is: "And you shall love the Lord your God with all your heart, and with all your soul, and with all your mind, and with all your strength" (Mark 12:30). We are to love God with our whole self: mind, heart, soul, and body. Thus the verbs of the worship vocabulary of the Bible all involve some particular use of the body.

"Bless" involves the hands and the knees. The Greek word is *eulogytos*, used to translate the Hebrew *barach*, a word involving the posture of kneeling. To bless is "to bring a gift to another while kneeling, while kneeling out of respect."[1] To "bless" means to come before another, go down on one's knees, stretch out one's hands, and offer a gift. To "bless God," therefore, means to come

---

1 Jeff A. Benner, "The Aaronic Blessing," at http://www.ancient-hebrew.org/12_blessing.html {accessed May 4, 2014}.

before His presence, kneel in adoration and submission, lift up our hands, and offer a gift. To offer the only gift we have to offer: to offer our whole selves.

We can thus paraphrase this phrase as: "May it be that people come before the God and Father of our Lord Jesus Christ, kneel, and with out-stretched hands offer their very selves."

Now we can appreciate the wonder of what the apostle Paul is declaring "Blessed be the God and Father of our Lord Jesus Christ, who has blessed us with every spiritual blessing..."

"Blessed us"! The same exact word is used as in "Blessed be..." We bless the God who has blessed us. God has come to us, knelt before us, stretched out His hands to us, and given us a gift—actually, lots of gifts! The Living God has come to us in Jesus Christ. He has gotten down on His knees in Jesus Christ. The Living God has opened His hands, and given us the gift of Himself in Jesus! And with Jesus, He has given us everything else we need to be all God made us to be. Mercy!

What Paul is celebrating in his theme sentence is the full implications of the benediction he heard all his life as a Jew. God instructs the priest to say over the people:

> The Lord [Yahweh] bless you, and keep you;
> The Lord [Yahweh] make His face shine on you,
> And be gracious to you;
> The Lord [Yahweh] lift up His countenance on you,
> And give you peace.
>
> Number 6:24-26

Then God says: "So they shall invoke My name on the sons of Israel, and I then will bless them" (Numbers 6:27).

LOCATION, LOCATION, LOCATION!

Do you see what is going on in that benediction? "Yahweh bless you..."

May Yahweh come to you, get down on His knees before you, and stretch out His hands to you with a gift. That is why He can keep you, He has come close to you, and stretched His hands out to take hold of you. "Yahweh make His face shine on you..." Not from way above you, looking down on you, but from right in front of you. "Yahweh lift up His countenance on you..." Since He is kneeling before you He has to "look up" to see you. An alternative reading of reality—big time! The God we bless blesses us. We bless God because He has blessed us. The great and awesome God, the Creator, has come to us in Jesus Christ, knelt down before us, and given us the greatest gift He could ever give. "God so loved the world, that He gave us His only begotten Son" (John 3:16). And with Him, "every spiritual blessing," every blessing the Spirit has to give.

"Blessed be the God and Father of our Lord Jesus Christ." We have to hear this in the context of Paul's whole life. For most of his life he would have addressed the Living God the way his fellow Jews did, as "the God of Abraham, Isaac, and Jacob." In Abraham, Isaac, and Jacob, God had revealed Himself, and revealed Himself as the God who blesses. To Abraham God had said, "I will bless you... and in you all the families of the earth will be blessed" (Genesis 12:2-3).

But in light of what God has done in Jesus Christ, Paul has to address God with a new name. For all the blessing God did in Abraham, Isaac, and Jacob, in Moses and in David, it doesn't hold a candle to the blessing God had done and is doing in Jesus.

"Blessed be the God and Father of our Lord Jesus Christ." Blessed be the God and Father Jesus knows and loves. Blessed be the God and Father revealed in the life and death and resurrection of Jesus. People flocked to Jesus when He lived visibly on earth, for in Jesus they experienced a kind of blessing they experienced nowhere else.

Let Paul's re-phrasing of the great blessing grab hold of your soul: "Blessed be the God and Father of our Lord Jesus Christ, who has blessed us with every spiritual blessing…"

In Christ

This brings us back to "location, location, location." We experience "every spiritual blessing" in a new location. We experience "every spiritual blessing" "in the heavenly places in Christ."

Paul is in Rome. His friends are in Ephesus. Paul is in jail. His friends are in all kinds of different circumstances. But Paul is also "in the heavenly places in Christ." And so are the believers in Ephesus. And so are we.

And what does all this mean?

Now, note carefully. Paul is not transported out of Rome in order to be "in the heavenly places in Christ." Paul is not taken out of jail. It is just that he is also "in the heavenly places in Christ." We are still located in the community in which we live, and we are still in the life circumstances in which we find ourselves. Some of these circumstances feel "blessed," and some do not. But that is not the whole story about our location; we are also "in the heavenly places in Christ." If you are like me you keep forgetting where we are located!

"In Christ." As noted in the last chapter, Paul uses the phrase or its equivalent some thirty-six times in Ephesians. It is the defining reality of his life. He is, as James S. Stewart puts it,

"A Man In Christ."[2] The phrase can be rendered "because of Christ." We are located "in the heavenly places because of Christ." We were "chosen before the foundation of the world because of Christ." We have been "predestined to adoption because of Christ." We have "redemption, the forgiveness of our trespasses because of Christ." We are "sealed with the Holy Spirit because of Christ."

But as you look at every place in Paul's writings where he uses the phrase "in Christ," his primary emphasis is locative—he is speaking of his and our new location. We live and move and have our being in Christ. It is what Jesus Himself promised us. On the night before going to the cross, He said to the first band of disciples, "Abide in Me, and I in you" (John 15:4). Dwell in Me, and I in you. Make your home in Me, and I will make My home in you. It is what Paul prays for later in his letter, "so that Christ may dwell in your hearts" (Ephesians 3:17). Christ in us, and we in Christ.

"Every spiritual blessing" the blessed God gives us is experienced, not only because of Christ, not only *with* Christ, but *in* Christ, in union *with* Christ. He is our true location no matter where else we might be located.

In the Heavenly Places

And, we are located "in the heavenly places."

But of course, for that is where Christ is. In order to be *in* Him we have to be where He is.

---

[2] James S. Stewart, *A Man in Christ: The Vital Elements of St. Paul's Religion* (London: Hodder & Stoughton, 1935).

Now, what does Paul mean by this phrase "heavenly places"? He uses it five times in his letter:

"Blessed be the God and Father of our Lord Jesus Christ, who has blessed us with every spiritual blessing in the heavenly places..." (Ephesians 1:3).

God "raised Him [Christ] from the dead and seated Him at His right hand in the heavenly places..." (Ephesians 1:20).

God has made us alive with Christ, "raised us up with Him, and seated us with Him in the heavenly places..." (Ephesians 2:6).

God makes known the mystery of the gospel "through the church to the rulers and the authorities in the heavenly places" (Ephesians 3:10).

Our battle is not with flesh and blood human beings, "but against the rulers, against the powers, against the world forces of this darkness, against the spiritual forces of wickedness in the heavenly places" (Ephesians 6:12).

What does this mean? I do not yet fully know the answer. I believe what Paul believes, I just do not yet fully understand what he believes!

In using this phrase Paul is taking us into the Biblical vision of the universe; he is taking us into the Biblical cosmology. In the Bible, reality is multi-dimensional or multi-layered. And the authors of the books of the Bible would tell us that we are not being "realistic" about our lives unless and until we take this seriously. The authors of the Bible would tell us that for all our "hard-nosed realism," most of us are not being "realistic" enough. Therefore, we do not really understand where we are located.

Most twenty-first century people have what we could call a two-dimensional vision of reality. The two dimensions are (1) the ego (the self), and (2) the environment (made up of the physical universe and other human selves). This reading of reality says that everything that happens in our lives can be explained in terms of these two dimensions. When something goes wrong in life, help, hope, or healing is to be found in one or both of these two dimensions.

But for the authors of the Bible, and for Paul in particular, reality is at least four-dimensional. In addition to (1) the self and (2) the environment, there is (3) the Living God and (4), there are "the heavenly places." We are not being hard-nosed realists unless and until we factor in the Living God (Father, Son and Holy Spirit), and unless and until we factor in the heavenly places.

I know this is hard for us modern and post-modern folks to really get a handle on. I became serious about following Jesus in the fall of 1967. I was studying Physics, so was understandably steeped in the world-view of professors I admired. At the time, one of the significant players in the theological world was the German scholar Rudolf Bultmann.

In 1941 Bultmann wrote an essay that resonated with many people, entitled, "The New Testament and Mythology." Bultmann argued that in light of all we have learned about the universe it is no longer possible to hold to the world-view of the Bible and the Christian creeds. He wrote:

> No mature person represents God as a being who exists above in heaven; in fact, for us there no longer is any 'heaven' in the old sense of the word.... Thus, the stories of Christ's descent and ascent are finished, and so is the expectation of the Son of

Man's coming on the clouds of heaven and of the faithful's being caught up to meet him in the air.[3]

Many theologians agreed with Bultmann and said so publicly. Many evangelical theologians disagreed with him and also said so publicly. But many of the theologians who disagreed with Bultmann lived their lives as though they agreed with him! "Heaven," and more specifically, "the heavenly places," made no practical difference in their lives; it did not seem to really matter. I would have put myself in that category. I saw the words on the pages of Ephesians, wondered what they meant, and went on living without taking the words seriously. And sometimes I think I still am in that category. I face the day as though this dimension does not exist. Can you relate?

Bultmann called his program "de-mythologizing." In light of all we now know about the universe, we simply have to strip our faith of all mythological elements—like "the heavenly places." I would never consciously agree with the program, but I have agreed with it in practice. I have lived as if what Paul is talking about does not really matter.

Thankfully, as I grew "in Christ" I began to experience things that could not be accounted for with a two-dimensional, de-mythologized reading of reality. Reality forced me to get serious about how Paul sees the world.

Then, a number of years ago, I came across the work of Andrew T. Lincoln, who earned his PhD at Cambridge University. In a book entitled, *Paradise Now and Not Yet*, he grapples

---

[3] Rudolf Bultmann, *New Testament & Mythology and other Basic Writings*, Trans. Schubert Ogden (Philadelphia: Fortress Press, 1984), 4.

with the heavenly dimension of Paul's thought. He argues that the need in Christian theology in our time is not to "de-mythologize" our cosmology, but to "re-mythologize" it. What we need is a thorough re-mythologizing of our everyday faith. This is how Lincoln puts it:

> It is not a question of whether modern people will interpret their lives by symbols or myths but rather the question is which symbols and myths they will accept or choose. Will it be those rooted in the Biblical perspective or those originating from some other world-view?[4]

Try this. Imagine a point.

Then imagine the point being dragged into a line.
One dimension.

Then imagine the line being dragged into a square.
Two dimensions.

Then imagine the square being dragged into a cube.
Three dimensions.

Then imagine the cube being moved in some way into some other configuration.
Four dimensions.

---

[4] Andrew T. Lincoln, *Paradise Now and Not Yet: Studies in the Role of the Heavenly Dimension in Paul's Thought with Special Reference to His Eschatology* (Grand Rapids: Baker Book House, 1981), 4-5.

Although such a new configuration is hard to conceive, it can be described mathematically. Indeed, as you may know, mathematicians claim they can write equations for up to eleven dimensions. When the apostle Paul speaks of "the heavenly places," he is speaking of another dimension, another layer, within, around, intersecting with our space-time reality. Christ is alive in this dimension. Christ is seated on the throne in this dimension. We are made alive with Christ in this dimension. We are seated with Christ in this dimension. We are "in Christ" in this dimension. It is our true location in the world.

And it is not "far away." I think that is what most of us think when we hear the words "heaven" or "heavenly places." But that is not the way the Bible thinks. The authors of the Bible regularly use the words in conjunction with "earth." On the first page of the Bible: "In the beginning God created the heavens and the earth" (Genesis 1:1). On the last pages of the Bible: "Then I saw a new heaven and a new earth" (Revelation 21:1). The Bible does not speak of heaven without referring to earth, nor of earth without speaking of heaven. Like earth, heaven is also a created dimension of reality. As there was a time when there was no earth, so there was a time when there was no heaven.

Heaven is not needed for God to be. Once there was only the Triune God.

And then God brought earth and heaven into being. God is "Maker of heaven and earth." Heaven is as inherently mortal as earth. Heaven is as dependent upon God as earth. Earth cannot sustain itself, and neither can heaven.

Like earth, heaven has also been affected by sin. God has not been affected by sin, but heaven has—by the sin of heavenly beings, fallen angels, and by the sin of earthly beings, fallen humans. "And there was war in heaven" (Revelation 12:7). "Our battle" is with the forces of darkness "in the heavenly places" (Ephesians 6:12). Life on earth is influenced by life in heaven, and vice-versa. What goes on "in the heavenly places" affects life on the earthly dimension.

The prophet Daniel had been praying for Israel. After many days, Michael, "the prince of Israel" comes to him and says he would have come earlier, but had been delayed by "the prince of Persia" and "the prince of Greece." What goes on "on earth" affects life in the heavenly dimension.

In the Gospel according to Luke, Jesus sends out disciples who announce in cities and villages, "The kingdom of God has come near" (Luke 10:9). When they return, Jesus says to them, "I was watching Satan fall from heaven like lightning" (Luke 10:18). Life on earth and life "in the heavenly places" are inextricably intertwined.

The most important thing is that Christ has ascended into that other dimension. And since we have been united to Him, somehow we too live in that other dimension.

We cannot make sense of our lives apart from being "in Christ." And we cannot finally make sense of our lives apart from being "in the heavenly places." This is why C.S. Lewis used to say that, contrary to popular opinion, those with heaven on their minds are of the most earthly good.[5] Those on earth with "heaven on their minds" have a more accurate cosmology, a more accurate view of the universe.

"Location, location, location." "View, view, view." In Rome, in jail. In Ephesus, in various human circumstances. In Vancouver,

---

5 C.S. Lewis, *Mere Christianity* (New York: Macmillan, 1952), 118.

in Shanghai, in New York, in Bangkok, in New Delhi, in all kinds of circumstances. And, by grace, also "in the heavenly places in Christ."

Living in and navigating our way around our true location is what the rest of the letter to the Ephesians is all about.

EPHESIANS 1:4-14

[4] just as He chose us in Him before the foundation of the world, that we would be holy and blameless before Him. In love [5] He predestined us to adoption as sons through Jesus Christ to Himself, according to the kind intention of His will, [6] to the praise of the glory of His grace, which He freely bestowed on us in the Beloved. [7] In Him we have redemption through His blood, the forgiveness of our trespasses, according to the riches of His grace [8] which He lavished on us. In all wisdom and insight [9] He made known to us the mystery of His will, according to His kind intention which He purposed in Him [10] with a view to an administration suitable to the fullness of the times, that is, the summing up of all things in Christ, things in the heavens and things on the earth. In Him [11] also we have obtained an inheritance, having been predestined according to His purpose who works all things after the counsel of His will, [12] to the end that we who were the first to hope in Christ would be to the praise of His glory. [13] In Him, you also, after listening to the message of truth, the gospel of your salvation—having also believed, you were sealed in Him with the Holy Spirit of promise, [14] who is given as a pledge of our inheritance, with a view to the redemption of God's own possession, to the praise of His glory.

CHAPTER 3

You're (Much) Richer than You Think

EPHESIANS 1:4–14

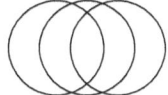

One of the deepest movements of the human heart is the longing to be rich. In the Broadway musical "Fiddler on the Roof," which became a now classic film, the lead character Tevye, an orthodox Jew living in Tsarist Russia, is talking to God while finishing the day's chores. "Dear God," Tevye prays, "You made many, many poor people. I realize, of course, that it's no shame to be poor. But it's no great honor either! So, what would be so terrible if I had a small fortune?"

Tevye then sings:

If I were a rich man,
Ya ha deedle deedle, bubba bubba deedle deedle dum.
All day long I'd biddy biddy bum.
If I were a wealthy man.
I wouldn't have to work hard.
Ya ha deedle deedle, bubba bubba deedle deedle dum.

> If I were a biddy biddy rich,
> Yidle-diddle-didle-didle man.

He goes on to sing of building a big tall house with dozens of rooms and long staircases; and of filling his farmyard with chickens and turkeys and geese and ducks; and of the joy his wife Golde would have, "with a proper double-chin." And of "the sweetest thing of all": having time

> To sit in the synagogue and pray.
> And maybe have a seat by the Eastern wall.
> And I'd discuss the holy books with the learned men,
> Several hours every day.

Then Tevye concludes by praying:

> Lord who made the lion and the lamb,
> You decreed I should be what I am.
> Would it spoil some vast eternal plan,
> If I were a wealthy man?[1]

The apostle Paul, who knows what it means to live as a sojourner in a foreign land, says to Tevye, and to every other human who wants to be wealthy: "Oh Tevye, I have good news for you. In Christ we are rich men and women! Tevye, in Messiah, 'You're richer than you think.'"

Many in Canada know the words "You're richer than you think" as one of the marketing slogans of Scotiabank. The

---

1 "If I were a Rich Man." Lyrics by Sheldon Harnick, Jerry Bock © 1964.

advertising department of the Bank produced a number of clever television commercials around these words, to which I think the Apostle Paul shouts, "Yes! You are richer than you think." Or, more faithful to what Paul opens up for us in his letter to the Ephesians, "In Jesus Christ, you are much richer than you think!" In relationship with Jesus, "in Christ, in the heavenly places," we discover that the "some vast, eternal plan" is all about making us very, very rich.

An Outpouring of Praise

In the original Greek, Ephesians 1:3-14 is one long sentence, one of the longest in the Bible. Paul will have other long sentences in his letter, but none as long as 1:3-14. It is 202 words in all, opening up for us "the every spiritual blessing" with which the God and Father of the Lord Jesus Christ has blessed us in Christ, in the heavenly places.

It is one long, compacted, compressed sentence. But it is not the type of rambling, run-on sentence that English teachers urge us to avoid. Andrew Lincoln in his commentary on Ephesians observes that "each thought builds on the previous one, sometimes explaining, sometimes elaborating, sometimes supplementing, sometimes contributing something new, and sometimes picking up again what had already been said."[2]

It is possible that the long sentence can be broken down into three parts. You will likely note the thrice repeated phrase "to the praise of…"

---

[2] Andrew T. Lincoln, *Ephesians* [Word Biblical Commentary] (Dallas: Word Books, 1990), 18.

Verse 6—"to the praise of the glory of His grace."
Verse 12—"to the praise of His glory."
Verse 14—"to the praise of His glory."

This tells us that, ultimately, everything God does for the world in Jesus Christ leads to worship. For it all ultimately manifests who God is, His glory; it all ignites and it all releases worship.

Many students of scripture see a Trinitarian structure (Father, Son, and Holy Spirit) in this three-fold breakdown of the long sentence:

- Up to the first "to the praise of..." (v. 3-6), Paul speaks of God the Father as the source, or origin, of "every spiritual blessing."
- From the first "to the praise of..." to the second (v. 7-12), Paul speaks of God the Son as the agent and the sphere, or location, of the "every spiritual blessing."
- From the second to the third "to the praise of..." (v. 13-14), Paul speaks of God the Holy Spirit as the seal of the "every spiritual blessing" and as the One who makes it all happen in our lives.

As attractive as that is, I do not think it is that neat. For one thing, God the Father is involved in all three supposed sections; indeed, God the Father is the subject of nearly all the finite verbs in the long sentence. And for another, God the Son, Jesus Christ, is involved in all three supposed sections. The phrase "in Christ' or some equivalent, is found in nearly every clause of the sentence:

Verse 3—"every blessing in Christ'
Verse 4—the Father chose us "in Him" (Christ)
Verse 5—the Father adopted us "through Christ"
Verse 6—the Father freely bestowed grace on us
   "in the Beloved," in Christ
Verse 7—"in Him" (Christ) "we have redemption"
Verse 7—"through His blood" (Christ's blood)
Verse 10—the Father is "summing up" all things "in Christ"
Verse 11—"in Him" (Christ) we "have obtained an inheritance"
Verse 12—We who were first to "hope in Christ"
Verse 13—We were sealed "in Him" (Christ)

So I do not think there is a single, neat structure to the long sentence. I think Paul is so caught up in the riches of the gospel that he is dictating a spontaneous, torrential outpouring of praise. He is so freshly captured by the wonder of being "in Christ," that the words simply tumble out of his mouth and heart.

This is like what happened to Zacharias, the father of John the Baptist, when he began to realize what God was doing in the birth of his son. He spontaneously broke out in song: "Blessed be the Lord God of Israel, for He has visited us and accomplished redemption for His people..." (Luke 1:67-79). And it is like what happened to the Virgin Mary, when she began to realize what God was doing in the birth of her son. She spontaneously broke out in an outpouring of praise: "My soul, exalts the Lord, and my spirit has rejoiced in God my Saviour..." (Luke 1:46-55).

But whereas both Zacharias and Mary focus on the blessing God was pouring out on Israel, Paul celebrates the blessings being poured out on the world. His vision goes beyond one nation to all the nations of the world, as he goes on to develop in the rest of his letter.

God "has blessed us with every spiritual blessing." New Testament scholar Gordon Fee argues that most of the time when Paul uses the word "spiritual" he has in mind God the Spirit.[3] Not all the time—in Ephesians 6:12 where he refers to "spiritual forces of wickedness in the heavenly places," clearly a different "spirit" is in mind! But in the long sentence that begins the letter, I think Dr. Fee is right. Paul is not simply juxtaposing "spiritual" blessings against "material," as though God is not concerned about material blessings; Paul is referring to the blessings God the Holy Spirit makes real in our lives.

In Christ, in the heavenly places, we are richer than we think or feel. Much richer! It's just that the riches are not obvious to the unaided intellect or emotions. We need a new set of glasses to see the riches. We need an alternative reading of reality, a reading shaped by the gospel of Jesus Christ.

While Paul is in prison in Rome, he is also in Christ in the heavenly places. And while under arrest in Rome, he is arrested by his true location ("in Christ") and his true state of being ("in Christ"), and is richer than anyone around him would think. Much richer!

In his long sentence, Paul celebrates just some of the "every blessing" with which we are blessed in Christ in the heavenly places. He names seven:

- chosen before the foundations of the world (4)
- predestined to adoption (5)

---

[3] Gordon D. Fee, *God's Empowering Presence: The Holy Spirit in the Letters of Paul* (Peabody, MA: Hendrickson, 1994), 32.

- redemption (7)
- forgiveness (7)
- insight into the mystery of history (9)
- an expansive inheritance (11)
- and sealed with the Holy Spirit (13)

Each of the blessings is worthy of numerous chapters!

Chosen Before the Foundation of the World

"Just as He [the God and Father of our Lord Jesus Christ] chose us in Him before the foundation of the world" (Ephesians 1:4). Paul begins by jumping into the deep end of the pool! Or, is it that he begins by emerging from the deep end of the pool?

The verb translated "chose" is *elexato*, which comes into our vocabulary as "election." Paul will use the word again half-way through his letter: "Therefore, I, the prisoner of the Lord, implore you to walk in a manner worthy of the calling with which you have been called [elected, chosen]" (Ephesians 4:1).

Why begin with this blessing? Why begin with being elected before the foundation of the world? Because for the apostle Paul this blessing expresses the wonder of the gospel.

Paul's salvation is not grounded in himself; Paul's salvation—and all that salvation means—is grounded in the free, sovereign, gracious choice of the Living God. This is what startled him in the encounter with Jesus on the road to Damascus. Paul, then Saul, was engaged in a terrorist campaign to wipe the name of Jesus off the pages of history. But to his surprise, the living Jesus came to him and claimed Paul for His own. From that day on Paul lived out of the deep and liberating realization that his salvation was not grounded in anything he did or did not do. His salvation was grounded in God's free, sovereign, gracious choice in Christ. This is the wonder of the gospel: "Chosen in Christ before the foundation of the world."

Now, I know that this blessing raises all kinds of questions! Questions that lead into issues with fancy words like double predestination, reprobation, supralapsarianism and eternal decree. Greater minds than mine have wrestled with the question over the centuries, and they have not yet resolved them all. People like Augustine of Hippo, Thomas Aquinas, John Calvin, Martin Luther, John Wesley, and Friedrich Schleiermacher. Karl Barth emphasized that we cannot understand "election" apart from Christ, and suggests that Christ is both the one who elects and the one who is elected; that Christ is both the God who elects and the human who is elected. There are so many nuances and caveats to the blessing of being chosen in Christ that one can get a severe headache trying to think it all into some coherent doctrine.

So I find I have to focus on what is clear about the first blessing Paul celebrates. For Paul, and the other Biblical authors who speak of it, God's election of us in Christ before the foundation of the world is good news. The truth of election causes Paul to bless God, to bow his knees and stretch out his hands, offering his whole self. This tells me that as I try to understand this blessing, if I go down an intellectual road that no longer stirs my soul to worship, something is off. A right understanding of divine election will engender an outpouring of praise.

We know that no one chooses God. No one, of their own will, chooses to know and love and follow the Living God. In his letter to the Romans, Paul quotes the psalmist: "There is none righteous, not even one; there is none who understands, there is none who seeks for God" (Romans 3:10-11; Psalm 14). Oh, we all seek for something to fill the emptiness of the human soul, for something to take away the existential ache. But no one of their own volition seeks the True and Living God.

So, unless God seeks, no one will find. Unless God chooses, no one will be saved. I like how New Testament scholar Harold Hoehner puts it: "Since human beings do not seek God, the only destiny is separation from God forever. It is the sheer grace of God that allows any person to have another destiny."[4] I know this raises all kinds of questions. But this we know; unless God chooses to win us, everyone would remain lost. The old hymn says it so well:

I sought the Lord, and afterward I knew
He moved my soul to seek Him, seeking me.
It was not I who found, O Saviour true;
No, I was found of Thee.[5]

What is also clear in Scripture is that God "choosing" does not necessarily imply God "rejecting." That may seem like a logical deduction. But Paul does not go down that road in the text. God chose Israel. But that choosing did not imply that God was rejecting other peoples, despising other nations. In fact, God chose Israel for the sake of other peoples, other nations! To Abraham, God said:

---

[4] Harold W. Hoehner, *Ephesians: An Exegetical Commentary* (Grand Rapids: Baker Academic, 2002), 188.
[5] "I Sought the Lord," words, anonymous (19th century). Jean Ingelow (1878).

> Go forth from your country and from your relatives and from your father's house, to the land which I will show you; And I will make you a great nation, and I will bless you,... and so you shall be a blessing... And in you all the families of the earth will be blessed.
>
> Genesis 12:1-3

God's choice of Abraham was unto the blessing of the whole world. When Jesus chose twelve disciples (Luke 6:13; John 13:18; 15:19), He was not thereby rejecting all the other people who were drawn to Him. He just chose twelve in whom He would uniquely work in order that they would bless others. When Paul says to the Corinthians that God chooses the foolish of the world and not the wise, God chooses the poor and not the rich (1 Corinthians 1:27), the intention is not to thereby reject the wise and rich, "but to show the world that one does not come to know God because of worldly status."[6] God's election has an outward, "other-directed" goal: chosen out of the world for the sake of the world.

Paul names "chosen before the foundation of the world" first because this is where our security lies. Our salvation is not grounded in ourselves. Our salvation is not grounded in anything we did or do, or in anything we did not do or do not do. It is not even grounded in God's foreknowledge of what we would do or not do, or what we will do or not do. Our salvation is grounded in God's free, sovereign, gracious choice in Christ to claim us for Himself. Blessed be His name!

Now, what Paul emphasizes in his long sentence is the reason

---

[6] Harold W. Hoehner, *Ephesians: An Exegetical Commentary* (Grand Rapids: Baker Academic, 2002), 187.

for election: "that we might be holy and blameless before Him" (1:4). "Holy." Many people bristle at the word because we are not, in and of ourselves, holy. But we need not bristle. "Holy" is what the Living God is. Three times the angelic choir repeats the word: "Holy, Holy, Holy" (Isaiah 6, Revelation 4). This is what God is, and it is what God made us to be. This is what we all, deep down in our souls, want to be even if we do not know the word.

Holy.

Pure.

Clean.

Clear.

Whole.

To be holy is to be whole. Like the whole God. Who does not want to be whole? The Holy One chose us in Christ before the foundation of the world to be holy and blameless before Him. It is the "vast eternal plan" to use the words of Tevye. We are to be holy.

Note carefully: God does not choose us in Christ because we are holy and blameless. God does not choose us in Christ because we are trying to be holy and blameless. God does not choose us in Christ because God foresees that one day we might be holy and blameless. Being holy is not the ground of our salvation, it is the goal. From before the world was made, the plan has been for us to be made like the Holy God... clean, clear, whole, full of light and beauty.

Steven Waldschmidt, an actor in Calgary, does a sketch involving Jesus and the disciple Peter. Jesus had told Peter to cast his fishing net on the other side of his boat. When Peter does so, he and his co-workers can hardly haul in the catch. This encounter with the Holy One made Peter feel his own unholiness. Peter falls down at Jesus' feet, and says, "Depart from me, for I am a sinful man, O Lord" (Luke 5:8). Steven has Peter say to Jesus: "Go away from me, for I will make you dirty." To which Steven has Jesus say: "No Peter, you will not make me dirty; I will make you clean."

"Chosen in Christ before the foundation of the world, that we should be holy and blameless before Him."

We are richer than we think or feel! Much richer.

Predestined to Adoption

"In love He predestined us as sons through Jesus Christ to Himself" (Ephesians 1:4-5).

"Predestined." Again, do not get hung up in all the questions the word raises. Hear Paul's fundamental declaration: in Christ we have a destiny. We have been destined for adoption!

In the Roman world a wealthy man would want to pass on his riches to an heir. If he had no son of his own, or if the relationship with his son or sons was broken in some way, he would select one of his trusted servants and adopt him as an heir. Can you imagine how that servant would feel? From rags to riches overnight! No longer "servant of Mr. Wealthy," but "son of Mr. Wealthy," "Heir of Mr. Wealthy's wealth."

Now, in this case, God the Father has a Son; "the Beloved," as Paul calls Him (Ephesians 1:6). God the Father is very pleased with His Son, so He does not need to go looking for someone else to be heir of His wealth. Out of sheer grace, the Father decides to make other sons and daughters and bring them into the deal with His beloved Son.

Theologian J.I. Packer argues in his classic book, *Knowing*

God, that adoption is "the highest privilege that the gospel offers."[7] Packer especially emphasizes what is surprising for a Reformed theologian, that adoption is a higher privilege than justification. Justification is a primary blessing of the gospel... no two ways about it. For in justification, God the Judge declares that sinners "are not, and never will be, liable to the death that their sins deserve, because Jesus Christ, their substitute and sacrifice, tasted death in their place on the cross."[8] Yet, says Packer, this is not the highest blessing. "Adoption is higher, because of the richer relationship with God that it involves."[9] Packer writes:

> Justification is a *forensic* idea conceived in terms of *law* and viewing God as *judge*.... Adoption is a *family* idea, conceived in terms of *love*, and viewing God as *father*. In adoption, God takes us into His family and fellowship, and establishes us as His children and heirs. Closeness, affection and generosity are at the heart of the relationship. To be right with God the judge is a great thing, but to be loved and cared for by God the father is a greater.[10]

There is so much involved in this blessing, that can be explored another time. For now, rejoice with Paul in the fact that in adoption we enter into and participate in the relationship at the centre of the universe. Before the foundation of the world there was a relationship between a Father and a Son. The relationship so pulsates with life that it itself is breathing, a spirit, a person,

---

7 J.I. Packer, *Knowing God* (Downers Grove: InterVarsity Press, 1973), 186.
8 Ibid., 187.
9 Ibid.
10 Ibid., 187-188.

the Holy Spirit. We were created to enter into and participate in the relationship! Jesus is the one natural Son, the one natural child of God. Out of love He brings us home with Him to the Father's house! And by His Spirit, He enables us to know His Father so deeply that we too pray as He does, "Abba, Father."

"According to the kind intention of His will" (Ephesians 1:5), says Paul. More literally, "according to His good pleasure." What pleases the Living God, what gives God great pleasure, is to bring human beings, not yet fully holy human beings, into the eternal relationship at the centre of the universe!

It will take the rest of our lives to live into this blessing!

We are richer than we think or feel! Much richer.

Redemption Through His Blood

"In Him we have redemption through His blood, the forgiveness of our trespasses, according to the riches of His grace" (Ephesians 1:7).

In Christ we have redemption. This is not just another synonym for salvation; the word has a very particular meaning.[11] As Leon Morris of Australia points out, whereas we hear the word "redemption" and begin to think in religious terms, people of Paul's day heard it and immediately thought in non-religious terms. The verb form of the word simply means to "loose" and was used of all kinds of loosening: loosening of clothing, loosening of tied up animals, and so on.[12] It was especially

---

11 Leon Morris, *The Apostolic Preaching of the Cross* (Grand Rapids: Wm. B. Eerdman Publishing, 1965), 11.
12 Ibid.

used of loosening human beings from captivity of one sort or another: loosening slaves, prisoners, political hostages, people from oppressive debt or oppressive governments. And loosening people by some kind of payment—releasing slaves and prisoners and hostages and debtors by someone paying the price of redemption.

Now, at first, naming this blessing may seem like a diversion from the flow of Paul's long-sentence-out-burst of praise. Chosen to be holy before God, adopted to be children, and then redemption. This initially feels like Paul has just randomly jumped to another blessing. But this is not the case at all.

"We have redemption" points to the human condition apart from the grace of God, to the fact we all know but seldom really face: apart from grace, we are in bondage. Unless we are loosened from the captivity, we cannot enter into and enjoy adoption and election. In order to actively live in the riches of adoption and election, we have to be set free.

This too is one of the deepest movements of the human heart, the longing to be free. Human beings long to be free. What Paul wants us to realize is that the bondage is much worse than bondage to dictators and corruption and injustice. We are held captive by much stronger forces and powers: by sin, by evil, by darkness, by death. What we need is redemption from this deeper captivity. What Paul is celebrating is that in Christ we have just the redemption we need.

Through the shed blood of Jesus Christ we have been redeemed. When Jesus Christ shed His blood on that Roman cross, we were redeemed from all that has held humanity captive. By His blood He has released us from the curse of the law, from the compulsion of sin, from the lordship of unseen powers in the heavenly places, from lies that have ensnared the human mind and heart, from the finality of death, and, therefore, from the fear of death. "For even the Son of Man did not come to be served, but to serve, and to give His life a ransom for many" (Mark 10:45). He came to pay the price that sets captives free!

And now we belong to Him. In Paul's day, what people redeemed they then owned. What Jesus redeems by His blood He now owns. He sets us free from all that holds humanity in bondage, so that we might belong to Him and live in the freedom of the children of God (Romans 8:15, 21; Galatians 5:1, 13).

Forgiveness of Our Trespasses

"We have... forgiveness of our trespasses" (Ephesians 1:7). Forgiveness is not just another word for redemption. Forgiveness is all about restoration of relationship. Theoretically, we could be released from bondage, but not be in relationship. Someone could come along and release captives from jail, and then walk on, not interested in any on-going relationship. Forgiveness is about establishing relationship with released captives!

"Of our trespasses," says Paul. The authors of the Bible use three different words for our condition apart from the riches of grace. They are sin, transgression, and iniquity (see Psalms 32 and 51):

> To sin is to miss the mark, like an archer, pulling back the arrow, letting it go and missing the target. We all sin—we all miss the mark in some way or other.

To transgress is to cross the line. We come upon a fence or gate with the sign "No Trespassing." We think about it for a few minutes... and then we do it anyway. We transgress, going ahead and crossing the line. We all do it—in one way or another. Iniquity is the thing in us that makes us miss the mark and cross the line, the twistedness in us, the perversion that makes us want to cross the line.

By His blood, Jesus rescues us from iniquity, releasing us from its horrible grip. By His blood, Jesus erases our sin, our missing the mark, wiping the slate clean. And by His blood, Jesus forgives our transgressions, choosing not to hold our willful disobedience against us! He takes the rap for us, and then brings us back into relationship with Him and His Father.

When we transgress, when we walk through the "no trespassing" sign, in whatever way, we suffer the consequences. God does not spare us the sting of our willful disobedience. But He does forgive, cancelling the indebtedness, and He does restore relationship.

I sometimes use a book entitled *A Dairy of Private Prayer* written by John Baillie in 1949, to help me pray; especially when I am too weary to pray, or feeling too guilty or ashamed to pray. In the book, Baillie has a prayer for each morning and evening of each day of the month. On January 18, I was deeply ministered to by the prayer for the evening of that day. Baillie has his reader pray this confession:

For my deceitful heart and crooked thoughts:
For barbed words spoken deliberately:
For thoughtless words spoken hastily:

> For envious and prying eyes:
> For ears that rejoice in iniquity and rejoice not in the truth:
> For greedy hands:
> For wandering and loitering feet:
> For haughty looks:
> Have mercy upon me, O God.[13]

And then Baillie has us pray: "Almighty God, Spirit of purity and grace, in asking Thy forgiveness I cannot claim a right to be forgiven but only cast myself upon Thine unbounded love."

> I can plead no merit or desert:
> I can plead no extenuating circumstance:
> I cannot plead the frailty of my nature:
> I cannot plead the force of the temptations I encounter:
> I cannot plead the persuasions of others who led me astray:
> I can only say, For the sake of Jesus Christ Thy Son my Lord. Amen.[14]

And wonder of wonders, He forgives. He wants the relationship! What a portfolio!

The Mystery of His Will

"In all wisdom and insight He made known to us the mystery of His will, according to His kind intention which He purposed in

---

[13] John Baillie, *A Diary of Private Prayer* (New York: Charles Scribner's Sons, 1949), 79.
[14] Ibid.

Him with a view to an administration suitable to the fullness of the times, that is, the summing up of all things in Christ, things in the heavens and things upon the earth" (Ephesians 1:8-10).

God has made known to us the mystery of history! This word "mystery" does not refer to something hidden which only those with the magic key can unlock. The word refers to "God's program for the world," which has been there for all the ages past, but which no one could have ever figured out on their own, which has to be revealed by God in order to be known.[15]

The mystery can now be known by all because the key to the mystery has come into the world. Jesus Christ is the key to the mystery of history. And what Paul celebrates in his long "every spiritual blessing" sentence is that in relationship with the Key we can know the mystery in all wisdom [practical skill], and in all insight [intellectual comprehension].

The mystery will all be summed up in Christ. All the lines of history—political, economic, scientific, moral—will all be summed up at a time determined by God who works all things according to His good pleasure. Everything in the universe will be summed up in Christ.

Paul uses an image-rich word to make the point. The verb "summed up" is built on the noun *kephale* which means "head." The literal rendering of the verb is "sum up under a head," which is why some translate the verb as "recapitulate," or "gather up under one head." More graphically, it is to "put the head back on." Recapitulate: that is the mystery none of us would have figured out on our own.

---

[15] Harold W. Hoehner, *Ephesians: An Exegetical Commentary* (Grand Rapids: Baker Academic, 2002), 214.

God is going to recapitulate all things. God is going to put the head back on all things. Apart from Jesus Christ, we are running around with our heads off!! All over the world right now, people are asking "what has gone wrong? What is wrong with us?" The Biblical answer is that we are running around with our heads off. We have capitulated to forces beneath our dignity. We have sought comfort in things that now hold us in bondage.

But the mystery, open for all to know, is that in His good pleasure God is going to recapitulate all things. God is going to put the head back on the human race. God is working even now, moving toward summing up all things under the crucified Lord as head. We know the mystery!

Obtained an Inheritance

"In Him also we have obtained an inheritance" (Ephesians 1:11).

Of course. The one long sentence has been moving toward this blessing from the beginning. We have been chosen, we have been adopted, we have been redeemed, we have been forgiven, we have been clued in on the mystery, all leading to obtaining an inheritance.

There is a debate about whose inheritance Paul is talking about. Is it ours, something we have obtained? Or is it God's, something He has obtained? Is it that we now possess something? Or is it that God now possesses something?

I wonder if Paul put it the way he did because he means both. That is, God now possesses something—namely us, men and women in Christ. Makes sense: God chose us, God adopted us, God redeemed us, God forgave us—for Himself, to make us His own. We are His inheritance. Imagine that! And He is investing all His wealth in us! Like a new home owner, investing everything they own to make her home all it can be, God has obtained an inheritance—us!

And we thereby have obtained an inheritance. We get to enjoy His inheritance. We get to enjoy His investments, all He is in His people. We get to enjoy His preparing a new place for His people, a new heaven and a new earth where we live with heads back on.

Sealed with the Holy Spirit

"You were sealed in Him with the Holy Spirit of promise, who is given as a pledge of our inheritance, with a view to redemption of God's own possession" (Ephesians 1:13-14).

When we believed, we were sealed. When we hear the gospel of our salvation and believe, we are sealed. This happens when we sign mortgage papers at the bank: the deed is sealed—to authenticate the deed and to secure the deed.

When we believe, we are sealed with the Holy Spirit! My goodness. God authenticates the deal in Christ with the Holy Spirit. God secures the deal in Christ with the third person of the Holy Trinity, Who, says Paul, is a pledge of the inheritance. The Greek word Paul uses is *arrabon*, a business term, referring to a down payment, or a first installment. An *arrabon* binds both parties in the deal, both the buyer and the seller. When the buyer puts down an *arrabon* as a down payment, but fails to pay the rest, he or she loses the down payment. When the seller puts down an *arrabon* as a first-installment but fails to deliver on the rest, he or she is obligated to pay double the first installment.

Oh my goodness! God is saying that if He fails to fulfill the promise—which will never happen given His character—He will pay twice the *arrabon*! God will pay twice His first installment. God will pay twice the Holy Spirit. God will pay twice Himself! What a portfolio! We are richer than we think we are. We are much richer than we think or feel!

- A solid anchor—chosen in Christ before the foundation of the world!
- A new identity—predestined to adoption as sons and daughters through Jesus Christ.
- Freedom—in Christ we have redemption.
- Restored relationship—through His blood, the forgiveness of our transgressions.
- Perspective—we know the mystery, everything summed up in Christ, the true Head of all things. We can keep our balance in times of change and turmoil.
- An inheritance—we share in God's own inheritance.
- And security—sealed, God Himself the first installment on our future!

Our son and his family worshiped with us when I was preaching through Ephesians, and afterwards David said, "You know what it [Paul's long sentence] means, Dad? It means God's got our back. It is going to be ok."

"To the praise of the glory of His grace." Amen.

EPHESIANS 1:15–19

¹⁵ For this reason I too, having heard of the faith in the Lord Jesus which exists among you and your love for all the saints, ¹⁶ do not cease giving thanks for you, while making mention of you in my prayers; ¹⁷ that the God of our Lord Jesus Christ, the Father of glory, may give to you a spirit of wisdom and of revelation in the knowledge of Him. ¹⁸ I pray that the eyes of your heart may be enlightened, so that you will know what is the hope of His calling, what are the riches of the glory of His inheritance in the saints, ¹⁹ and what is the surpassing greatness of His power toward us who believe. These are in accordance with the working of the strength of His might

CHAPTER 4

Gospel-Shaped Praying

EPHESIANS 1:15–19

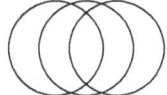

We now come to one of my favourite paragraphs of the letter to the disciples living in Ephesus. We come to one of my favourite parts of any of Paul's letters! We come to the first of two prayers that Paul prays for disciples of Jesus living in the Roman Empire.

The Preaching of Paul

I love to hear Paul preach. Where would we be without his preaching? Where would we be without what he preaches in his letter to the Romans?

> Therefore, having been justified by faith, we have peace with God through our Lord Jesus Christ.
>
> Romans 5:1

> ...where sin increased, grace abounded all the more, so that, as sin reigned in death, even so grace would reign through righteousness to eternal life through Jesus Christ our Lord.
>
> Romans 5:20-22

> Therefore there is now no condemnation for those who are in Christ Jesus.
>
> Romans 8:1

> For I am convinced that neither death, nor life, nor angels, nor principalities, nor things present, nor things to come, nor powers, nor height, nor depth, nor any other created thing, will be able to separate us from the love of God, which is in Christ Jesus our Lord.
>
> Romans 8:38-39

Where would we be without what Paul preaches in his letter to the Colossians?

> He [Jesus Christ] is the image of the invisible God, the firstborn of all creation. For by Him all things were created, both in the heavens and on earth, visible and invisible, whether thrones or dominions or rulers or authorities—all things have been created through Him and for Him. He is before all things, and in Him all things hold together.... For it was the Father's good pleasure for all the fullness to dwell in Him, and through Him to reconcile all things to Himself, having made peace through the blood of His cross.
>
> Colossians 1:15-17, 19-20a

Where would we be without what Paul preaches in his letter to the Philippians?

> Have this attitude in yourselves which was also in Christ Jesus, who, although He existed in the form of God, did not regard equality with God a thing to be grasped, but emptied Himself, taking the form of a bond-servant... He humbled Himself by becoming obedient to the point of death, even death on a cross. For this reason also, God highly exalted Him, and bestowed on Him the name which is above every name, so that at the name of Jesus every knee will bow, of those who are in heaven and on earth, and under the earth, and that every tongue will confess that Jesus Christ is Lord, to the glory of God the Father.
>
> Philippians 2:5-11

Where would we be without what Paul preaches in the letter through which we are making our way? Where would we be without his great "Blessing"?

> Blessed be the God and Father of our Lord Jesus Christ, who has blessed us with every spiritual blessing in the heavenly places in Christ.
>
> Ephesians 1:3

Chosen. Adopted. Redeemed. Forgiven. Sealed by the Holy Spirit. I love to hear Paul preach!

The Praying of Paul

But as much as I love to hear Paul preach, I especially love to hear Paul pray. Listen:

> [I pray] that the God of our Lord Jesus Christ, the Father of glory, may give to you a spirit of wisdom and of revelation in the knowledge of Him. I pray that the eyes of your heart may be enlightened, so that you will know what is the hope of His calling, what are the riches of the glory of His inheritance in the saints, and what is the surpassing greatness of His power toward us who believe.
>
> Ephesians 1:17-19

No one prays as expansively as Paul, except, of course, the Lord Jesus Himself in the prayer He prayed just before going to the cross, recorded in John 17. But no one else in all of Scripture prays like Paul—no king, no priest, no prophet, no psalmist. And no one else in all of Church history prays like him—not Augustine, not Luther, not Calvin. No one prays with the "emotional depth" or the "extravagant expectations" with which he prays.[1] I love to hear Paul pray!

What amazes me, and challenges me, is that his expansive praying emerges from crummy circumstances. Crummy is putting it mildly! He is not on a retreat on the slopes of beautiful Mt. Hermon. He is not in a vacation villa on the Italian seacoast. He is in prison, going on five years: three in Caesarea, and now

---

1 David Crump, *Knocking on Heaven's Door: A New Testament Theology of Petitionary Prayer* (Grand Rapids: Baker Academic, 2006), 241.

two in Rome. His emotionally deep, extravagantly expectant, intellectually rigorous praying takes place in jail.

Not that the only prayers Paul prayed are those recorded in his letters. I do not want to idealize Paul's spirituality. He must have also prayed for release from his crummy circumstances. Before he ended up in jail in Rome, he had written to the Roman church in anticipation of his visit to Jerusalem, where he sensed he would be arrested. "Strive together with me in your prayers to God for me," he wrote, "that I may be rescued..." (Romans 15:30-32). He asked the same of the believers in Corinth (2 Corinthians 1:10-11).

And Paul very likely asked God in prayer, "Why? Why are You letting this happen to me?" He was, after all, taught to pray by praying the Psalms, many of which are laments: "O Lord, you are the Sovereign One. You are good and faithful. Then why? Why is this happening to me? How long O Lord?" (See Psalm 3-13 for example.)

Paul surely felt free to pray in the biblical way. It is just that, by grace, he realized his true location in the world. Yes, in Rome, and yes, in jail. But also, and precisely, in Christ, in the heavenly places (Ephesians 1:3). And in his true location in the world, he was gripped by the gospel. If I were to write a book on Paul, that would be the title: *Gripped by the Gospel*.

And gripped by the gospel, Paul prays gospel-shaped prayers! I love to hear Paul preach the gospel. But I especially love to hear him then pray the gospel, shaking me out of my limited perspective, stirring me to pray more boldly.

A Prayer for Knowledge

"I want you to *know*," says Paul. That is the major burden of his first prayers in his letter to the Ephesians—twice he uses the verb "know." In his second prayer in this letter, in Ephesians 3, he will pray "I want you to be filled."

"I want you to *know* God." Not just "know *about* God," but to *know* the Living God: first-hand, intimately, deeper than you know anyone or anything else. "And I want you to know the benefits of knowing God," Paul says. "I want you to know the hope of God's calling, the riches of the glory of God's inheritance, the surpassing greatness of God's power being exercised toward you right now."

Notice how Paul addresses God while in the prison cell: "The God of our Lord Jesus Christ." As I pointed out in a previous chapter, this reflects a huge change in Paul's understanding of God. All his life he had prayed using the title "The God of Abraham, Isaac, and Jacob," or "The God of Israel." He had prayed on the basis of God's revelation to the great patriarchs of the people of God. And what wonderful revelation it was (and is) that God gave (and gives) in the life of Abraham, Isaac, and Jacob. But it is nothing compared with the revelation given in "our Lord Jesus Christ."

In Jesus, God gives us a fuller self-revelation. And Paul has to change the way he addresses God. He prays now to the God we meet in Jesus. He prays now to the God whom Jesus knows; the God whom Jesus loves; the God whom Jesus trusts.

"The Father of glory" is what Paul also calls God. The Father who is all-righteous, and who has manifested His glory in Jesus; the glory that lays itself down for the life of the world.

"I want you to know *this* God," Paul is saying. "And I want you to know the benefits of *knowing* this God."

In order for us to know, two things must happen. And it is for these two things Paul prays: God must open up to us, and God must open us up to what God has opened up. In order to know God more intimately, we need a double work of grace.

This is the case in any relationship. In order for me to know you, you must open up to me. I can make certain deductions about who you are from the way you act, speak, and spend your time and money. But I cannot know the real you unless you open up your heart and mind to me. But then I must open up to what you have opened up. A double opening. In order for us to know God as God truly is, God must open God's self to us, and God must then open our eyes to apprehend what God has opened up.

So Paul prays, may the God of our Lord Jesus Christ "give you a spirit of wisdom and of revelation" (1:17). He is not here asking God to give disciples of Jesus the Holy Spirit. That God does when we believe; as he says just in the text before his prayer, "you were sealed in Him [Christ] with the Holy Spirit of promise" when you believed (1:13). Rather, Paul is praying for a particular work of the Holy Spirit. He is asking the Holy Spirit to give the Ephesians, and us, wisdom and revelation.

Wisdom: skill, concrete know-how to live in this world in relationship with "the God of our Lord Jesus Christ." And revelation: the word Paul uses is "apocalypse." This is one of Paul's favourite words—and one of my favourite words! It is a word that is wrongly used in our time to refer to awful, cataclysmic events—"an earthquake struck Christchurch with apocalyptic vengeance," "huge fires are burning out of control in the central interior of the Province," etc.

In the first century *apocalypsis* simply meant "opening up." It referred to the opening of a door, the opening of a curtain, or the lifting of a cover off a box. People wanted apocalyptic moments! Paul is asking the Holy Spirit to pull back the curtain so we may know more fully the God Jesus knows and is. Yes, dear God, yes! Pull back the curtain—we want to know You as Jesus knows you!

And then Paul asks that the eyes of our hearts be enlightened to know what is being made known. In the Bible, "the heart" is the centre of our personhood. Yes, it is the seat of emotion, the place where we feel. But it is also the seat of intellect, the place where we think. And it is the seat of volition, the place where we make decisions. "Enlighten the eyes of their hearts." "Get hold of the central centre of their very being," Paul is praying, "and help them know You and the great benefits of knowing You."

Everyone who believes the gospel has experienced this double work of grace. Do you believe there is a Creator? Do you believe that somehow this Creator spoke the universe into being? You did not figure that out on your own. Do you believe that the Creator came to earth in and as Jesus of Nazareth? Do you believe that in Jesus' death God has somehow accomplished reconciliation with the world?

Had you and I been there in AD 33, standing beneath the cross as Jesus died, there is no way we would have known that on our own. We would have concluded that here is yet another victim of injustice. We would never, on our own, have concluded that God was saving the world. Do you believe God then raised Jesus from the dead? Do you believe God then exalted Jesus and seated Him on the throne of the universe? You believe because God gave you the spirit of revelation; God gave you an apocalypse. And, you believe because God has opened the eyes of your heart to apprehend the apocalypse. God has, in His mercy, enlightened the control centre!

This is why Paul began his prayer with thanksgiving. I "do not cease giving thanks" (Ephesians 1:16) "having heard of the faith in the Lord Jesus which exists among you" (Ephesians 1:15). The disciples in Ephesus used to put their faith in the gods and goddesses, in the lords and ladies of their culture. They used to put their faith in actions. They used to put their faith in Caesar as Lord. They used to bank it all on Wall Street and Bay Street and the Hong Kong Stock Exchange. But now they were banking it all on Jesus. Paul does not cease giving thanks for the double work of grace that made possible the shift in faith!

Paul wants us to know God, the God who comes to us in Jesus. And he wants us to know the benefits of knowing the God who comes to us in Jesus.

Knowing the Hope of God's Calling

So he goes on: "I pray that the eyes of your heart may be enlightened, so that you will know what is the hope of His calling" (1:18). We cannot live without hope. Paul wants us to know, to live, the hope we have in knowing "the God of our Lord Jesus Christ."

What is this hope? Recapitulation: putting the Head back on. As Paul declares in the opening blessing, "According to His kind intention," as Paul puts it, "He [God] made known to us the mystery of His will" (Ephesians 1:9): God is going to sum up everything in Christ. God is going to put the head back on the human race! The hope of the gospel is that one day God is going to restore all things... in a new heaven and in a new earth with a new humanity.

The hope of the gospel is that before that day, God is taking all that happens to us, and is using it toward the end of our becoming more like Jesus. The hope of the gospel is that what God has begun in Jesus Christ He will complete in the day that Jesus Christ comes again (Philippians 1:6). The hope of the gospel is that Jesus is coming. So Eugene Peterson can say: "If the future is dominated by the coming again of Jesus, there is little room left on the screen for projecting our anxieties and fantasies. It takes the clutter out of our lives."[2]

O God... open our eyes to see Jesus coming! Help us be alive in gospel hope!

Knowing the Riches of God's Glory

Paul goes on: "I pray that the eyes of your heart may be enlightened, so that you will know... what are the riches of the glory of His inheritance in the saints" (Ephesians 1:18). In Christ, God has claimed us for Himself: We are His inheritance. Imagine that! God creates and sustains the universe. He has at His disposal planets and stars and galaxies, but chooses as His prized possession the people He has redeemed in Christ!

And God invests everything He is in His inheritance. That is what Paul wants us to know: God, "the Father of Glory," is investing all His glory to make His inheritance altogether glorious.

"The riches of the glory." The idea is that the riches are

---

[2] Eugene Peterson, "Introduction to 1 & 2 Thessalonians," in *The Message: The New Testament in Contemporary English* (Colorado Springs: NavPress, 1993), 428.

inexhaustible. The Living God is rich beyond our imagining, and is investing it all in His people. He always gives us everything we need to be His people.

This is what Paul himself experienced in prison. He was given all he needed to be the kind of person who reflected the glory of God in a dark place. It is what we are promised—all we need to be the new humans God has claimed us to be in Christ. The Father of glory is making sure His prized possession becomes all He desires us to be.

O God... open our eyes to see how much we mean to you!

Knowing the Greatness of God's Power

And "I pray that the eyes of your heart may be enlightened so that you may know... what is the surpassing greatness of His power toward us who believe" (Ephesians 1:19). Power "toward us" means, "to our advantage." Paul prays that we know the kind of power, the extent of power, God is exercising toward us.

The apostle heaps up "power words" to convey "the surpassing greatness": "... in accordance with the working of the strength of His might" (Ephesians 1:19). Each term he uses can be translated "power": "So that you may know the surpassing greatness of His power... which is according to the power of the power of the power."[3] Paul wants us to know the power that exceeds all bounds; excessive, enormous power exercised toward us who believe.[4]

---

[3] Harold W. Hoehner, *Ephesians: An Exegetical Commentary* (Grand Rapids: Baker Academic, 2002), 269.
[4] Frank Thielman, *Ephesians* [Baker Exegetical Commentary on the New Testament] (Grand Rapids: Baker Academic, 2010), 100.

No one prays like Paul!

"Power." The word is *dunamis*, which comes into English in words like "dynamite" and "dynamism." It refers to the capacity to do whatever needs to be done.

"Working." The word is *energia*, which comes to English as "energy". It refers to the ability to do whatever needs to be done. "It is active energy as opposed to potential energy."[5]

"Strength." The word is *kratos*, which comes into English in words that end with "-cracy." Theocracy, the rule of God; democracy, the rule of the people; autocracy, the rule of self; plutocracy, the rule of the wealthy. It refers to the authority to exercise power, the right to work.

And "might" (*ischus*) refers to "inherent strength," the "inherent ability to overcome resistance."[6]

I pray that the eyes of your heart be enlightened to know the power, working strength, might… toward us who believe. Overcoming obstacles, overcoming resistance, so that we can be all God calls us to be in Christ.

O God, open our eyes to see how much power is at work to our advantage!

To help us begin to comprehend His power, Paul goes on in his prayer to show us how it works.

- It is the power that God exerted in Christ.
- It is the power that raised Christ from the dead.

---

[5] Harold W. Hoehner, *Ephesians: An Exegetical Commentary* (Grand Rapids: Baker Academic, 2002), 269.

[6] Frank Thielman, *Ephesians* [Baker Exegetical Commentary on the New Testament] (Grand Rapids: Baker Academic, 2010), 101.

- It is the power that seated Christ on the throne far above any and all other powers at work in the universe.
- It is the power that put all things in subjection under Christ's feet.
- It is the power that gave Christ as Head of the Church.

Do you see all the resistance God overcame? His power overcomes the resistance of death. His power overcomes the resistance of cosmic forces: no god or goddess, no spirit or demon, can remove Christ from the throne of the universe. And God's power overcomes the resistance of the human heart to the Lordship of Jesus. That any of us today surrenders to Christ as Head is a huge triumph of divine power.

And living in the victory of that power is what the rest of Paul's letter is all about:

- It is the power we need to stand in the conflict with the powers that still try to resist the gospel.
- It is the power we need to stand against evil.
- It is the power we need to be the new humanity in Christ.

"Therefore, I, the prisoner of the Lord, implore you to walk in a manner worthy of the calling to which you have been called" (Ephesians 4:1). How? "with all humility and gentleness"—it takes great power to choose humility and gentleness. And "with patience, showing tolerance for one another in love" (Ephesians 4:2)—it takes great power to be patient; it takes great power to forbear in love—especially in crummy circumstances.

Oh God... open our eyes to know the surpassing greatness of Your power toward us who believe.

I love to hear Paul preach the gospel, but I especially love to hear Paul pray the gospel. Because Paul is an apostle of Jesus, a sent one of Christ, we know that what he preaches pleases the Living God. Because Paul is Jesus' sent one, we know that what he prays pleases the Living God. God delights in gospel-shaped praying. We can pray Paul's prayers with great confidence that they will be heard... and answered!

So, let me paraphrase...

O Living God, God of our Lord Jesus Christ, we want to know You. Grant us a spirit of revelation/apocalypse... and enlighten the control centers of our lives. And in knowing You, we want to know and live the hope of Your calling. We want to know and live the riches of the glory of Your possession of us, and we want to know and live the greatness of the power... of the power... of the power... of Your power toward us. In Jesus' name. Amen.

EPHESIANS 1:20-23

[20] which He brought about in Christ, when He raised Him from the dead and seated Him at His right hand in the heavenly places, [21] far above all rule and authority and power and dominion, and every name that is named, not only in this age but also in the one to come. [22] And He put all things in subjection under His feet, and gave Him as head over all things to the church, [23] which is His body, the fullness of Him who fills all in all.

CHAPTER 5

Look Who is on the Throne Now

EPHESIANS 1:20–23

Paul prays two times in his letter to the believers in Ephesus: in the second half of chapter one, and in the second half of chapter three. As he does so, he prays us into the "alternative reading of reality" shaped by Jesus' life, death, resurrection, ascension, and coming again.

I invite you to focus on just one section of his first prayer, on Ephesians 1:20-22. New Testament scholar Timothy Gombis identifies these verses as "the thesis statement of the letter."[1] I want to focus on Paul's amazing and audacious claim that the crucified and resurrected carpenter now sits on the throne of the universe.

---

[1] Timothy G. Gombis, *The Drama of Ephesians: Participating in the Triumph of God* (Downers Grove: IVP Academic, 2010), 89.

The Structure of Ephesians

But before we do, I want to go back to the observation about the letter as a whole we made in the Introduction to this book. As you read Ephesians, you discover that the letter is written in two halves: chapters one to three and chapters four to six. The turning point is chapter four, verse one: "Therefore I, the prisoner of the Lord, implore you to walk in a manner worthy of the calling with which you have been called." In chapters one to three, Paul preaches and prays God's call upon our lives. Then in chapters four to six, Paul shows us how to live God's calling in this world.

Or, to put it another way: in chapters one to three, Paul gives us the indicative of the gospel—the "is." Then, in chapters four to six, he gives us the imperative of the gospel—the "do." In chapters one to three, Paul develops the expansive scope of the gospel; in chapters four to six, he spells out the behavioural implications of the scope of the gospel, implications for every arena of our lives. Or, to put it more simply: in chapters one to three we have good news; in chapters four to six we have good advice.

This is typical of Paul: good news comes before good advice. In this he is simply following the Lord Jesus. As Jesus does, before Paul gives us any good advice about how to live as disciples of Jesus in this world, he lays out the good news—for the simple reason that the good advice is impossible to live without the good news.

You may have noticed that in this book I have not been telling anyone to do anything, except to listen to the text and trust the Lord of the text. This is very intentional! I am following the Apostle Paul's pattern. Before he gives us any good advice he makes sure we first understand and live in the good news.

Many thoughtful Christian leaders in our day are lamenting the fact that for all the preaching that takes place, North America appears to be drifting further and further away from the gospel. May I be so bold as to suggest why? Most of the preaching in North America is good advice, not good news. Good advice without good news changes no one. Only heavy doses of good news changes us!

Paul will give a lot of good advice in his letter. Beginning with verse one of chapter four—"Therefore I, the prisoner of the Lord"—the Apostle will develop a number of "therefores":

- "Therefore... walk in a manner worthy of the calling with which you have been called." (4:1)
- "[Therefore...] walk no longer just as the Gentiles also walk, in the futility of their mind." (4:17)
- "Therefore, laying aside falsehood, speak truth each one of you with his neighbour,... be angry, and yet do not sin;... do not grieve the Holy Spirit of God." (4:25, 26, 30)
- "Therefore be imitators of God..." (5:1)
- "Therefore... walk as children of Light." (5:8)
- "Therefore, be careful how you walk, not as unwise men but as wise... be filled with the Spirit." (5:15,18)
- "Finally, be strong in the Lord... put on the full armour of God..." (6:10-11)

But before we can do the good advice we have to be gripped by, and changed by, the good news.

And the heart of the good news Paul preaches and prays in the letter to the Ephesians is here:

> I pray that the eyes of your heart may be enlightened, so that you will know... the surpassing greatness of His [God's] power toward us who believe... in accordance with the working of the strength of His might, which He brought about in Christ, when He raised Him from the dead and seated Him at His right hand in the heavenly places, far above all rule and authority and power and dominion, and every name that is named, not only in this age, but also in the one to come. And He put all things in subjection under His [Christ's] feet, and gave Him as head over all things to the church, which is His body, the fullness of Him who fills all things.
>
> Ephesians 1:18-23

All the "therefores" of chapters four to six only make sense in light of this good news. Indeed, the "therefores" of chapter four to six are impossible to live without living in the good news of these verses from chapter one.

The God of Our Lord Jesus Christ

Notice how Paul addresses God in his prayer; Paul prays to "the God of our Lord Jesus Christ" (Ephesians 1:17). Explosive words for a life-long Jew and for a life-long Roman citizen. Had he prayed that way at a civic gathering he would have been in big trouble! "Our Lord Jesus Christ, Messiah."

Here we have to remind ourselves of the historical context. The Roman Empire revolved around the word "Lord." *Kurios* is the actual term: Sovereign one, final authority, last word. The words "Caesar is *Kurios*" were the glue that held the Empire together.

Our Lord Jesus Christ [Messiah]" has huge implications for every arena of life: the political, the economic, the relational, the spiritual, and the sexual. You could get crucified for saying the words, "the crucified Jesus is Lord."

In his first prayer in the letter to the Ephesians, the Apostle of the Lord Jesus prays that we might "know... the God of our Lord Jesus Christ." Paul wants us to know this God who comes to the world in Jesus, the God who comes to the world as Jesus; he prays that we might know the One whom God has installed as Sovereign of the cosmos.

In doing this, God is fulfilling the two Psalms the New Testament quotes the most, Psalm 2 and Psalm 110. In Psalm 2, God says to the nations and their kings who want to run the world their way: "As for Me, I have installed My King upon Zion, My holy mountain" (Psalm 2:6). And in Psalm 110, King David says: "The Lord says to my Lord: 'Sit at My right hand until I make Your enemies a footstool for Your feet'" (Psalm 110:1). The God of Abraham, Isaac and Jacob, the God of Moses and of David, of Isaiah and Jeremiah, has installed Jesus of Nazareth on the throne above all thrones. This is the heart of the gospel. It is the drumbeat of the good news that swept through the Roman Empire.

Interestingly, the English word "church" declares this news. "Church" comes from the Scottish word *kirke*. And *kirke* came from the Greek word *Kuriokos*, meaning "of the *Kurios*," "of the Lord." To be the church in the world is to be the people in the world who belong to, swear allegiance to, and love and obey the Lord of the universe.

So Paul prays that we might know this Lord, and that we might experience the benefits of knowing this Lord. "I pray that the eyes of your heart [the control centre of your very being] may be enlightened, so that you will know the hope of His calling, what are the riches of the glory of His inheritance in the saints, and what is the surpassing greatness of His power toward [being exercised to the advantage of] us who believe" (1:18-19a).

Paul especially wants us to know God's "power toward us who believe," the power we need to actually live the gospel in the world. It's the power that raised Jesus from the dead. It's the power that seated Jesus on the throne. It's the power that places everything under Jesus' feet. It's the power that appoints Jesus, the Head of the cosmos, as the Head of the *Kirke*, the church.

Focus on the phrase "seated Him" in verse 20—"seated Him at His right hand... far above all rule and authority..." This is the "news" undergirding the "advice" to come in the rest of the letter. Timothy Gombis, in his book *The Drama of Ephesians*, puts it this way: "The basic thrust of Paul's story is that God has defeated the fallen powers and authorities in Christ Jesus and has installed Christ Jesus as cosmic ruler over all of reality."[2] Isn't that a magnificent title? Jesus—friend of sinners, healer of broken bodies and minds—has been installed as the "cosmic ruler over all of reality"! It makes me want to dance! Gombis goes on: "God is manifesting His victory by creating the church, in which He is overcoming the effects of evil powers on His world."[3]

Here is the amazing thing: Paul preaches and prays this news about Jesus and His church in circumstances that seem to call the news into question! Paul is in prison, waiting to stand trial before Caesar, who calls himself *"Domine et Deus,"* "Lord and

---

2 Ibid.
3 Ibid.

God." Caesar demands that all citizens of the Empire call him "Lord and God." Caesar decreed that all citizens regularly go to worship—that they go to a temple dedicated to Caesar, take a pinch of incense, throw it on the altar, and say the words, "Caesar is Lord." One could believe just about anything else, as long as one said, "Caesar is Lord."

Disciples of Jesus could not obey the edict. Respect Caesar, yes. Work with Caesar, yes. Pray for Caesar, of course. Even if Caesar treated them badly, they could treat him with dignity. But confess him as Lord? No. For that is not true. Caesar is only Emperor, not Lord. Only Jesus is Lord.

Powers and Dominions

Jesus is exalted "far above all rule and authority and power and dominion, and every name that is named" (1:21). To what is Paul referring?

These terms were used in reference to human beings: human rulers, human authorities, human powers, human dominions. But they were also used in reference to extra-human, supra-human rulers, authorities, powers, and dominions. At the end of his letter Paul uses the terms in this way. He speaks of the nature of our struggle in the world, saying, "our struggle is not against flesh and blood"—humans only—"but against the rulers, against the power, against the world forces of this darkness, against the spiritual forces of wickedness in the heavenly places" (Ephesians 6:12).

French sociologist Jacque Ellul names some of the supra-human forces at work in our world: "Mammon, the prince of this world, the prince of lies, Satan, the devil, and death."[4] Ellul points out that these names are "all characterized by their functions: money, power, deception, accusation, division, and destruction."[5] And we all experience these forces at work in our part of the world.

The person who helps me the most to understand this "alternative reading of reality" is Walter Wink. He is known for his series of books, *Naming the Powers*, *Unmasking the Powers*, and *Engaging the Powers*. While I do not agree with everything he develops, Wink helps me begin to understand how the human and supra-human interact.

Dr. Wink uses the little equation: $P = O + I$.

P = the powers at work in the world
O = the outward human dimensions
I = the inward spiritual dimensions

Here is how he puts it:

$P = O + I$. Remember that simple formula and you can avoid the confusion of centuries about the principalities and powers.... The powers (P) are not spiritual spooks inhabiting the air and leaping on the unwary. That was an earlier way of putting it. Nor are they merely institutions, political or economic systems, ideologies, or social structures. That has been the modern way of coming at it. Neither is adequate, though both contain some

---

[4] Jacques Ellul, *The Subversion of Christianity*, trans., Geoffrey W. Bromiley (Grand Rapids: William B. Eerdmans, 1986), 176.
[5] Ibid.

truth. The powers consist, it turns out, of an outer manifestation (O) and an inner spirituality (I).[6]

Dr. Wink continues:

As the inner aspect of material reality, the spiritual powers are everywhere around us. Their presence is real and inescapable. The issue is not whether we believe in them but whether we can learn to identify our actual, everyday encounters with them—what Paul called 'discerning the spirits'.... The powers, whether benign or satanic, always consist of an outer, visible form (constitutions, judges, armies, leaders, buildings) and an inner, invisible spirit that provides its legitimacy, credibility, and clout.[7]

Makes sense does it not?
Wink then speaks to us in the Western world:

We in the West are so individualistic that we have ceased to regard corporate entities as anything more than the mere aggregates of their parts. But an institution is more than the sum of its visible parts.... Our incapacity to recognize the spirituality of institutions has left us tinkering with their parts while ignoring their essence. I am suggesting, in short, that the spiritual and material aspects of the powers are the inseparable but

---

[6] Walter Wink, "The Powers Behind the Throne: An Election-Year Equation for Discerning the Spirits," *Sojourners* Vol. 13, no. 8 (September 1984), 23.
[7] Ibid., 24.

distinguishable components of a single thing—power in its manifestations in the world. $P = O + I$.[8]

So, take for example something we all know and have to deal with every day: money. "No one can serve two masters," says Jesus, "for either he will hate the one and love the other, or he will be devoted to one and despise the other. You cannot serve God and wealth" (Matthew 6:24). Many of us, of course, think we know better, and are trying to prove Jesus wrong! But that is another story.

Money. Coins—mere metal. Bills—mere paper. Right? Debit cards, credit cards—mere plastic. Right? Banks—buildings, vaults, employees just trying to make a living, advertisements, monetary policies, Boards of Directors. The "O"—the outer, visible manifestations of mammon. And the "I"—the inner, spiritual dynamics at work. A real force, a real power, a god, if you will, who wants to be lord of our lives, seeking to keep us captive. This is why Jesus spoke so much about money: It is not a neutral player in our lives, or in the world. $P = O + I$.

Another example: pornographic magazines and films, seemingly harmless in a free and "enlightened society." "O"—photographers, editors, models... all trying to make a living. Human bodies... elegant, appropriately praised as works of beauty. Corporate investors. "I"—exploiting women and children, engendering lust, giving a false sense of comfort, slowly taking the soul captive.

Gaming. Casinos... you get the point.

"I pray that the eyes of your heart may be enlightened...

---

[8] Ibid.

so that you will know..." that in Jesus Christ, God defeated the powers and is setting the captive free.

The powers that crucified Jesus. Yes, on one level ["O"] it was Caiaphas the High Priest and Pilate the Roman Governor who were responsible for Jesus' death. But on another level ["I"] it was the spirit of religion-gone-off-the-rails, and the spirit of politics-gone-off-the-rails, who were responsible. $P = O + I$. And God won the victory over both the "O" and the "I."

And He won by losing! At the cross, it looked like Jesus lost. But He had not. He was winning. And those who thought they were winning, were losing.

That is the gospel Paul wants us to know. It is not always obvious. It does not always appear to be the case. I know! That is why Paul prays: "God of our Lord Jesus Christ... enlighten the eyes of our hearts." Help us realize and live Your victory over the powers!

Living the Victory

So, what do we do? We co-operate with the victory. How?

Live in the Book that declares the victory. If we only read the newspaper or CNN or Fox on our iPhones, if we only read fashion, decorating, and travel magazines, if we only read technical journals and political essays, we are not going to understand what is going on in our world. Soak in the Book that opens up the mystery of Jesus' Lordship.

And live in community with other believers who are also trying to live in light of the gospel. Sunday morning is not enough! We have to be part of a group of disciples with whom we share the specific nature of our struggle to live in Christ.

We also co-operate with God's victory in Jesus by treating people in light of the victory. We refuse to gossip. We refuse to accuse. We refuse to speak ill of anyone for whom Jesus died. What stifles the gospel is not just the "big sins" like sexual and financial scandals, but gossip and accusation.

And we co-operate with the victory by sharing our money. The pull on us is to keep our money—and to think that our money is ours! It is not. It is the Lord's. The first 10% is unequivocally His. Giving the tithe, the first 10%, breaks the spell wealth weaves in our souls. That is why giving the offering in a worship service is a very powerful moment. It is when we give thanks, yes. But it is also when we once again declare that Jesus, not money, is Lord. In parts of Africa, worshippers dance at offering times, because they are celebrating Jesus' victory over money!

And we follow the lead of Paul and pray. Walter Wink reminds us how disciples of Jesus living in the Roman Empire dealt with injustice and immorality of their day. Unlike us, they had no access to political process, they had no financial resources. Wink says:

> But this seems to have done little to prevent the church from impacting the Roman Empire with devastating force. When the Roman magistrates ordered the early Christians to worship the imperial spirit or *genius,* they refused, kneeling instead and offering prayers on the emperor's behalf to God. This seemingly innocuous act was far more exasperating and revolutionary than outright rebellion would have been. Rebellion simply acknowledges the absolute and ultimate nature of the emperor's power, and attempts to seize it. Prayer denies that ultimacy altogether by acknowledging a higher power. Rebellion focuses solely on

the physical institution or its current incumbents, and attempts to displace them by an act of superior force. Prayer, on the other hand, challenges the very spirituality of the empire itself, and calls the emperor's "angel," as it were, before the judgment seat of God.[9]

Finally, we co-operate with God's victory in Jesus by eating the meal we call the Lord's Supper, a profoundly transformative act. Every time we do it, we again declare that He who was crucified is alive, is coming again, and even now is seated on the throne.

I love to hear Paul preach the gospel. But I especially love to hear him pray the gospel: "Oh God, open the eyes of their hearts that they may know who is on the throne!"

---

[9] Ibid.

EPHESIANS 2:1-3

¹ And you were dead in your trespasses and sins, ² in which you formerly walked according to the course of this world, according to the prince of the power of the air, of the spirit that is now working in the sons of disobedience. ³ Among them we too all formerly lived in the lusts of our flesh, indulging the desires of the flesh and of the mind, and were by nature children of wrath, even as the rest.

CHAPTER 6

Rescued Out of a Deep Pit

EPHESIANS 2:1–3

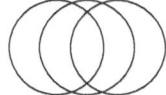

"But God." This little phrase is the gospel in the simplest form. It could be the title for the whole Bible, stamped on the cover. From the beginning of the Great Story, all through the middle, and at the end: "But God."

Especially in the middle of the Great Story! Jesus of Nazareth, Friend of sinners, Healer of broken bodies and minds, is crucified on a Roman cross. "But God," thundered the early preachers of the gospel, "raised Him from the dead" (Acts 13:30).

So too, in the middle of our stories. We were dead in our sins. We had fallen into a very deep pit, from which we could not free ourselves. "But God." That little phrase takes us into the heart of the gospel of Jesus Christ.

We can understand why some translators of the Bible move the good news forward into the text before us, beginning the text with "but God." But, the good news comes at verse 4: "But God, being rich in mercy, because of His great love with which He loved us, even when we were dead in our transgressions, made us alive together with Christ..." (Ephesians 2:4-5). Paul begins with awful news: "And you were dead in your trespasses and sins..." But some translations (like the King James Version or the Revised Standard Version), eager to get to the gospel, have Paul begin: "God made us alive when we were dead."

Amen! This is the good news. But Paul does not announce it until he speaks the bad news. The good news is so good because the bad news is so bad. Yes, the good news is good enough on its own without any reference to the bad news. "But God" made us alive together with Christ. But God raised us up with Christ. But God has seated us with Christ in the heavenly places. Really good news! But all the more so, in the face of the really bad news. So, before he announces the really good, good news, Paul takes us through the really bad, bad news.

So in this chapter, I invite you to focus with me on Ephesians 2:1-3. The words are not politically correct. I am keenly aware of that. I realize that most people in the part of the world from which I am writing would find these verses offensive. But as politically incorrect as they are, they help us make sense of the world today. And these verses make us realize how really, really, good is the really good, good news of Jesus Christ!

Observations about the Text

A couple of observations about the text before we dig in.

In the English translation of Ephesians 2:1-3, we have two sentences: there is a period at the end of verse 2, and a period at the end of verse 3. In the original Greek, however, they are commas. That is because verses 1-3 are part of one sentence that goes through verse 7. Another of Paul's long sentences!

Paul began the letter with a 202-word sentence: "Blessed be the God and Father of our Lord Jesus, who has blessed us with every spiritual blessing in the heavenly places in Christ"... going on to name the blessings. He then shares his prayer for the Ephesians, and for us, in a 167-word sentence: "that the God our Lord Jesus Christ, the Father of glory, may give to you... that the eyes of your heart may be enlightened, so that you will know..." And then in 2:1-7, in a 124-word sentence, Paul announces the good news in the face of bad news. I will say more about the structure of the long sentence in the next chapter.

One other observation before we get to the bad news: In the long sentence Paul uses a cluster of inter-related words, a cluster he uses in just about every letter he writes. The words are: justice, mercy, and grace. And here is how they are inter-related:

Justice is God giving us what we deserve.

Mercy is God not giving us what we deserve.

Grace is God giving us what we do not deserve.

Apart from God's actions in Jesus Christ, we were (or are?) in a pit, a very deep pit—justly so. Humanity made, and continues to make, the decision to go it alone, to live without the Living God, and we end up in a pit. It would be perfectly just of God to leave us in the pit—it is what we deserve.

But God, "being rich in mercy" (2:4)—blessed be His name!—does not want us to stay in the pit. In His mercy God does not want to give us what we deserve. So God rescues us out of the pit.

And then, wanting to "show the surpassing riches of His grace" (2:7), God not only does not give us what we deserve, God gives us what we do not deserve. God makes us alive together with Christ! God raises us up with Him! And God seats us with

Christ in the heavenly places! We will focus on all this in the next chapter.

The Bad News

Now let us make our way through Paul's description of life apart from Jesus' mercy and grace. It is not the whole story, for even in what Paul develops, he would still offer that we are created in the image of God, which has huge implications for human goodness. It's just that something has gone wrong. Terribly wrong.

> And you were dead in your trespasses and sins, in which you formerly walked according to the course of this world, according to the prince of the power of the air, of the spirit that is now working in the sons of disobedience. Among them we too all formerly lived in the lusts of the flesh, indulging the desires of the flesh and of the mind, and were by nature children of wrath, even as the rest.
>
> Ephesians 2:1-3

Sobering.

In 1960, J.B. Phillips of England paraphrased Paul this way:

> [You] were spiritually dead all the time that you drifted along on the stream of this world's ideas of living, and obeyed its unseen ruler (who is still operating in those who do not respond to the truth of God)... We all lived like that in the past, and followed the impulses and imaginations of our evil nature, being in fact under the wrath of God by nature, like everyone else.

In 1993, Eugene Peterson paraphrased Paul in *The Message*:

> It wasn't so long ago that you were mired in that old stagnant life of sin. You let the world, which doesn't know the first thing about living, tell you how to live. You filled your lungs with polluted unbelief, and then exhaled disobedience. We all did it, all of us doing what we felt like doing, when we felt like doing it, all of us in the same boat. It's a wonder God didn't lose his temper and do away with the whole lot of us.

I realize that hardly anyone outside of the church believes Paul. Indeed, even inside the church, very few take Paul seriously. Yet, I hear hints of agreement with Paul when I listen to people struggle with what they want to be, but are unable to be.

Paul is describing the pit from which we cannot free ourselves. Really bad, bad news.

Dead

We were dead. Paul repeats it twice: "you were dead in your trespasses and sins" (Ephesians 2:1), "when we were dead in our transgressions" (Ephesians 2:5).

Sin means to miss the mark. We all have done it, says Paul. Trespassing, transgressing, crossing the line, stepping over clear boundaries. We all have done it, says Paul, and it has resulted in death. O, our physical bodies are alive—for a while. But even they pay the price for sin, and one day they return to dust.

"Dead" is no mere figure of speech. Because of sin we were dead in the only sphere of life that finally matters. We were dead in relationship with the Source of Life; we were dead in relationship with the Living God.

We were "the walking dead" as some refer to our state apart from mercy and grace. We were as interested in the things of God and His kingdom as a corpse is interested in the things above the ground.

And we could not make ourselves alive. Try as we might, nothing gives us the life for which we were originally created. "You were dead." "We were dead." All of us... dead. Doing our jobs, buying and selling, relating to people. But, at the core, dead.

The Course of This World

The pit is deeper still. We were simply going with the flow of the "walking dead." We were walking, says Paul, "according to the course of this world."

The word for world here is *cosmos*. In the New Testament, *cosmos* does not refer to the physical universe. Rather, it refers to the world rejecting the presence and lordship of God. *Cosmos* refers to "human society organizing itself without God."

We used to go with the flow of "human society organizing itself without God," says Paul:

- We took our cues on how to live from it.
- We let our sense of identity and worth be determined by it.
- We let our careers and livelihoods be determined by it.
- We let our understanding of how communities and cities and nations work be shaped by it.
- We let our understanding of sexuality and marriage and family be formed by it.

Our values were set by a God-less way of life, shaped by a God-less vision of reality. As Eugene Peterson paraphrased it: we "let the world, which doesn't know the first thing about living, tell us how to live."

Following Spiritual Powers

The pit is deeper still. We were not only going with the flow of God-less humanity, we were going with the flow of spiritual powers that despise the name of Jesus. Paul refers to "the prince of the power of the air" and to "the spirit that is now working in the sins of disobedience" (2:2), whom Paul later in his letter identifies as the devil, Satan, the archenemy of God. In our sin we were unwittingly cooperating with powers opposed to the Giver of Life.

Again, I know how crazy this sounds to the contemporary world. But according to the authors of scripture, we will never understand life on this planet unless we take this dimension of reality into consideration. Walter Wink exhorts us:

> The spiritual powers are everywhere around us. Their presence is real and inescapable. The issue is not whether we believe in them but whether we can learn to identify our actual, everyday, encounters with them—what Paul called "discerning the spirits."[1]

The bad news Paul is telling us is that we did not recognize the powers, and we inadvertently fell into their web. We

---

1 Ibid., 24.

inadvertently ended up living in ways that were inspired by the spirit that nurtures disobedience to the ways of the Living God.

Do you think that human trafficking is just the work of humans? Do you think the stranglehold pornography has on our culture is just the work of humans? Do you think the grip gangs have on people is just the work of humans? Do you think the power wielded by dictators is just the work of humans? Do you think the chokehold of consumerism is just the work of humans? Do you think conspiracy theories—lies—are just the work of humans? Paul explains that we used to walk according to the "prince of the power of the air," who messes with human sin to bring us down into the pit.

In the early days of the church, people began to sell their property and give the proceeds for the work of the gospel. One couple, Ananias and Sapphira, sold theirs. No one was expected to give all they made on the sale but, for whatever reason, they pretended to give all they made. They lied and they unknowingly co-operated with the prince of lies. The apostle Peter says: "Ananias, why has Satan filled your heart to lie to the Holy Spirit...?" (Acts 5:3)

Judas Iscariot did not like the way Jesus was acting in the face of opposition from the religious establishment. He did not like the way Jesus was being Messiah. He decided to force Jesus' hand to give him up to the powers that be. And Luke in his Gospel says: "Satan entered into Judas... he went away and conferred with the chief priests and captains how he might betray [Jesus]..." (Luke 22:3-4).

You went with the flow of "the prince of the air," says Paul. Every one of us... in one way or another.

"Working in the sons of disobedience," says Paul (2:2). The word "disobedience" is made up of two words: the word "belief" and the letter alpha which serves to negate that to which it is attached. Not believing. Paul is telling us that at the root of disobedience is disbelief; the root of non-obeying is non-believing.

That is the goal of the "prince of the power of the air"—non-believing. Everything he does "in the air," in the atmosphere in which we humans live, is unto the one great end of unbelief. This is what we see going on in the desert at the beginning of Jesus' ministry (Matthew 4:1-11; Luke 4:1-13). The spirit of disobedience was working on Jesus' mind to get Him to disbelieve, and then disobey the Father's plan. It is what he is doing with everyone on this planet. Working to get us to not trust the God and Father of the Lord Jesus Christ. For once we do not trust, we are then prone to not obey. And then we fall deeper into the pit.

Lust of Our Flesh

The pit is deeper still. "We too all formerly lived in the lusts of our flesh." Paul knows no exceptions. "We too all formerly lived in the lusts of our flesh, indulging the desires of the flesh and of the mind" (2:3). I told you the bad news was really bad!

"Flesh" sometimes refers to our physical flesh, like in the expression "flesh and blood." But most of the time in the Bible, "flesh" refers to human nature as it is apart from the Living God.

- Cosmos/world = human society organizing itself without God.
- Flesh = human nature trying to live apart from God.

Flesh is human nature turned away from the Creator and then turned in on itself.

Flesh is humanity with self at the centre. We all know what Paul means: self-oriented, self-driven, self-empowered, self-grounded. This, as Paul told the Galatians, issues in the "deeds of the flesh... immorality, impurity, sensuality, idolatry, sorcery, enmities, strife, jealousy, outbursts of anger, disputes, dissensions, factions, envying, drunkenness, carousing..." (5:19-21). Ghastly. The inherent consequences of the self turned in on the self—and we all have lived in it.

It affects the mind, says Paul. The self turned in on itself is no longer able to reason clearly. Oh, the mind is able to think great thoughts; the mind is able to do art and science and philosophy and medicine. But since the core of the self has turned away from the source of all truth, the mind is unable to see reality as it really is.

"Flesh" is an awful reality. The "flesh" resists God; it finds the things of the kingdom of God odious. The "flesh" fights God; it does everything it can to keep Jesus out of the picture. The "flesh" rejects God; "I will be the captain of my soul," ending up in alienation and loneliness.

Children of Wrath

The pit is deeper still: "[We] were by nature children of wrath," says Paul, "even as the rest" (2:3).

For most people, the word "wrath" conjures up the picture of someone in a fit of rage, out of control. Some people speak of natural disasters as the wrath of God. It is not, even if the insurance companies label it an "act of God"! In many readings of reality such calamities are thought to be the work of angry gods, and people turn to trying to placate the gods so such tragedies do not happen again. Not so in the biblical "reading of reality." Natural disasters say something is "off" in the created order. But they are not the work of an angry God.

Then what does Paul, and other biblical authors, mean by the "wrath of God"? The wrath of God is God's controlled, relentless, righteous reaction to all that is not righteous.

Leon Morris of Australia has, in my opinion, done the best work on understanding God's wrath. In his book *The Apostolic Preaching of the Cross*, Morris writes:

"The wrath of God is often confused with that irrational passion we so frequently find in man and which was commonly ascribed to heathen deities."[2] But, thank God, that is not what the Bible means. The wrath of God, says Morris, "denotes not so much a sudden flaring up of passion which is soon over, as a strong and settled opposition to all that is evil arising out of God's very nature."[3]

And the worst expression of God's opposition to all that is contrary to His very nature is not thunderbolts from heaven, but letting us have our own way. "Handing us over," as Paul writes (in Romans 1:24), to the sin we choose, to the cosmos we prefer, to the powers we are enamoured with, to the flesh we indulge. "You want to keep crossing the boundaries. You want to go with the flesh of God-less-ness. You want to co-operate with the forces that oppose My way. You want to live with 'self' at the center. I grant you your wish." This is the wrath of God.

---

[2] Leon Morris, *The Apostolic Preaching of the Cross* (Grand Rapids: Wm. B. Eerdman Publishing, 1965), 149.
[3] Ibid., 180.

C.S. Lewis said that there are two kinds of people in the world: "those who say to God, 'Thy will be done,' and those to whom God says, in the end, 'Thy will be done'!"[4] "By nature, children of wrath, even as the rest" (2:3). Justice—giving us the natural consequences of our sin.

The Good News

"But God"!

God does not leave us in "Your will be done." His will will be done. His will for His creatures and creation will be done.

In Jesus, God comes all the way down. And in Jesus, God becomes one of us, a full "flesh and blood" human, and enters the pit! Down, down, down, down,... all the way down. He grabs hold of us, and rescues us. This is the essential meaning of the biblical word "salvation." The Living God rescues us out of the pit. Mercy!

And grace. For God then makes us alive with Christ. He raises us up with Christ. And He seats us with Christ in the heavenly places.

Really, really good, good news!

I invite you now to take some time to personally respond to God's word. In the quiet, confess any ways we still live in the pit. Be honest... be brutal. Confess. And then ask for greater freedom from the pit. Name the places of your soul where you want to be freed.

---

4 C.S. Lewis, *The Great Divorce: A Dream* (San Francisco: Harper Collins, 1946), 75.

EPHESIANS 2:4-7

⁴ But God, being rich in mercy, because of His great love with which He loved us, ⁵ even when we were dead in our transgressions, made us alive together with Christ (by grace you have been saved), ⁶ and raised us up with Him, and seated us with Him in the heavenly places in Christ Jesus, ⁷ so that in the ages to come He might show the surpassing riches of His grace in kindness toward us in Christ Jesus.

CHAPTER 7

Look Who Else is on the Throne Now!

EPHESIANS 2:4–7

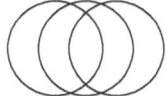

The letters of Paul are not an easy read. This is partly because nearly every word and phrase is jam-packed with rich theology. And it is partly because Paul uses long, complex sentences to express this rich theology!

In this chapter, we are going to focus on Ephesians 2:4-7 and, in particular, on the verbs "made alive," "raised up," and "seated." In most English translations it appears that these verses are a new and separate sentence. But as we saw in the last chapter, in the Greek in which Paul wrote, they are part of one long sentence. Verses 1-7 are a 124-word sentence, one of the many long sentences in the letter to the Ephesians.

Whenever I read Paul, I take time to try to understand how his long sentences go together, how each part relates to the other parts. And the first thing I try to do is get down to the one basic affirmation in each sentence that holds it all together.

Gospel Grammar

The language in which Paul wrote his letter, Koine Greek, works a lot like English. (Of course, it is more historically accurate to say that English works a lot like Koine Greek.) The building blocks of an English sentence are: subject, verb, object. And they are usually found in that order: subject, verb, object. Sometimes the verb precedes the subject: "Down came the rain." But for the most part, it is subject, verb, object: "The Vancouver Canucks win the Stanley Cup." (One has to dream once in a while.)

When I was learning to read Paul in Greek, my mentor at the time was Daniel Fuller, son of Charles E. Fuller of "The Old Fashioned Revival Hour" radio program, and founder of Fuller Theological Seminary. He taught us to do sentence diagramming, and I am so grateful! The discipline has helped me again and again make my way through complex sentences to their basic, fundamental gospel affirmation.

The basic structure of an English, and most Greek sentences is diagrammed like this:

SUBJECT / VERB / OBJECT

Take as an example the sentence "God loves us."

The subject is God. All the great sentences of history have God as the subject! Indeed, we will never finally understand history unless we use sentences with God as the subject. So, too our own lives: all the significant sentences of our lives have God as the subject, "the God and Father of our Lord Jesus Christ," as Paul calls Him. When I pass on to the other side, I want the first and last sentence spoken at my memorial service to begin with

"God…" not "Darrell." A good discipline is to periodically take out a piece of paper and write ten sentences with God as the subject.

"GOD LOVES US."
SUBJECT / VERB / OBJECT
GOD / LOVES / US

"Because of His great love with which He loved us," as Paul puts it (2:4).

Now, to this simple "God loves us" can be added all kinds of elaborations, qualifications, and implications:

- "God… who made heaven and earth… who holds all things together… loves us."
- "God loves us because…" or "God loves us although…"
- "God loves us… who were not even looking for God," or "who did nothing to deserve it."

But it will all still come down to the basic: God / loves / us.

Ephesians 2:1-7 is one long, complex sentence, with many elaborations, yet it comes down to:

SUBJECT / VERB / OBJECT

Actually, there are three verbs:

SUBJECT / THREE VERBS / OBJECT

All three verbs have the same subject and object, and each verb is complemented by the same phrase, "with Christ."

```
                    MADE ALIVE
     GOD    /      RAISED UP     /   US   /   WITH CHRIST
                     SEATED
```

The preposition "with" is actually built into the verbs. Each verb begins with *sun*, meaning "with." Paul takes existing verbs: make alive, raise up, seat, and attaches *sun* to each one. This is typical of Paul! He likes to make up new words to convey the new thing God has done for the world in Jesus.

- To the verb "make alive" he adds *sun*, so that the new verb is literally, "with-made-alive."
- To the verb "raise up" he adds *sun*, so that the new verb is literally "with-raised-up."
- To the verb "seat" he adds *sun*, so that the new verb is literally "with-seated."

And he adds the prepositional phrase "in Christ" to locate the new reality:

- with-made-alive in Christ
- with-raised in Christ
- with-seated in Christ

When we diagram the whole sentence, the gospel leaps off the page!

And when did God do the three verbs? When we "were dead"(2:1). And why did God do the three verbs? "Being rich in mercy" (2:4) and in order to "show the surpassing riches of His grace" (2:7).

Gospel Verbs

So let us now focus on the three verbs: "made alive," "raised up," and "seated." Note that it is not "will make alive," "will raise up," and "will seat." Paul is not here referring to the future. All three verbs are in the past tense: "made alive," "raised up," and "seated." And alive, raised up, seated now. Now!

We have met the second and third of these verbs earlier in Paul's letter, in Paul's first prayer. Paul prays that we might know "the surpassing greatness of His [God's] power... which He brought about in Christ, when He raised Him from the dead and seated Him at His right hand in the heavenly places, far above all rule and authority and power and dominion..." (Ephesians 1:19-21).

Jesus of Nazareth had been crucified. He was lying in a tomb. "But God" raised Him from the dead. And then God seated Him on the throne of the universe.

Do you see what Paul wants us to see? Do you hear the good news Paul wants us to grasp? What the Living God did for and with Jesus of Nazareth, He now does for and with all who believe in and belong to Jesus of Nazareth.

God raised up and seated Jesus on the throne to demonstrate His power. God raised up and seated those who belong to Jesus to demonstrate His grace.

Here, then, is the gospel being proclaimed in the three verbs: when we enter into relationship with Jesus Christ we somehow begin to share in what is true about Jesus Christ right now. Remember, Paul is proclaiming this good news while imprisoned, chained day and night to a Roman soldier! Paul is telling us that no matter what our circumstances, we share in what happened to Jesus Christ. We share in what happened to Jesus Christ because we are now "in" Jesus Christ.

It seems to me, therefore, that in order for us to understand what it all means for us to be made alive, raised up, and seated, we need to understand what it means for Christ to be made alive, raised up, and seated. When we understand more of what happened to Him, we can better understand what has happened to us in Him.

And the simplest way to express it is that Jesus' death, resurrection, and ascension changed the way the universe goes together, altered the basic structure of the universe. Something real, objective, measurable—and revolutionary!—happened when Jesus died, rose from the grave, and ascended to the throne.

As Jesus died, the grasp sin had on the world was broken. "He made Him who knew no sin to be sin on our behalf" (2 Corinthians 5:21). And Jesus took upon Himself all that sin deserved, and thereby broke sin's grip. As Jesus died, the grip death had on the world was broken. Matthew tells us that as Jesus died, "the tombs were opened" (27:52). In the moment Jesus died, death lost its finality and had to release its captives. And, therefore, evil lost its greatest weapon: the fear of death. Evil can no longer frighten people with death because death is no longer what it once was; it no longer has the last word.

When Jesus was raised from the grave, a new reality emerged in the midst of the old. Jesus' resurrection is not just one man returning to life after dying. It is not a returning to life; it is a going through death into a whole new order of life. When Jesus emerged from the grave, it was the emergence of a New Creation, a New Human, the second and last Adam. Easter morning is the first day of a whole new world!

When God the Father seated His Son on the throne, all the powers that think they rule the world were placed under Him, under Jesus. The powers do not like it. They fight it. No matter: the universe goes together in a new way. Jesus of Nazareth is now on the throne above all thrones. And there is no force in all the universe that can remove Him.

And all of this—His death, resurrection, and ascension—removes all the barriers between heaven and earth. At the moment Jesus died, the veil in the temple in Jerusalem was torn in two, signaling that all the walls have come down, and there is now free and full access into the heavenly realm of our existence. This is what Jesus announces in His gospel: "The kingdom of God has come near."

I like how New Testament scholar Andrew Lincoln sums it up for us:

> Christ's death was a death to the old order, to the powers of this age, including sin, and His resurrection was a coming alive to a new order, in which He functioned as Lord with the power of God. Christ's death and resurrection changed the power structures in history.[1]

And here is the gospel in Paul's three verbs: In relationship with the crucified, risen, and ascended Jesus, we enter into the new order resulting from His crucifixion, resurrection, and enthronement. Right now! Even while we still live in these decaying bodies, while still on a profoundly fragile planet, while

---

1 Andrew T. Lincoln, *Ephesians* [Word Biblical Commentary] (Dallas: Word Books, 1990), 108.

sin, evil, and death still hang around. Even now we share in Jesus' new order, in Jesus' victory, in Jesus' dominion, and in the union of heaven and earth.

We know Paul is not saying that in relationship with Jesus we are freed from trouble. For one thing, Paul is chained to a soldier awaiting trial before Caesar, who still thinks he rules the world. For another, in chapter six of his letter, Paul will call us to stand firm against the powers that have not yet surrendered to the new configuration of the universe.

What Paul is saying is that in union with the resurrected, ascended Christ, death is not final and need not be feared; sin is not final, and we therefore need not live in bondage and shame; evil is not final, and we therefore need not play the game on evil's terms; the walls have come down between heaven and earth, and the resources of heaven are available on earth now.

Made Us Alive

"He made us alive with Christ." He enlivened us. Only God can. Dead people—as Paul describes what we were in 2:1-3—cannot enliven themselves. But the God who made Jesus alive can, and does... now. Jesus says in John that whoever "hears My word and believes Him who sent me, has eternal life, and does not come into judgment, but has passed out of death into life" (5:24). Now... before the grave. God has made us alive in the life of Jesus who is alive.

And the "vital signs" are not hard to detect. Those made alive with Christ:

- Those made alive with Christ love Christ and want to love Him more;
- Those made alive with Christ love His word and want to understand and live it more;
- Those made alive with Christ love His friends, the church, with all our warts and blemishes and brokenness;
- Those made alive with Christ love the world for which He died and want neighbours and co-workers to find Him too;
- Those made alive with Christ love His appearing. They long for His return not only because He then heals the broken world, but because they finally see His face.

Raised Us Up

"He has raised us up with Christ."

Not only are we made alive, but we are brought into a qualitatively different life... now. We receive an indestructible life which the grave cannot destroy. Again, Jesus says: "whoever believes... has eternal life." Now. "Eternal life" is not just long life, it is the life God has and is. We have been transferred into the new order of life, even while still in the old. And the old cannot destroy the new.

I have been with a number of Christian people as they were dying. Some were so physically frail, outwardly decaying. But at their core there was this different quality of life which clearly could not be taken away.

Seated Us with Christ

He "seated us with Christ in the heavenly place in Christ." Christ is on the throne. And so are all who belong to Him. Now.

The prophet Daniel saw this centuries ago. In the seventh chapter of his book, he sees the Son of Man—Jesus' favourite self-designation—on the throne (7:13-14). And Daniel sees what he calls "the saints of the Highest One" joining the Son of Man on the throne (7:18). In relationship with the One on the throne, we too are on the throne! Mercy—not given what we deserve. Grace—given what we do not deserve.

What does it all mean? I do not yet fully know. I know of no one who fully understands! I know it means we are to finally live what we were created to live... God's original design that we rule with Him in the world (Genesis 1:26-28).

What is clear is that we need not fear other powers and dominions, which means we need not live by the values and agendas of other powers and dominions. Flex their muscles as they might, strut across the stage of history as they might, they are no match for the true Ruler of the Universe.

And this too is clear. The true Lord is a very different kind of Lord. The true King has a very different understanding of royalty. He is the Servant King, who washes the feet of His subjects! And He invites the world to join Him in the very different way He rules the world!

You see, it is the Jesus we meet in the pages of the four Gospels who is seated in His new humanity on the throne. He did not become a different person when the Father raised Him up and seated Him far above all rule and authority. He is the same Jesus: Friend of sinners and tax collectors, Healer of sick bodies and troubled minds. He is the same Jesus: gentle and compassionate, entering into the world's pain and sorrow, making it His own.

His dominion, which stretches from sea to sea, is all about servant-love. It is about choosing the way of costly servanthood. It is about entering into the brokenness of earth and being a channel of the resources of heaven. It is a very different kind of kingdom led by a very different kind of King.

Ever since that day when God seated Jesus of Nazareth on the throne, it has been servants who have "made the world go around." No society, no nation, no city, no corporation, no church, can make it without the servants. As the world saw big time during the Covid-19 pandemic. This is why the world's leaders were drawn like magnets to Mother Teresa: in her they saw true royalty.

Made alive, raised up, seated, all because of the riches of God's mercy, in order to show the surpassing riches of God's grace.

Made alive, raised up, seated, to live in the riches of God's mercy and in the surpassing riches of God's grace.

Made alive, raised up, seated, to be part of God's program of extending the riches of mercy and the surpassing riches of grace to the world.

Please dear God, help us truly live in the reality of the three verbs: alive, raised up, and seated, with Jesus Christ who is alive, raised up, and seated. Please!

EPHESIANS 2:8-10

⁸ For by grace you have been saved through faith; and that not of yourselves, it is the gift of God; ⁹ not as a result of works, so that no one may boast. ¹⁰ For we are His workmanship, created in Christ Jesus for good works, which God prepared beforehand so that we would walk in them.

CHAPTER 8

Poetry in Motion

EPHESIANS 2:8–10

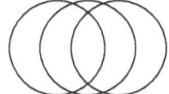

In Ephesians 2:8-10 we have one of the clearest articulations of the gospel of Jesus Christ. After a series of long, complex, exquisitely crafted sentences, the Apostle Paul sums it up in two simple sentences. Many of us committed Paul's articulation of the gospel to memory when we first came to life in Christ:

> For by grace you have been saved through faith; and that not of yourselves, it is the gift of God; not as a result of works, so that no one may boast. For we are His workmanship, created in Christ Jesus for good works, which God prepared beforehand, so that we would walk in them.

It is about as clear and concise as it can be. Yet, for reasons that will become clear, easily forgotten.

Clearly the text is about salvation in Jesus Christ. Verse 8 ("By grace you have been saved through faith") echoes the earlier outburst of the gospel in verse 5 ("By grace you have been saved"). I want to explore this salvation by simply asking a series of questions.

But before I do, let me say a bit more about reading and preaching Paul's letters. No one gets it all on the first reading—or on the second, third, fourth... or tenth reading! Is this not part of the reason why the Holy Spirit saw fit to have God's Word written? There is no way anyone would have listened to Paul speak his articulation of the gospel and get it all right away. People of the first century would get it quicker than we do, for they lived in an oral culture; they were able to listen with much greater comprehension than we can. But even they would not have been able to take in everything Paul was announcing and developing on first hearing. They too needed the words on parchment, so they could go over them again and again.

So if you happen to be finding Ephesians too much to process, it is okay. No one gets it all right away. I want to free you from the sense that one ought to be able to take everything in at once. Take in what you can. Even little bits of the word of God work wonders in the human soul. Besides, the function of the word of God is not just to inform, but to transform. As we soak in the word, written and spoken, something is happening even if we do not get it all.

So, to the series of questions.

Question 1: What does it mean to be saved?

Someone asks you, "Are you saved?" what do they mean? When we say, "I have been saved," what do we mean? What does it mean to be saved?

- It means to be forgiven of all our sins.
- It means to be cleansed of our sins.
- It means to be justified before the Judge of the universe.
- It means to be reconciled to the Creator.
- It means to be adopted into the family of God; into the Family that is God; into the Friendship of God as Father, Son and Holy Spirit!

We could go on and on... and we would finally come to what Paul is announcing in the text before us: to be saved is to become a new creation!

Where does Paul say that in the text? In verse 10: "For we are His workmanship, created in Christ Jesus..." The actual word Paul uses for "workmanship" is *poiema*, from which we get our English word poem. Not that the word was used only for poems; it meant handiwork of all kinds—with the particular nuance of rhythm, orderliness, and beauty.[1] Poems were one expression of this, but paintings too, and gourmet meals, and buildings, and administrative systems. "For we," we who were once dead in sin, sold out to ways of life that brought disorder and bondage, "we are His *poiema*, His handiwork, created in Christ Jesus." That is what it means to be saved.

The word *poiema* is used only two times in the New Testament, both by Paul. The first use is in his letter to the Romans, referring to God's first work of creation, Romans 1:20, "For since the creation of the world His invisible attributes, His eternal

---

[1] G. Campbell-Morgan, "His Workmanship," a sermon on Ephesians 2:10. From http://www.gcampbellmorgan.com/sermons/199.html {accessed 23 July 2013}.

power and divine nature, have been clearly seen, being understood through what has been made..." The phrase "what has been made" is a translation of the word *poiema*.

In the beginning God wrote a poem, through which He made Himself known. God made the world and we who dwell in it. The world and we were His first work expressing rhythm, orderliness, and beauty. God's first poem got ruined, a fact with which everyone on this planet is painfully aware.

So God wrote a new poem and made a new creation. God made us... people alive in Jesus Christ. We are His new work, expressing rhythm, orderliness, and beauty. So Paul can say to the church at Corinth: "If anyone is in Christ, he is a new creature; the old things passed away; behold, new things have come" (2 Corinthians 5:17). That is what it means to be saved!

Paul will develop this further in the fourth chapter of his letter as the basis for Christian ethics. He will appeal to us: "lay aside the old self, which is being corrupted in accordance with the lusts of deceit... and put on the new self, which in the likeness of God has been created in righteousness and holiness of the truth" (Ephesians 4:22-24). To be saved is to become a new creation.

We have been saved *from*:
- the stronghold of sin,
- the finality of death,
- bondage to the powers of evil,
- the wrath of God.

And we have been saved *for*:
- being alive with Christ,
- being raised up with Christ,

- being seated with Christ,
- living as new creations!

That is what it means to be saved. We are God's handiwork, created in Christ Jesus.

Question 2: Who does the saving?

Who makes this all happen? Who does the saving in the world and in the church?

Why we do, of course. Right?

We make ourselves into new creations. Right?

We make ourselves into rhythmic, orderly, beautiful poems and works of art. Right?

We free ourselves from the stronghold of sin; we break the hold a rebel world has on us; we overcome the power of death; we avert the wrath of God. Right?

We make ourselves alive with Christ; we raise ourselves up with Christ; we seat ourselves with Christ in the heavenly places. Right?

NO!

But we act as though we do. What else accounts for all the striving and agonizing?

We do not make it happen.

Ah, but pastors do, right? They make it happen. They pull us out of the pit. Right? The pastor makes us alive, raises us up, seats us. As a kind of junior-advisor, the pastor creates the new creation. Right?

NO!

Who does the saving around here? The Living God, the God

and Father of our Lord Jesus Christ, as Paul delights to call Him. If we are really going to be saved we have to get this clear. No one can write the poem of the new creation but the Re-Creator. "His" workmanship, says Paul. God's, not "ours." Only one Person does the saving: the God who comes to us in and as Jesus Christ.

Question 3: Why does he do it?

Why does God do it? Why does He save us?
    Because we deserve it. Right?
    Because we have done so much good. Right?
    Because we are, after all, inherently good people. Right?
    NO!
God does it because of His grace. "You are saved by grace." Paul says it twice, and he needs to say it a hundred times! God saves us by unmerited favour, undeserved kindness, unearned blessing: Grace.

This is both good news and offensive news, which is why it takes so long for us to really get it. Jacques Ellul says, "Grace is odious."[2] We want to be able to say we made it on our own. Grace humbles us. It then lifts us, but first it humbles us. We cannot make it on our own.

Jesus tells a parable about two men who went to the temple: one a Pharisee, the other a tax-collector. One thought himself quite the godly man, the other knew himself to be broken and helpless. The Pharisee stood off by himself, our usual posture when we do not know grace. "God," says the Pharisee, "I thank

---

[2] Jacques Ellul, *The Subversion of Christianity*, trans., Geoffrey W. Bromiley (Grand Rapids: William B. Eerdmans, 1986), 159.

You that I am not like other people: swindlers, unjust, adulterers, or even like this tax-collector. I fast twice a week; I pay tithes of all that I get" (Luke 18:11-12). These are not bad things to do! But they do not earn God's favour. The tax-collector, says Jesus, was "standing some distance away." He could not even lift up his eyes to heaven, says Jesus, "but was beating his breast, saying, 'God be merciful to me, the sinner'" (Luke 18:13). Who goes away a new creation? The tax-collector... because of grace.

I have a friend who is processing having done something very hurtful. The person keeps going around and around the deed. The person keeps saying, "But I am basically a good person. You believe that of me, don't you Darrell?" During the most recent session I simply said, "Don't go there. Whether or not you are a good person is not helpful right now. Accept the grace of God. Only grace sets you free."

Church historian Richard Lovelace says that too few of us believers know how to take our stand on the gospel of grace:

> [Many professing Christians are] drawing their assurance of acceptance with God from their sincerity, their past experience of conversion, their recent religious performance or the relative infrequency of their conscious, willful disobedience. Few know enough to start each day with a thoroughgoing stand upon Luther's platform: you are accepted, looking outward in faith and claiming the wholly alien righteousness of Christ as the only ground for acceptance.[3]

---

[3] Richard F. Lovelace, *Dynamics of Spiritual Life: An Evangelical Theology of Renewal* (Downers Grove: Inter-Varsity Press, 1979), 101.

"Saved by grace," says Paul. "That no one should boast," says Paul. It all comes down to grace.

> Amazing grace, how sweet the sound;
> That saved a wretch like me.
> I once was lost, but now I'm found;
> Was blind, but now I see.[4]

Was dead but now I live! God saves us by grace.

Question 4: So, what is our role in this salvation?

So, what do we do? What is our role in this salvation?

Faith, says Paul. We are "saved by grace through faith." Our role is to believe, to trust, to bank it all on God's grace. That is all it can be. When we are given a gift, all we can do is accept it. It is the only way to honor the giver.

And what is faith? I used to say, "Faith is reaching out and taking the gift." But the verb "reaching out" comes too close to "works." We are not saved by works, says Paul, and "reaching out" can too easily become a "work." So I started saying, "Faith is throwing oneself on God and His grace." But the verb "throwing" also comes too close to "work." So now I say, "Faith is falling into grace. Faith is giving in to the new reality shaped by grace, and simply falling into the new reality."

You see, the good news is not that the Saviour came to the side of the pit into which we had fallen, and extended His hand, calling us to take hold. The good news is that the Saviour dove

---

[4] "Amazing Grace," words by John Newton, first published in 1779.

into the pit, all the way down to the bottom. And at the bottom, He calls us to fall into His arms! Faith is collapsing into grace; after all the striving and agonizing, faith is simply stopping and collapsing into the new creation.

"Saved by grace through faith." Christ alone. Grace alone. Faith alone.

"And that not of yourselves, it is the gift of God" (Ephesians 2:8). To what is the "that" referring? What is not of yourselves? What is the gift of God? Salvation? Grace? Faith? It could be that Paul is referring to each, or to all. Many take it to refer to faith, maintaining that even faith is God's gift; that anyone believes at all is a gift. That is theologically true. But it does not seem to be what Paul is emphasizing in Ephesians. The word "that" is neuter. The word "faith" is feminine. So is the word "grace." So it is most likely that "that" refers to the whole package: "saved by grace through faith." "Saved by grace through faith"—that is the gift of God.

Question 5: Where is (faith in) grace taking us?

We just sit around and wait for Jesus to come. Right?

We just wait for Him to bring in the new heavens and the new earth. And when He brings in the new heaven and the new earth, we just sit around on clouds singing songs of praise. Right?

NO!

Grace picks us up and puts us to work. We begin to walk in good works, says Paul. We are not saved by good works, but we are saved for good works. "We are His workmanship, created in Christ Jesus for good works, which God prepared beforehand so that we would walk in them" (Ephesians 2:10).

You see, salvation is not just a new state of being, a new status. Salvation is a vocation not a vacation. To be saved by grace through faith is to be given a new, glorious vocation. New creations walk in good works God has designed for them.

We "walk." We used to walk in the death of our sins, and according to human society organizing itself without God, and according to the prince of the power of the air, and according to the lusts of our flesh. Awful! Now we walk a new walk. This is the major verb used to describe the Christian life in the rest of the letter to the Ephesians:

- "Walk in a manner worthy of the calling with which you have been called" (4:1).
- "Walk no longer just as the Gentiles also walk, in the futility of their mind" (4:17).
- "Walk in love" (5:2).
- "Walk as children of Light" (5:8).
- "Walk... filled with the Spirit" (5:15,18).

And here in the text before, "walk in good works" which God has prepared for us.

To what is Paul referring to? He is referring to a wide range of good works in which all new creations are created to walk in.

- As a lifelong Jew, he would certainly have in mind the Ten Commandments. We are not saved by keeping the commandments, but we are saved to walk in them.
- As a lover of Jesus, Paul would certainly have in mind Jesus' Sermon on the Mount. We are not saved by living the new, radical kingdom commands Jesus speaks:

"Love your enemies, pray for those who persecute you; do unto others what you want them to do to you." We are not saved by doing those good works, for no one can do them perfectly, but we are saved to walk in them.
- As a disciple of Jesus, as a witness to the works of the Spirit in the early church, Paul would also be thinking of Jesus' works of healing and deliverance that the Spirit continues to perform in the world. We are created in Christ Jesus to do the works of Christ Jesus!

This is how Paul puts it in a letter to his friend and colleague Titus. "Our great God and Saviour, Christ Jesus... gave Himself for us to redeem us from every lawless deed and to purify for Himself a people for His own possession, zealous for good deeds" (Titus 2:13-14).

I think Paul also has in mind God's unique and specific call upon each new creation.

Of all the possible good works in which all disciples walk, He calls us to particular ones for which He uniquely equips us. No one disciple can be engaged in all the good works of God's people. Each of us is wired for a few good works.

We are not to expect everyone to be doing the same work. We are to encourage one another to do one or two or three of the works of the kingdom of God.

We see this being worked out in the early church. A dispute arose about the feeding of widows; a very good work in which the church was walking. Things were getting out of hand, taking up a lot of the apostles' time and energy. They say to the church, "it is not desirable for us to neglect the word of God in order to serve tables" (Acts 6:2). They were not saying it was not good to wait on tables, not at all. No one worthy of the name of Jesus would ever say or feel that. They were saying that they could not do the good work of waiting on tables AND do the good work of teaching and preaching the word. Just as those waiting on tables could not do the good work of the word AND do the good work of table service well. We are each called to do the good work uniquely prepared for us. And we are to encourage and free others to do the good work uniquely prepared for them.

I bless you who are called to the good work of administration. I bless you who are called to the good work of nursing. I stand in awe of those of you called to the good work of caring for children, and those of you called to the good work of engineering, and the good work of counselling, and the good work of serving in government..

We are not saved by doing the good works. But we are saved for walking in the good works of the kingdom of God.

And do you know what the reward is for walking in the good work? A surprising reward: the joy of being given more of the good work to do!

I like how Dallas Willard developed this in his *The Divine Conspiracy*. Speaking of the coming new heavens and new earth, he writes:

> We will not sit around looking at one another or at God for eternity but will join the eternal Logos, "reign with him," in the endlessly ongoing creative work of God. It is for this that we were each individually intended, as both kings and priests (Exodus 19:6; Rev. 5:10).... A place in God's creative order has been reserved for each one of us from before the beginnings of cosmic existence. His plan is for us to develop, as apprentices to

Jesus, to the point where we can take our place in the ongoing creativity of the universe. [5]

Isn't that cool? Willard continues:

In due time... we will begin to assume new responsibilities. "Well done, good and faithful servant," our magnificent Master will say, "you have been faithful in the smallest things, take charge of ten cities," "five cities," "many things," or whatever is appropriate (Luke 19:17; Matt. 25:21). I suspect that there will be many surprises when the new creative responsibilities are assigned. Perhaps it would be a good exercise for each of us to ask ourselves: Really, how many cities could I now govern under God? If, for example, Baltimore or Liverpool were turned over to me, with power to do what I want with it, how would things turn out? [6]

New creations... created to do good works to do.

No, I did not quote Paul accurately. Paul does not say, "good works that we would do them." He says, "good works that we walk in them." A big difference. For the good works are not our good works! They are God's good works, works God is doing. And we are invited to join Him in His good works. It is not that we are working FOR God in the world; we are working WITH God in the world.

---

[5] Dallas Willard, *The Divine Conspiracy: Rediscovering our Hidden Life in God* (New York: HarperCollins, 1998), 378.
[6] Ibid., 398.

Question 6: How do we live saved?

How do we live as God's workmanship in the world?

By pulling up our boot-straps and exerting all the human energy we can muster. Right?

We do it by working harder. Right?

NOT!

We are beginning to understand that we do not save ourselves, that we do not make ourselves new creations. But we still think that we live the saved life by our own effort. Right?

Here is the good news. We do not live the new creation ourselves. "In Christ Jesus," says Paul. Created *in* Christ Jesus. As we have already noted, he uses the little preposition "in" 36 times in his letter. In intimate relationship with a Person.

"Abide in Me, and I in you," Jesus says. We need to hear it again and again. So clear, yet so easily forgotten. "Abide in Me, and I in you... for apart from Me you can do nothing" (John 15:4-5).

- Apart from Christ we cannot save ourselves.
- Apart from Christ we cannot live the life for which He saves us.
- Apart from Christ we cannot become new creations.
- Apart from Christ we cannot live as new creations.

It is as we live in Him that He equips us for walking in His good works. He goes before us, preparing the good work in which He calls us to walk. He fills us with the Holy Spirit, the doer of good works. We are created for good works and good works are created for us. Not to work them, but to walk in them...

by walking in the Saviour.

This explains the rhythm, orderliness, and beauty of the letter to the Ephesians. Paul is in prison, in Rome, chained to a soldier. But he is also, and primarily, in Christ. You know he wanted to be "out there," proclaiming the gospel in the cities of Ephesus. But instead he is locked up in a room somewhere in downtown Rome. Yet, "in Christ" he was still able to walk in the good work which had been prepared for him. Indeed, it turns out that locked up in a room, he fulfilled his call to proclaim the gospel in ways he could never have imagined!

It is in relationship with the Master Poet that the poems begin to emerge. When we live in the Master Poet, wherever else we live, we begin to walk like Him, like "poetry in motion."

I conclude with the prayer by D.T. Nils of Sri Lanka, which I have written on the first page of my journal.

> Jesus, Master Carpenter of Nazareth, who on the Cross through wood and nails has wrought man's full salvation, wield well Thy tools on us, that we who come to Thee rough-hewn may by Thy Hand be fashioned to a truer beauty; for Thy Name's sake. Amen.[7]

---

[7] D.T. Niles, *Living with the Gospel* (London: Lutterworth Press, 1957), 8.

EPHESIANS 2:11-22

[11] Therefore remember that formerly you, the Gentiles in the flesh, who are called "Uncircumcision" by the so-called "Circumcision," which is performed in the flesh by human hands— [12] remember that you were at that time separate from Christ, excluded from the commonwealth of Israel, and strangers to the covenants of promise, having no hope and without God in the world. [13] But now in Christ Jesus you who formerly were far off have been brought near by the blood of Christ. [14] For He Himself is our peace, who made both groups into one and broke down the barrier of the dividing wall, [15] by abolishing in His flesh the enmity, which is the Law of commandments contained in ordinances, so that in Himself He might make the two into one new man, thus establishing peace, [16] and might reconcile them both in one body to God through the cross, by it having put to death the enmity. [17] And He came and preached peace to you who were far away, and peace to those who were near; [18] for through Him we both have our access in one Spirit to the Father. [19] So then you are no longer strangers and aliens, but you are fellow citizens with the saints, and are of God's household, [20] having been built on the foundation of the apostles and prophets, Christ Jesus Himself being the corner stone, [21] in whom the whole building, being fitted together, is growing into a holy temple in the Lord, [22] in whom you also are being built together into a dwelling of God in the Spirit.

CHAPTER 9

Look What is Being Built in the City

EPHESIANS 2:11–22

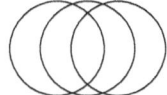

It is happening all over the city in which I live, nearly everywhere I turn: building, building, building. In the downtown core there is constant daily activity. Dump trucks, construction cranes, jackhammers, electric saws, pneumatic nail guns. And also in residential neighbourhoods like the one Sharon and I lived in for eleven years. Old houses being demolished, replaced by newer, bigger homes. So-called Lane-way houses are under construction in nearly every alley. All over the city: building, building, building.

This is nothing, of course, compared to what is happening in the great cities of Latin America and Asia. For miles and miles in every direction... building, building, building. Now that I have been to New York City, one of my heart's desires is to go to Shanghai! New York may still be the media and advertising centre of the world, but everyone knows that the financial centre has shifted to Shanghai. Building, building, building.

And in the midst of it all, in every city of the world, another kind of building is taking place. Through Ephesians 2:11-22, Paul helps us realize that in the midst of all the building going on in the world, the Living God is actively building something else. In every village, in every town, in every city of the world, the Living God is, through Jesus Christ, building a new human race who constitute a new commonwealth, who together are given access into the Presence of God, and who (amazingly!) constitute a new dwelling place for God in the world.

The Flow of Ephesians

When focusing on one section of any of Paul's letters, it is good to see and hear it in the larger context. Let us step back for a moment and recall the flow of Paul's letter to the Ephesians.

Chapter two of this letter flows out of Paul's prayer recorded in chapter one. In that prayer, Paul asks "the God of our Lord Jesus Christ, the Father of glory" (1:17) to enlighten the eyes of our hearts "so that you might know what is the hope of His calling, what are the riches of the glory of His inheritance in the saints, and what is the surpassing greatness of His power toward us who believe" (1:18-19). Paul then heaps up all kinds of "power words" to describe the power God is exercising toward us: "These are in accordance with the working of the strength of His might" (1:19)—a LOT of power! This power, says Paul, was first exercised in Jesus Christ when God raised Him from the dead and seated Him at His right hand in the heavenly places far above all rule and authority and dominion (1:20-21)! This power, says Paul, was then exercised, and is now being exercised, by taking us who were dead in sin and captive to powers of evil and slaves to our own lust, and making us alive with Christ, raising us up with Christ, and seating us with Christ in the heavenly places in Christ (2:1-7). This power, says Paul, was exercised, and is now being exercised, by making us into new creations in Christ who are called to participate in God's good works in the world.

God's Building Project

And then in the text before us, Paul is telling us that this power is at work building a new human race who constitute a new commonwealth, who together are given access into the Presence of God, and who (amazingly!) constitute the new temple where the Creator of all things fulfills His desire to come and live in the world.

Paul is in jail, awaiting trial before Caesar, the most powerful human being alive at that time. And yet, in jail he can see that all around him God is building something no one else can build.

This "alternative reading of reality" that Paul sees is nothing short of revolutionary, especially coming as it does from a life-long Jew. There simply is no way for us Gentiles to feel how revolutionary a vision it is.

It is this vision of God building something new in the world that got Paul into jail! Paul is not locked up in Rome because he offended Rome; he is in jail because he had offended his fellow Jews who then wanted to kill him. Paul is in jail in Rome because as a Roman citizen he had appealed to Caesar to protect him against the desire of some of his fellow Jews to have him wiped off the face of the earth. In the next chapter of his letter, Paul will speak of himself as "the prisoner of Christ Jesus for the sake of you Gentiles" (3:1). He is in trouble because he preached what he called "the mystery of Christ" (3:4), the mystery of Messiah, that "Gentiles are fellow heirs and fellow members of the body, and fellow partakers in Christ [Messiah] Jesus through the gospel" (3:6).

The vision of this new human race constituting a new dwelling place of God in this world is also what got Stephen, one of the first deacons of the church, in trouble. Standing before the great Sanhedrin, the ruling council in Jerusalem, meeting in the great temple, Stephen dared to say "the Most High does not dwell in houses made by human hands" (Acts 7:48). The leaders gnashed their teeth, driving him out of the temple to the edge of the city, pelting him to death with rocks. Standing by approving of the action was Saul, who would become Paul, and who would expand Stephen's vision, and end up in jail for proclaiming and acting on it.

I hear Paul saying through the text: "Look! Look at what is being built in the city!" A new human race constituting a new commonwealth who, together as Jews and Gentiles, have access into the Holy Presence of the Holy God and who constitute a new temple, a new dwelling place of God in the Spirit.

As you can see and hear in the text, Paul is working with many different metaphors. Underneath them all is the architectural metaphor of "temple."

Temples and the Temple

People living in the Roman Empire of the first century knew all about temples! Everywhere you traveled you found temples. Ephesus was especially proud of its temples. The biggest one was built for the goddess Artemis, as the Greeks called her, or

Diana, as the Romans called her. At the time Paul wrote his letter to the Ephesians, the temple of Diana was one of the Seven Wonders of the World. It was built on a platform measuring more than 100,000 square feet, twice the size of a football field! Built with 100 stone columns, all made of marble, each 55 feet high, Ephesus was also one of the centres for the worship of the goddess Roma, and one of the centres for the emperor cult. Rome honoured Ephesus for its loyalty to the Empire by granting the city permission to build a temple to the emperors. The Ephesians knew all about temples! Life revolved around temples.

What Paul expressly has in mind in Ephesians 2:11-22 is the temple of Jerusalem, built by Herod the Great. It too was one of the great wonders of the world. It no longer stands, as it was destroyed by Rome in 70 AD, in the most devastating event in the history of Judaism.

There simply is no way to exaggerate the role the Jerusalem temple played in the life of first century Jews. It was thought to be the place where the Living God dwelled. Everything else in Jewish life revolved around the temple. It was for many, literally, the centre of the cosmos. This is why Jesus' actions in the temple, especially on Palm Sunday, were so problematic. Jesus was messing with the cosmic center of the universe!

The temple was made up of four courts. From the outside moving inward they are:

- the court of the Gentiles
- the court of the women
- the court of the priests and
- the Holy Place or the Holy of Holies.

The Court of the Gentiles was so named because that was as far in as the Gentiles could go and, even then, they would face much disdain from hyper-strict Jews. Gentiles were, as Paul says in the text "far off" (2:13), "far away" (2:17) from the presence of God. This is the court where Jesus cracks the whip, driving out the money-changers and sellers of sacrificial animals, crying out, "My house shall be called a house of prayer for all the nations" (Mark 11:17; quoting Isaiah 56:7).

The court of the women was so-named because that was as far in as Jewish women could go. And even then, they too faced much disdain from the hyper-religious.

The court of the priests was so named because that was where the priests offered up the daily sacrifices and prayers.

And the Holy Place or the Holy of Holies was so-named because it was thought that it was there the Holy God chose to dwell in all His Holiness. Only one person, the High Priest, was allowed to enter that space; and only once a year on Yom Kippur, the Day of Atonement. He could enter only after a long, elaborate process of purification, and even then a rope would be tied around his waist so that should he displease the Holy God and die, his body could be retrieved.

You can see, then, that the temple was thought to be the centre of the cosmos. And you can see, then, why what the Apostle Paul declares as "the mystery of Messiah" is so revolutionary and why it got him in such trouble.

Paul, the life-long Jew, is declaring that Jesus the Messiah has changed everything through two primary actions: By His blood, Jesus "broke down the barrier of the dividing wall" (v. 14), and in His flesh, He "abolished the enmity" (v. 15).

Broken the Barrier

Jesus has "broken down the barrier of the dividing wall," or "the middle wall" or "partition," as some translate it (v.14). To what is Paul referring?

Here we need to know more about the Jewish temple. Gentiles, standing in the outer court—"far off" or "far away"—could look up at the real temple, the real dwelling place of God, but could not "draw near." That is putting it mildly! The Jewish historian Josephus tells us that the Jewish part of the temple was "encompassed by a stone wall for a partition with an inscription, which forbade any foreigner to go in under penalty of death."[1] The wall was three cubits, four and a half feet, high. On the wall were the words "law of purity," and in Greek and Latin the words "no foreigners." In 1871, archaeologists found the exact wording. It goes like this: "No foreigner may enter within the barrier and enclosure round the temple. Anyone who is caught doing so will have himself to blame for his ensuing death."[2] As John Stott points out, the sign did not say, "'Trespassers will be prosecuted' but 'Trespassers will be executed'"![3]

Jesus broke this wall of partition down! Can you hear the gasping in Paul's voice? Stunning. Revolution of revolutions! The Jewish Messiah broke down the dividing wall! Not a Gentile invader but the Jewish Messiah broke down the wall of partition.

This is what we see Jesus doing from day one of His ministry.

---

[1] "The Antiquities of the Jews" in *The Works of Josephus,* trans. William Whiston (Lynn, MA: Hendrickson Publishers, 1980), Book XV, chapter xi, section 5.
[2] John R.W. Stott, *God's New Society: The Message of Ephesians* [The Bible Speaks Today] (Downers Grove: InterVarsity Press, 1979), 92.
[3] Ibid.

He breaks down all kinds of walls to offer a drink to a Samaritan woman. He breaks down all kinds of walls to go to the house of a Roman office whose child is sick. He breaks down all kinds of walls to touch those with leprosy and other kinds of "uncleanness." Jesus is always jumping over and breaking down walls to seek and save sinners… to "draw near" those who are "far off." The actual dividing wall would stand until 70 AD. But it was broken down in 33 AD by Jesus on the cross. No more wall!

Abolished the Enmity

And, says Paul, Jesus abolished in His flesh the enmity. Or, as some translate it, "He put to death the enmity." To what is Paul referring? "The Law of commandments contained in ordinances" (v. 15). The enmity that kept people apart was the Law.

Now, here is where we have to be careful. To what law is Paul referring? Jesus has abolished in His flesh the enmity which was the law. What law has been abolished? The so-called moral law as chiefly embodied in the Ten Commandments? Or the so-called ceremonial law, prescribing and describing all the sacrificial and purity ordinances? Which law has Jesus put to death?

Paul cannot be referring to the moral law. He knows what Jesus taught, especially in His Sermon on the Mount: "Do not think that I came to abolish the Law or the Prophets; I did not come to abolish but to fulfill" (Matthew 5:17). In jumping over all kinds of walls to seek and save us, Jesus did not put the moral law to death. In the rest of His Sermon on the Mount, Jesus draws out the inherent goodness of the law, and expands it, deepens it, calls us to the fundamental reasons it was first spoken. The moral law is not the enmity.

Yes, when we encounter the law, we realize how far short we fell from God's good will; and we realize we are to keep God's good will. But in order to seek and save us, in order to draw us near, Jesus did not have to abolish the moral law. He takes away the curse for our disobedience (Galatians 3:10,13). He cancels the debt of our disobedience (Colossians 2:13-14). He breathes His Holy Spirit into us, enabling us to live in sync with God's good will (Romans 8:1-11). But He does not abolish the moral law.

He abolishes the ceremonial law, all the supposed ways humans were to cleanse themselves so they could approach the Holy God. Jesus puts it all to death for it is no longer needed. Jesus has fulfilled it through His death on the cross. He is the final sacrifice that makes all other sacrifices unnecessary. By offering up His life on the cross, there is no longer any need for the sacrificial system. No more blood needs to be shed. His blood is enough. By His blood we are made clean.

> What can wash away my sin?
> Nothing but the blood of Jesus.
> What can make me whole again?
> Nothing but the blood of Jesus.[4]

And as a consequence of Jesus' work—broke down and abolished—God is building something new in the city. God is building a new human race who constitute a new commonwealth who together have direct access into the Holy of Holies and who (amazingly!) constitute the New Temple of the Living God in the world.

---

4 "Nothing But the Blood," written by Robert Lowry.

A New Human Race

"For He Himself is our peace, who made both groups into one" (v. 14). Do you hear the gasping in his voice? "That in Himself He might create the two into one new man" (v. 15). Hear the gasp again? Hear the thrill in his voice? Both… into one. The two… into one new human. Remember that it is a lifelong Jew who is saying this. "Circumcised the eighth day, of the nation of Israel, of the tribe of Benjamin, a Hebrew of Hebrews," as he tells the Philippians (3:5). Yet he sees that because of the Messiah's work on the cross, Jews and Gentiles are brought together as a new human race. Jesus is the new human and in Him we become the new human race, incorporating both Jews and Gentiles, and transcending both Jews and Gentiles. A third race, as some call it.

So Paul can tell the believers in Colossae, not far from Ephesus, "Put on the new self who is being renewed to a true knowledge according to the image of the One who created it—a renewal in which there is no distinction between Greek and Jew, circumcised and uncircumcised, barbarian, Scythian, slave and free, but Christ [Messiah] is all, and in all" (3:10-11). And he can tell the believers in Galatia, "there is neither Jew nor Greek, there is neither slave nor free, there is neither male nor female; for you are all one in Christ Jesus" (3:28).

God is building a new human race who constitute a new commonwealth among the nations. Apart from the Jewish Messiah, Gentiles were "excluded from citizenship in Israel" (v. 12). Citizenship, often translated as "commonwealth," is *politeia*, from which we get the English words "polity," "politics," and "political." It refers to a whole way of life shaped by common vision and values. In the case of the Jews, it was a *politeia* shaped by the great covenants God made with the patriarchs: the covenant with Noah, the covenant with Abraham, the covenant with Daniel, and the promised New Covenant. To which, says Paul, Gentiles were strangers. But now, in Messiah, they are no longer strangers and aliens, but "fellow citizens with the saints." The phrase "fellow citizens" is *sum-politeia*, with-*politeia*. In Jesus Christ and because of Jesus Christ, Gentiles get in on the *politeia* God has been shaping for centuries.

They are members "of God's household" (v. 19). The term "household" (*oikeios*) is used in the Greek version of the Old Testament for "blood relation." Mercy! Gentiles in Christ are now "blood relatives" with Jews in Christ. The blood of the Jewish Messiah brings Gentiles and Jews together in Himself.

All this is why John Stott entitles his commentary on Ephesians, *God's New Society*.[5] God is building a new *politeia*—a new commonwealth in the world—centered in the One who is our peace (2:14).

Who Have Access

"Who together have access," says Paul (2:18). Access is a life-giving word. In Paul's day it was used of those who are granted "an audience" with the emperor. We both—Jews and Gentiles—have been granted an audience with the Great Emperor. In terms of the architectural metaphor, we both have been given access into the Holy of Holies! We all get to go all the way in! Through the court of the Gentiles, through the court of the women, through

---

[5] John R.W. Stott, *God's New Society: The Message of Ephesians* [The Bible Speaks Today] (Downers Grove: InterVarsity Press, 1979).

the court of the priests, all the way into the Holy of Holies! Can you handle it? Free, full, unhindered access into the Presence of the Holy God!

"For through Him (Christ) we both have our access in one Spirit to the Father" (2:18). It is the foundational text for a theology of prayer, and for a theology of relationship into the Triune God:

Through, in, to:

- *Though* Jesus Christ: God the Son, who makes peace between human and human, and between human and God.
- *In* the Spirit: God the Holy Spirit, who carries us into the Presence.
- *To* the Father: God the Father, who so loved the world He sent the Son to make life with God possible.

Never again do we meet any sign that says "restricted access." All the walls are down. We have full, free access into the very life of the Triune God!

And then, in a morphing of the metaphor, we not only have access into the Holy of Holies; the new human race becomes the Holy of Holies! "In whom (Christ) the whole building, being fitted together, is growing into a holy temple in the Lord" (v. 21). Remember, it is a lifelong Jew who is saying this, for whom the temple was the centre of the cosmos. Jew and Gentiles together in Christ are the new temple!

There are two words the New Testament uses for temple. One (*hieon*) refers to the whole temple area, all four courts. The other (*naos*) refers just to the Holy of Holies, and it is this word Paul uses here. "Growing into a holy *naos*," a holy Holy of Holies. We, broken, sinful human beings, being redeemed, becoming new creations, we constitute the new Holy of Holies in the world! We do not just *go to* the Holy of Holies; we *are* the Holy of Holies. It takes my breath away!

Built on the foundation of apostles and prophets, like Paul and Peter and Priscilla, who just announce the good news. The cornerstone is Jesus Himself. The cornerstone determines the size and shape of the rest of the building. Given who He is, the building can be very big and it will be very beautiful!

Implications

So what are the implications for us in this city?

First, and foremost, we invite the city to join the building project! We invite everyone we can to get in on what the Living God is building in the midst of all the building.

And then we make sure that we do not create new forms of the "barrier of the dividing walls." Jesus' work on the cross levels all barriers. So we need to make sure not to lift them up again in any form.

And we treat each other in light of the building project. We treat each other as the new humans we are, as the new society we are, as the Holy of Holies we are. We treat each other with the reverence deserving of holiness.

And most of all we do everything we can to grow in sensitivity to the Presence of the Holy One. In all we do we live aware that the Triune God of grace is dwelling among us and in us!

A reading from C.S. Lewis captures for me the message of Ephesians 2:11-22.

Imagine yourself as a living house. God comes in to rebuild that house. At first, perhaps, you can understand what He is doing. He is getting the drains right and stopping the leaks in the roof and so on: you knew that those jobs needed doing and so you are not surprised. But presently he [sic] starts knocking the house about in a way that hurts abominably and does not seem to make sense. What on earth is He up to? The explanation is that He is building quite a different house from the one you thought of—throwing out a new wing here, putting on an extra floor there, running up towers, making courtyards. You thought you were going to be made into a decent little cottage: but He is building a palace. He intends to come and live in it Himself.[6]

---

6 C.S. Lewis, *Mere Christianity* (New York, MacMillan, 1952), 174.

EPHESIANS 3:1-13

¹ For this reason I, Paul, the prisoner of Christ Jesus for the sake of you Gentiles— ² if indeed you have heard of the stewardship of God's grace which was given to me for you; ³ that by revelation there was made known to me the mystery, as I wrote before in brief. ⁴ By referring to this, when you read you can understand my insight into the mystery of Christ, ⁵ which in other generations was not made known to the sons of men, as it has now been revealed to His holy apostles and prophets in the Spirit; ⁶ to be specific, that the Gentiles are fellow heirs and fellow members of the body, and fellow partakers of the promise in Christ Jesus through the gospel, ⁷ of which I was made a minister, according to the gift of God's grace which was given to me according to the working of His power. ⁸ To me, the very least of all saints, this grace was given, to preach to the Gentiles the unfathomable riches of Christ, ⁹ and to bring to light what is the administration of the mystery which for ages has been hidden in God who created all things; ¹⁰ so that the manifold wisdom of God might now be made known through the church to the rulers and the authorities in the heavenly places. ¹¹ This was in accordance with the eternal purpose which He carried out in Christ Jesus our Lord, ¹² in whom we have boldness and confident access through faith in Him. ¹³ Therefore I ask you not to lose heart at my tribulations on your behalf, for they are your glory.

CHAPTER 10

When Grace Grabs Hold

EPHESIANS 3:1-13

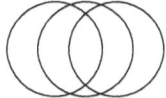

Paul has been vilified over the centuries. He has been accused of all manner of ills: oppressing women, supporting slavery, and nurturing anti-Semitism. Gary Wills, the author of *What Paul Meant*, notes:

> Many people think that Judas was the supreme betrayer of Jesus. But others say Paul has a better right to that title. Judas gave Jesus' body over to death. Paul, it is claimed, buried his spirit.[1]

Thomas Jefferson, for instance, argued that Paul was "the first corrupter of the doctrines of Jesus."[2] Playwright Bernard Shaw argued in the preface of one of his works: "There has never been a more monstrous imposition perpetrated than the

---

[1] Garry Wills, *What Paul Meant* (New York: Penguin Books, 2006), 1. I want to make it clear that this is not Wills' opinion!
[2] Ibid.

imposition of the limitations of Paul's soul upon the soul of Jesus."³ Friedrich Nietzsche called Paul "the Dysangelist," the "bad-news bearer."⁴

As we work through Paul's letter to the Ephesians, I have to wonder what Paul Jefferson, Shaw, and Nietzsche were referring to? Not the Paul who wrote this letter so full of Jesus and so full of grace! Jefferson and company simply could not have spent any serious time with Paul.

They are reacting to texts in Paul's letters that they have read out of context. Paul, an oppressor of women? Not when you read Paul in context, especially in his cultural context. Paul, advocating slavery? Ever read his letter to Philemon? Paul, anti-Jewish? Not when you read Romans 9-11; not when you read Ephesians 2.

Working through Paul's letter to the Ephesians, I have come to agree with the claim: If you want to know Jesus, get to know Paul. For when you really get to know Paul you realize that no one knows Jesus the way Paul does.

That is quite a statement coming from me! Throughout the past fifty years of pastoral ministry, I would have said: if you want to get to know Jesus, get to know John! The apostle John had the privilege of sharing the closest relationship with Jesus during Jesus' earthly ministry. John is the one whose head literally rested on Jesus' heart at the supper in the upper room. No one else had that privilege! When you read John, whether his Gospel, his letters, or the Revelation, you can feel that intimacy oozing out of the pages. But as a result of living in the letter to the Ephesians, I can now add: if you want to get to know Jesus,

---

3 Ibid.
4 Ibid.

get to know Paul.

As far as we know, Paul never met Jesus during Jesus' earthly ministry. He might have seen or heard Jesus from a distance during one of the three or four Passovers that Jesus was in Jerusalem. But Paul did not have the opportunity to meet Jesus in the way the original disciples did. However, Paul was, by the grace of God, given one encounter with the risen Jesus, an encounter which changed not only Paul, but the course of history. While on his way to the city of Damascus to arrest and punish followers of Jesus, Paul was knocked off his horse by a blazing light. "Who are you?" asked Paul from his knees. "I am Jesus whom you are persecuting" (Acts 9:5). What grace! Jesus loves His enemy! Jesus seeks out the persecutor and makes him His friend, His disciple, His ambassador. From that day on everything was about Jesus. "For to me, to live is Christ," Paul declared (Philippians 1:21).

I agree with those who believe that Paul is history's greatest interpreter of Jesus' thought. No one else knows the mind of the crucified and risen Jesus as Paul does. No one else knows the heart of Jesus as Paul does. No one else knows the grace of Jesus as Paul does. No one else knows what it means to be grabbed hold of by grace as Paul does. You want to see what it looks like when grace breaks through and takes hold of a person? Look at Paul. Yes, look at John, Peter, Mary, and Priscilla. But especially look at Paul.

This is what is going on in the text of Ephesians before us. Paul is telling us what grace does in a human life. Three times he refers to grace:

- "God's grace which was given to me..." (3:2)
- "God's grace which was given to me..." (3:7)

- "To me, the very least of all saints, this grace was given..." (3:8)

If you want to get to know the grace of Jesus, get to know Paul. If you want to get to know what grace does in a human life, get to know Paul.

Up to this point in his letter, Paul has been developing an alternative reading of reality shaped by the grace of God. He has been describing the new life into which Jesus calls us, a life shaped by "the surpassing riches of His grace," as Paul puts it (2:7). Then, in chapter 3 verse 1, he says "For this reason I, Paul..." and seems to move forward praying for the Ephesians (and us) in light of the riches of grace. But he stops, and shares more of his own experience of grace. He does eventually pray, (beginning at 3:14), but he first shares more personally what happened to him when grace grabbed hold of his heart and mind.

The major theme of Ephesians 3:1-13 is "the mystery of Christ." Not "mystery" as something to be solved. But "mystery" as something that needs to be revealed. Three times Paul uses the word:

- "by revelation there was made known to me the mystery" (v. 3)
- "my insight into the mystery of Christ" (v. 4)
- "the administration of the mystery which for ages has been hidden in God..." (v.9)

The mystery is that in Christ (the Jewish Messiah), and because of Christ (the Jewish Messiah), we Gentiles have been included in what God has been doing in the world through the family of Abraham and Sarah!

What I want to focus on in this chapter is Paul's identity in Jesus Christ. I want to focus on who he became when the grace of Jesus grabbed hold. And I want to do so because, although Paul is a unique individual upon whom God placed a unique call, who Paul became because of grace is who we also become because of grace.

Prisoner

Verse 1 says "I, Paul, the prisoner of Christ Jesus for the sake of you Gentiles," and Paul will repeat this word in chapter 4, verse 1: "Therefore I, the prisoner of the Lord." Because of grace, Paul ends up a prisoner!

He is speaking on a number of levels here. Historically, Paul is in prison in Rome because grace drove him, as a Jew, to take grace to the Gentiles. In the Damascus road encounter, Paul was called by Jesus to take the gospel to the nations (Acts 26:17), and Jesus warned Paul that he would find himself in trouble for doing so. That is putting it mildly!

In the book of Acts, we see how this act of grace triggered hostility in some of Paul's fellow Jews who then wanted to kill him. They hounded him to such a degree that in order to save his life Paul appealed to Caesar, seeking the protective justice of the empire. Paul is in jail in Rome in hopes that Caesar will defend him.

But Paul speaks of being a prisoner on a theological level. Historically he is a prisoner of Nero, but theologically he is a prisoner of Jesus Christ. This is not just because Paul believes Jesus is sovereign, and that he would, therefore, not be in prison if Jesus had not allowed it. Paul sees himself as a prisoner of Jesus because Paul had placed himself at Jesus' disposal, for Jesus to use him in any way Jesus wanted. Long before he became Caesar's prisoner, he became Jesus' prisoner. Long before he was taken captive to Nero, he had been taken captive by Jesus. Grace broke through and grabbed hold of Paul. And for the rest of his life he speaks of himself as the "the prisoner of Christ Jesus."

Can you say that of yourself? Can I? That He has us wholly—hook, line, and sinker? "I am captive to Jesus Christ. All I have and am is His to use for His good pleasure."

Steward

Paul also sees himself as a steward, a trustee, of what God has given him: "...if indeed you have heard of the stewardship of God's grace which was given to me for you" (v. 2).

In particular, he is a steward of the mystery that Gentiles are included in the covenants with the covenant people. This mystery was hinted at for centuries, especially at the beginning of Jewish history in the call of Abram and Sarah. God had told Abram he would become a blessing to "all the families of the earth" (Genesis 12:1-3). God's choice to bless one man and one family was, from the beginning, all about blessing the whole world.

By the first century, the universal scope of God's grace had been lost for all kinds of reasons. In Jesus, because of Jesus, the mystery is now revealed. It is now an open secret for all to know. Gentiles are now "fellow heirs and fellow members of the body, and fellow partakers of the promise" (3:6), as Paul puts it.

But that particular mystery is part of the even greater mystery. God "made known to us the mystery of His will," says Paul

(Ephesians 1:9). God plans the "summing up of all things in Christ, things in the heavens and things on the earth" (1:10). As I pointed out in chapter four, the verb "sum up" is literally "recapitulate," "to put the head back on." The great mystery revealed to Paul (3:3-5) is that in Jesus, God is putting the head back on the human race; making a new human race which is neither Jew nor Gentile, but one new humanity in Jesus, the new Human.

And Paul sees himself as a steward of that mystery: a protector of the mystery, a guardian of the mystery, one who passes on the mystery so others can know it and live in it.

Of what have you been made a steward? What has God given to you or made known to you that you are passionate to protect and pass on? "Given to me for you," Paul says: "grace given to me for you." That is how it always is with grace. It is given to us for others.

I believe I have been given stewardship of a number of treasures revealed to me through study of the Word:

- I am a steward of Jesus' gospel of the kingdom, of what He has shown me—especially while in the Philippines—about the nature of the kingdom, and how the kingdom comes into the world.
- I am a steward of Jesus' "I AM" sayings recorded in the Gospel of John; of what He has shown me about who He is relative to the Jewish feasts.
- I am a steward of Jesus' prayer recorded in John 17; of what He has opened up to me as He opens up His heart to His Father.

- I am a steward of Jesus' teaching on His easy yoke (Matthew 11:28-30).
- I am a steward of Jesus' making it possible for us to enter into and enjoy the inner life of the Trinity.
- And, I am a steward of the last book of the Bible, "the Revelation of Jesus Christ"; of what He has shown me about how the book goes together and, thus, its clear message, changing the way we see Him and His place in history.

Of what has He made you a steward? What have you been given to protect and pass on to others?

Minister

Grace made Paul a minister: "of which I was made a minister, according to the gift of God's grace…" (v. 7). The word Paul uses is *diakonos*: deacon, servant. Grace made Paul a servant. Grace always does. Grace makes servants of the gospel in and for the world.

In Paul's case, grace made him a minister to the Gentiles. It was his reason for being. Specifically, as Paul puts it, "to preach to the Gentiles the unfathomable riches of Christ" (v. 8). Is that not a great phrase: "the unfathomable riches of Christ"? The "beyond-searching-out riches of Christ." The "untraceable riches of Christ." The "never-to-be-exhausted riches of Christ."

So, too, everyone grabbed hold of by grace: we too want others to know the unfathomable riches of Christ. We want our family, friends, and co-workers to know the Jesus of Matthew, the Jesus of Mark, the Jesus of Luke, the Jesus of John. Right? We want the world to know the Jesus of the book of Hebrews, the Jesus of the letters of Peter, the Jesus of James. We want the city to know the Jesus of Isaiah, and of Jeremiah, and of Amos and Jonah. We want the whole of humanity to know the Jesus of Revelation, the Lamb of God slain for the redemption of the world, the King of Kings and Lord of Lords, the Alpha and Omega, the source and end of all things. And we want others to know the Jesus of Paul! All of us are servants, ministers of the unfathomable riches of Christ to everyone we encounter.

And in Paul's case, minister to the "rulers and authorities in the heavenly places"(v. 10). Paul serves so that Gentiles may know Christ, and so that the spiritual powers at work in the world would know Christ. He is on a mission to the Gentiles, and to the angelic powers that seek to influence cities and nations.

Paul says that "the manifold wisdom of God," the wisdom that made the world, planned salvation history, and unites Jews and Gentiles into one new human race, is made known to the spiritual realms "through the church" (v. 10). Through the multi-racial, multicultural, multi-gifted church, God's multi-dimensional wisdom is revealed to the powers behind the scene.

More is going on in being the church than meets the eye! Something cosmic is happening. In sharing the unfathomable riches of Christ, and in living those riches in the new community centered in Christ, "principalities and powers" are hearing the gospel. And things begin to change. This is why I have said to some: if no one shows up at our church's Sunday morning service, I am still going to preach! When anyone preaches the gospel, the angelic powers in the heavenly places are being informed about the true nature of reality. And things begin to change in the city.

God makes all of us ministers of the gospel to the human realm and to the angelic realm. All of us who belong to Jesus are ministers, bringing the mystery to light for others.

Least

God made Paul "least of all saints": "To me, the very least of all saints, this grace was given" (v. 8). Literally, Paul says that he is "less than the least of all saints."

Is Paul suffering from a poor self-image? Not that we know of. Indeed, given his privileged upbringing and education and massive intellectual capacities, he probably suffered from the opposite, from an inflated sense of self. Hence his attempt to wipe out the early church! But grace healed him. Grace brought him to his senses—"less than the least of all saints."

Over the centuries, people have pointed to Paul's "progress" in grace:

- In AD 55, in his letter to the Corinthians, he refers to himself as "least of the apostles" (1 Corinthians 15:9).
- Then in AD 62, in his letter to the Ephesians, he refers to himself as "the very least of all saints" (3:8).
- Then in AD 66, in his letters to his dear friend Timothy, he refers to himself the foremost of sinners: "Christ Jesus came to the world to save sinners, among whom I am foremost of all" (1 Timothy 1:15).

When grace grabs hold we see ourselves as we are apart from grace. And we then throw ourselves on grace all the more.

"Least of all saints." There may be a play on words going on here. Paul's name before grace got hold of him was Saul, in honor of Israel's first king, whose pride was his downfall. In his life following Jesus, Saul became Paul, meaning "little." From Saul ["big shot"] to Paul ["little"]. This is in line with one of the great themes of the great Story: God is always choosing and working through "little."

King David, of the little tribe of Judah, and smallest of his brothers. Mount Zion, smallest of the mountains. The kingdom of God is like a mustard seed, says Jesus; "smaller than all other seeds," He adds (Matthew 13:32). Grace helped Paul be small. And then through small Paul, grace did a mighty work.

Grace is doing the same thing with each of us: bringing us to the place where we understand the mystery of God's (little) ways in the world.

Participant in Tribulation

"I ask you not to lose heart at my tribulations on your behalf, for they are your glory" (v. 13). When grace got hold of Paul he began to experience "tribulations."

The word Paul uses has a particular nuance. It does not refer to the troubles we all experience in a broken world. It refers to the kind of trouble that comes when the kingdom of God begins to break into the world. The word literally means "pressure," and it refers to the kind of pressure that is generated at the interface of clashing kingdoms. As one kingdom comes up against another, there is pressure, sometimes crushing pressure. It is unavoidable, and it comes with the coming of the kingdom of God.

Paul experienced it. And so do we.

"They are your glory," he tells the Ephesians. Paul's experience of tribulation is their glory, meaning that Paul's experience of tribulations is all part of the process of God bringing the gospel to life in the world. The tribulations are there because God is there, bringing His rule of justice and mercy. Paul gladly bears the pressure, because he knows the pressure is leading to the redemption of others.

Grace enabled Paul to bear tribulations. Grace enables us to do so too! Grace enables us to choose to suffer that others might be brought into grace. Grace enables us to give up creature-comforts and be inconvenienced so that others may encounter Jesus Christ.

Debtor

One more thing: Grace made Paul a debtor. Paul became a debtor to grace. He is where he is, doing what he is doing, being who he is, all because of grace. As the old hymn puts it: "O to grace how great a debtor, daily I'm constrained to be!"[5] I owe it all to Him. You owe it all to Him. The world owes it all to Him.

If you want to get to know Jesus, get to know Paul. If you want to understand what the grace of Jesus does, get to know Paul. And we will be like Paul.

- Prisoners of Christ Jesus, and therefore truly free.
- Stewards of the mystery.
- Ministers of the gospel.
- Least of all saints, living in the power of littleness.

---

5 "Come, Thou Fount of Every Blessing," words by Robert Robinson, adapted by Margaret Clarkson.

- Participant in tribulation so that others get in on the kingdom.
- And growing deeper and deeper into debt… to the grace that only gets richer and richer.

EPHESIANS 3:14-21

[14] For this reason I bow my knees before the Father, [15] from whom every family in heaven and on earth derives its name, [16] that He would grant you, according to the riches of His glory, to be strengthened with power through His Spirit in the inner man, [17] so that Christ may dwell in your hearts through faith; and that you, being rooted and grounded in love, [18] may be able to comprehend with all the saints what is the breadth and length and height and depth, [19] and to know the love of Christ which surpasses knowledge, that you may be filled up to all the fullness of God.

[20] Now to Him who is able to do far more abundantly beyond all that we ask or think, according to the power that works within us, [21] to Him be the glory in the church and in Christ Jesus to all generations forever and ever. Amen.

CHAPTER 11

Praying the Gospel into Our Hearts

EPHESIANS 3:14-21

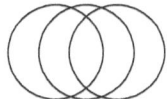

After studying all of Paul's prayers in all of Paul's letters, New Testament scholar David Crump observes that Paul "asks for nothing in moderation."[1] Says Dr. Crump, Paul's prayers are marked by "blatant extravagance... superlatives become the lingua franca" of all of Paul's praying.[2]

"That he would grant you, according to the riches of His glory..." (Ephesians 3:16).

"Now unto Him who is able to do far more abundantly beyond all we ask or think..." (Ephesians 3:20).

Paul is in prison; in Rome, the capital city of the greatest empire on earth. He is awaiting trial before Caesar, the most powerful human being alive. A Roman soldier guards Paul day and night. He is allowed some contact with his friends, like with

---

[1] David Crump, *Knocking on Heaven's Door: A New Testament Theology of Petitionary Prayer* (Grand Rapids: Baker Academic, 2006), 233.
[2] Ibid.

the man named Tychicus who, at the end of the letter to the Ephesians, Paul calls "the beloved brother and faithful minister in the Lord" (Ephesians 6:21). Tychicus is serving Paul as a kind of secretary, writing down what Paul is dictating.

By the time Paul and Tychicus get to the text before us, Paul is on his knees praying. As a number of commentators have observed, this is not the normal posture for Jews to take when praying. Kneeling was the norm for Gentiles, but not for Jews. Jews usually stood to pray, lifting their hands to God. But this time Paul gets down on his knees, partly to identify with Gentiles, but mostly because kneeling expresses a deeper reverence and a new fervent longing.

On his knees, Paul, as it were, takes the hearts of the believers in Ephesus into his hands and lifts them to the Living God, asking the Lord Jesus Christ to do in their hearts what only the Father can do in human hearts.

Extravagant Praying

Remember the note on which Paul began his letter, the note he sustains throughout Ephesians? "Blessed be the God and Father of our Lord Jesus Christ, who has blessed us with every spiritual blessing in the heavenly places in Christ" (Ephesians 1:3).

Talk about extravagance! And superlatives! Every spiritual blessing; every blessing of the Spirit in the heavenly realm in Christ. He goes on to identify some of the "every":

- chosen before the foundation of the world
- adopted into the family of God
- redeemed

- forgiven
- invited into the mystery of God's purpose in the world
- given an inheritance in God's future
- sealed with the Holy Spirit

How did Tychicus keep up with Paul's dictation?

Paul then reports how he has been praying, asking "the God of our Lord Jesus Christ" to open the eyes of our hearts so that we might know:

- the hope of God's calling
- the riches of the glory of His inheritance in His people; and
- the surpassing greatness of God's power toward us who believe—the power God exercised when He raised Jesus from the dead, and seated Him far above all other powers.

Paul then proclaims the gospel of God's power. God takes people who were dead in their sins and held captive by evil, and makes us alive together with Christ, raising us up with Christ, and seating us with Christ in the heavenly places in Christ. As a result of the work of God's power we have become new creations, God's handiwork in the world.

Paul then puts all this in the context of God's massive building project: creating a new human race, made up of Jews and Gentiles:

- who together constitute a new human society in the world, centered in the One who is our Peace;

- who are granted access into the very Presence of the Holy God, and
- who constitute a new dwelling place for God on earth, the new temple of the Living God in the world.

Then (Ephesians 3:1) Paul seems to begin to pray ("For this reason...") but he stops to share more personally, telling us about his own experiences of grace, about how by grace God revealed the mystery of His plans, and called Paul to proclaim "the unfathomable riches of Christ" (Ephesians 3:8). And he shares how the crushing pressure he experiences in doing gospel ministry has served for the sake of the advancement of the gospel.

Then, in the midst of that pressure and in light of the gospel, Paul gets down on his knees and prays (Ephesians 3:14). In chapter one he reports that he has been praying; in chapter three, he actually prays the gospel into our hearts. In chapter one he prayed that we might *know* the good news; in chapter three he prays that we might *experience* the good news. More exactly, in chapter one he prayed that we might *know* the God of the gospel; in chapter three he prays that we might *experience* the God of the gospel, the Triune God: Father, Son, and Holy Spirit.

This has to be one of the most moving scenes in all of Scripture. Paul the prisoner, gets down on his knees, takes our hearts into his hands, and prays the gospel he preaches into our hearts. He does not want the gospel to get stuck in our heads, as mere theory. He wants the gospel to be a living reality, so he boldly asks the Father to make it so.

That Paul prays is in and of itself one of the clearest signs that Paul really believes the gospel. Because of Jesus' death and resurrection, the way into the presence of the Living God has been opened. As Richard Foster puts it in his book on prayer: "The Father's heart is open wide—you are welcome to come in."[3]

Paul has used the word "access" two times before this point in his letter. "For through Him [Jesus Christ] we both [Jews and Gentiles] have our access in one Spirit to the Father" (Ephesians 2:18), and "in whom [Christ Jesus our Lord] we have boldness and confident access..." (Ephesians 3:12). At the moment Jesus died on the cross, the huge curtain (60 feet high, 30 feet wide, 12 inches thick) in the Jerusalem temple was torn in two from top to bottom. This was clearly an act of God, signaling that the way into the Holy of Holies, the way into the very presence of the Creator and Redeemer, is open wide and we are welcome to come in.

That Paul prays what he prays says he really believes what the gospel declares about the God of the gospel.

To Whom Paul Prays

"I bow my knees before the Father" (Ephesians 3:14). Paul speaks of God as Father a lot in his letters to the Ephesians. After decades of walking with Jesus Christ, Paul is still stunned by the good news. The gospel declares that those who belong to Jesus are brought into the same relationship with the Father that Jesus has! Jesus lives for His Father. Jesus loves His Father. Jesus trusts His Father. Jesus basks in the goodness of His Father.

Paul delights to call God "Father" because he realizes the unspeakable privilege: *We* have been granted the *same* status with

---

[3] Richard J. Foster, *Prayer: Finding the Heart's True Home* (SanFrancisco: HarperSanFrancisco, 1992), 2.

God that Jesus has! We too are brought in on the intimate relationship Jesus enjoyed with the Father in His earthly ministry. Jesus' Father relates to us as He relates to Jesus! Jesus' Father loves us as He loves Jesus! Can you hear the wonder in Paul's words? The Father of Jesus, who, because of what Jesus did for us in obedience to His Father, is now *our* Father. Paul is taking seriously what Jesus taught us: "Pray, then, in this way," He says in His Sermon on the Mount, "Our Father..." (Matthew 6:9).

It is one of the greatest blessings of the gospel: to address the awesome, holy, Living God as "Father." To address Him the way the Father's only begotten Son does. Paul really believes the gospel: In and because of Jesus Christ, we have been adopted by Jesus' Father and have been granted the same status before the Father that Jesus has! Jesus' Father, whom Jesus loves and trusts, is now *your* Father and *my* Father. The Father delights in you as He delights in Jesus. The Father delights in me as He delights in Jesus.

"From whom every family in heaven and on earth derives its name" (Ephesians 3:15). It is not clear what Paul is referring to here. I do not think he is saying here that the Father of Jesus is the model of "fatherhood." That is true, but it is not what Paul is emphasizing here.

The term "family" (*patria*) refers to a group of people related to a common ancestor or leader.[4] It can refer to a family, a clan, a movement, or a nation. I think Paul is saying that any grouping of people—in heaven or on earth—finds its true life in the Father of Jesus. The nuclear family and the new family (the church)

---

4 John A. Allan, *The Epistle to the Ephesians: Introduction and Commentary* (London: SCM Press, 1959), 97.

both find true life in the Father, through the Son, by the Spirit.

"I bow my knees before the Father who is able." Massively able! Paul expresses it in his doxology from the prison cell: "Now to Him who is able..."

Able to do.

Able to do what we ask.

Able to do what we think.

Able to do all that we ask or think.

Able to do beyond all that we ask or think.

Able to do abundantly beyond all that we ask or think.

Able to do far more abundantly beyond all that we ask or think.

What are you facing today? The One before whom Paul bows his knees is able!

And He acts "according to the riches of His glory." Glory is a way of saying, "All that makes God be God." "Riches of His glory" are the unfathomable riches of God's very essence: wisdom, power, mercy, grace, justice, love, and creativity. The Father of the Lord Jesus acts toward us out of the inexhaustible wealth of His very being!

So Annie Johnson Flint can write in her song "He Giveth More Grace":

> He giveth more grace when the burdens grow greater,
> He sendeth more strength when the labors increase;
> To added affliction He addeth His mercy,
> To multiplied trials He multiplied peace.
>
> His love has no limit, His grace has no measure,
> His power has no boundary known unto men;

For out of His infinite riches in Jesus,
He giveth, and giveth, and giveth again."[5]

Then this verse:

When we have exhausted our store of endurance,
When our strength has failed ere the day is half done,
When we reach the end of our hoarded resources,
Our Father's full giving is only begun.[6]

Paul bows his knees before the Father of Jesus, who is able to do more than any of us can yet imagine, who gives out of the treasures of His inexhaustible glory. And remember, Paul is saying all of this from a prison cell. The gospel works in prison cells!

Paul takes our hearts into his hands, lifts them up to the Living God, and prays: Father... good and gracious Father of Jesus... You are able to do way beyond anything any of us can ask or dream. Will You, out of the bottomless well of what makes You be You, invigorate our inner persons with the power of Your Spirit, with the power that raised Jesus from the dead, so that Jesus may freely dwell in every nook and cranny of our being.

Strengthened

And on his knees, Paul prays the gospel further into our hearts: "[May the] Father... grant you... to be strengthened with power through His Spirit in your inner person" (Ephesians 3:16).

---

5 "He Giveth More Grace," written by Annie Johnson Flint, © 1941.
6 Ibid.

The verb "strengthen" can be rendered "fortify" or "invigorate." O Father, fortify these people with power; invigorate them with power.

We know from his prayer in chapter one, that the power Paul has in mind is the power that raised Jesus from the dead and seated Him above all other powers. O Father, invigorate them with resurrection power. You are able. Please Father, fortify us with your life-giving power.

"In the inner person." In the deepest recesses of our being.

In his second letter to the Corinthians, Paul speaks of the outer person and the inner person. The outer person is decaying, says Paul. Tell me about it! But, says Paul, the inner person "is being renewed day by day" (2 Corinthians 4:16). Father, strengthen our inner person with the power You exercised when You raised Your Son from the grave.

"Through His Spirit." I pray that He would grant you, "according to the riches of His glory, to be strengthened with power through His Spirit in the inner person." The Spirit, like the Father, and like Jesus the Son, is a person. The Spirit, like the Father, and like Jesus the Son, is God. The third person of the Holy Trinity in the beginning hovered over the dark nothingness and brought the universe into being. In the middle of history He hovered over the emptiness of the virgin's womb and brought the God-Man, Jesus of Nazareth, into being. In this moment in history, the Spirit hovers over our lives, bringing resurrection life to our inner persons even as our outer persons decay. As Gordon Fee puts it, "The living God is a God of power; and by the Spirit the power of the living God is present with and for us."[7] And *in* us!

So J.B. Phillips paraphrased Paul's prayer for us: "that out of the glorious richness of his resources he will enable you to know [experience] the strength of the spirit's inner reinforcement."

Dwelling

"So that Christ may dwell in your hearts by faith" (Ephesians 3:17).

Paul is not asking here that Christ comes to dwell in our hearts. Christ has already done that; He has already come to believers, to live with us and in us. That is what makes a person a Christian, a Christ-in-one. Earlier he says of believers that we "are being built together into a dwelling of God in the Spirit" (Ephesians 2:22). The indwelling is already happening.

Paul has taken our hearts into his hands and is praying that we be strengthened by the power of the Holy Spirit, so that the indwelling might be all Christ intends it to be. Paul is praying that Christ might completely dwell in our hearts.

"Hearts" and "inner person" are related. Yet heart goes a bit deeper. If "inner person" is the center of our personhood, "heart" is the control center. Paul is praying that Christ dwell at the control center of our inner person.

The basic Greek word for "dwell" is *oikeo*, related to the noun *oikos*, meaning home. *Oikeo* is to dwell in a home. Now, in the Greek language, one can add different prepositions to the same verb, creating words with different meanings. So one can add

---

7 Gordon D. Fee, *God's Empowering Presence: The Holy Spirit in the Letters of Paul* (Peabody, MA: Hendrickson, 1994), 8.

to *oikeo* the preposition *para*, meaning "around," or "alongside." The resulting word *paroikeo* would then mean to "dwell beside," or "dwell alongside." It came to mean "dwell as a visitor, guest, or sojourner." *Paroikeo* comes into English in the word "parish." The apostle Peter uses this word for the church (1 Peter 1:17, 2:11). The church dwells in the world as a visitor, as a guest, as a sojourner, never settling down in the world because the world is not yet our home.

Now, here is what I want you to see about what Paul is praying. In Paul's day one could also add to *oikeo* [dwell] the preposition *kata*, meaning "down." The resulting world *katoikeo*, would then mean "dwell down," or "settle down," that is, to move in and permanently reside. This is the word Paul uses in his prayer: Father, invigorate their inner persons with the power of Your Spirit, so that Christ may *katoikeo* in their hearts (not just *paroikeo*). May He dwell in their hearts not as a visitor, but as a permanent resident, not as guest, but as Master.

In the evangelical world, we speak of "receiving Christ," and invite people to "receive Christ" in their heart. In the Middle East, to receive someone into your home, is to welcome them as a guest. But it also, and primarily, means to now treat the guest as master of the home. Everything in the home now revolves around the guest-treated-as-master.

I had the opportunity in 1999 of spending a few days in Beirut, Lebanon. My host was a History Professor at Arab Baptist Theological Seminary. My host took me to a fabulous restaurant, overlooking the Mediterranean Sea. My father-in-law was with me on this trip, but was not able to come to the restaurant, so when I saw him later, I said to him in the presence of the host, "I wish you could have been there." The professor, on a limited budget, then took my father-in-law and me that night to the same restaurant. I was a guest, but I was treated as master; my slightest whim was now his order. That is what it means to "receive someone in the home."

Do you see now why Paul prays for power? It takes power to alter everything around a new person in the home. It takes power to change routines, to change attitudes, to switch from living as one's own master, to living at the beck and call of the new Master.

And it takes power to remodel the home. Christ comes to take up residence; He comes to take over the place and make it His own. I commend to you the little booklet *My Heart—Christ's Home* by Robert Boyd Munger (who took me under his wing while in seminary 40 years ago).[8] Dr. Munger works with the imagery inherent in *katoikeo*, "dwelling down" and encourages us to think of our hearts as a house, and then to think of all the "rooms" of our homes; and then, one by one, to welcome Christ into each of the rooms.

Munger encourages us, as Paul would:

- To let Christ go beyond the living room, where many want Christ to stay.
- To invite Christ into the kitchen/dining room and transform our eating;
- Into the family room and transform our relationships;
- Into the recreation room to transform the way we spend our free time;

---

[8] Robert Boyd Munger, *My Heart—Christ's Home* [Expanded edition] (Downers Grove: InterVarsity Press, 1986). This was first published in 1954, and is available in different formats.

- Into the study and transform what we read and allow into our minds;
- Into the bedroom to transform the most intimate of spaces;
- and into all the secret closets, cleansing and healing and freeing.

In prison, the Apostle Paul gets down on his knees, takes our hearts into his hands, and prays the gospel into them: Father, the good and gracious Father of Jesus, you who are able to do way beyond anything we can ask or think. Will you, out of the inexhaustible riches of your very essence, strengthen our inner persons with power by Your Spirit so that Christ may freely live in us in all His fullness!

Rooted and Grounded

"That you, being rooted and grounded in love, may be able to comprehend with all the saints what is the breadth and length and height and depth, and to know the love of Christ which surpasses knowledge, that you may be filled up to all the fullness of God" (Ephesians 3:17b-19).

This part of the prayer is one of the boldest prayers ever prayed, maybe second only to the bold prayer Jesus prays in John 17.

The second half of Paul's prayer begins with an exclamation. As is typical of Paul, right in the middle of an exquisitely crafted sentence, he breaks out with an exclamation: "You are rooted and grounded in love."

He is not praying that we become rooted and grounded. That is already the case, even if we do not realize it yet. Because of all that God has done for us in Jesus, because Jesus has come and taken up residence in us, Paul can exclaim, "You are rooted and grounded in love."

As is typical of Paul, he mixes metaphors: Rooted—an agricultural metaphor; grounded, or founded—an architectural metaphor. He did this earlier in the letter, in chapter two with "building" and "growing": "... in whom the whole building being fitted together is growing into a holy temple" (2:21). He does this in his first letter to the Corinthians, where he speaks of disciples as both God's building and God's field (3:6-17). And he does this in his letter to the Colossians, saying that we are "firmly rooted and now being built up in Him [Christ]" (2:7).

Whether we realize or not, love is the soil in which we are growing; love is the foundation on which we are standing. You are rooted and grounded in love.

Breadth, Length, Height, Depth

Then Paul returns to praying: that you "may be able to comprehend with all the saints what is the breadth and length and height and depth..." "May be able" is better translated as "may be strong enough." Paul recognizes that we are facing a challenge, and prays that we be made strong enough to press through.

The challenge? To comprehend the breadth and length and height and depth! "Comprehend" (*katalambano*) is to catch, grasp, seize, or lay hold of. This is the same word Paul uses in his letter to the Philippians when he says: "I press on so that I may lay hold of that for which also I was laid hold of by Christ

Jesus" (3:12). I press on that I may *catch* that for which I was caught by Christ Jesus, that I may *grasp* that for which I was grasped by Christ Jesus, that I may *seize* that for which I was seized by Christ Jesus.

This is the same verb the Apostle John uses in the prologue to his gospel: "The Light shines in the darkness, and the darkness did not comprehend it" (John 1:5). The light shines in the darkness—praise God!—and the darkness did not *catch* it. The darkness did not *grasp* the light. The darkness did not *seize* the light. The darkness did not *grasp* the light. The darkness did not *lay hold* of the light. Indeed, the light laid hold of the darkness!

Paul takes our hearts into his hands, and asks the Father to make us strong enough to catch, grasp, seize, lay hold of "the breadth and length and height and depth." To what do those terms refer? What does Paul have in mind?

Throughout church history, different opinions have been offered.[9] The oldest known view is that the terms refer to the four points of the cross.

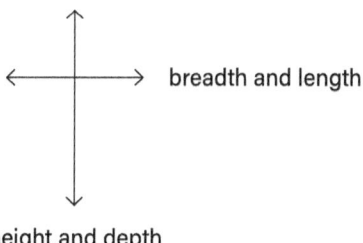

breadth and length

height and depth

---

[9] Helpfully summarized by Frank Thielman, *Ephesians* [Baker Exegetical Commentary on the New Testament] (Grand Rapids: Baker Academic, 2010), 234-237.

This is the view of significant church thinkers like Origen and Irenaeus of the second century, and Gregory of Nyssa and Augustine of the fourth century.

Later in the fourth century, a prevailing view was that "the four terms referred to the dimensions of a perfect sphere, which, in turn, stood for the perfection of the God Paul wanted his readers to know."[10] In the eighteenth and nineteenth centuries, some leading commentators believed the terms refer to the dimensions of the new temple made up of believers, which Paul describes in chapter two of his letter. Paul wants us to grasp the totality of the church Jesus Christ is building. In the twentieth century, a number of scholars suggested that the terms refer to the dimensions of believers' "inheritance" in heaven, which Paul describes in chapter one of his letter.

A view to which many have leaned throughout the centuries is that "breadth and length and height and depth" refer to God's wisdom. In Ephesians 1:8-9, Paul says that "in all wisdom" God made known the mystery of His will. In 1:17, Paul prays that we be given "a spirit of wisdom." In 3:10, Paul says that through the church "the manifold wisdom of God" is being made known to the principalities and authorities in the heavenly places. So, many argue that Paul is praying that we be made strong enough to comprehend God's wisdom—its breadth, length, height, and depth.

There is Biblical precedence for this line of thought. In the book of Job, one of Job's friends (Zophar) says: "But would that God might speak, and open His lips against you, and show you

---

[10] Ibid., 234. See also *Ancient Christian Commentary on Scripture, Vol. VIII: Galatians, Ephesians, Philippians*, ed. Mark J. Edwards (Downers Grove: InterVarsity, 1999), 154-156.

the secrets of wisdom!" (11:5-6) And then he asks Job:

> Can you discover the depth of God? Can you discover the limits of the Almighty? They are high as the heavens, what can you do? Deeper than Sheol, what can you know? Its measure is longer than the earth and broader than the sea. (11:7-9)

In his letter to the Romans Paul cries out: "Oh, the depth of the riches both of the wisdom and knowledge of God! How unsearchable are His judgments and unfathomable His ways" (11:33).

So it is possible that in his prayer in Ephesians 3 Paul is asking the Father to help us comprehend, lay hold of, the vastness of God's wisdom. Please, Father!

But it seems to me that the majority of believers through church history, including John Chrysostom, Martin Luther, and John Calvin, are right when they argue that the terms "breadth, length, height, depth" refer to love. Just before Paul uses the terms he speaks of "being rooted and grounded in love." And right after using the terms he speaks of knowing the love of Christ which surpasses knowledge. Paul asks the Father of the Lord Jesus to make us, by the Holy Spirit, strong enough to lay hold of the "breadth and length and height and depth" of the love of God in Jesus!

"May be strong enough." Why pray this? Because Paul knows our hearts. He knows we all face external circumstances and internal dynamics that keep us from laying hold of the love of God in Jesus:

- Some of us experienced things in childhood that keep haunting us, drowning out the knowledge of the love of God.

- Some of us have tapes playing in our minds about how unworthy we are of the love of anyone, let alone God.
- Some of us have done things in our past that we cannot forget that keep us from expressing the love of God.
- Some of us are facing circumstances right now that seem to call the love of God into question.
- Many of us look around at all the misery in the world right now and wonder where the love of God is.
- Some of us are disappointed with God; we feel let down by God, and are not sure we can trust the claim that He loves us.
- Some of us have tried to be "good Christians" all our lives; we have "kept the rules" so to speak, but God is not acting in ways we think we deserve God to act, and we are deeply angry with God; the anger keeps us from experiencing any love, let alone God's love.
- And there is the enemy of Jesus, the enemy of our souls, who does not want any human being to know and experience God and His love, the enemy who fuels our own sense of unworthiness, who lies to us, telling us that our sin disqualifies us from relationship with God.

Oh, Father, make them strong enough to press through all the obstacles, to overcome any and all lies and confusion; and help them grasp the "breadth and length and height and depth" of your love for us in Jesus Christ.

- Father, help us seize the breadth of Your love—broad enough to include millions upon millions of sinners, from every race and every clan.

- Father, help us seize the length of Your love—long enough to last through all the ages, and long enough to reach to the farthest places. No one can escape the reach of your love!
- Father, help us seize the height of Your love—love that opens the door into heaven. Love that raises us up with Jesus, and seats us with Him in the heavenly places.
- Father, help us seize the depth of your love—love that comes down in Jesus. Love that comes all the way down into the depths of our sin and sickness, into the depths of our darkness and death. You came all the way down to lay hold of us!

Oh, Father, make us strong enough to lay hold of the "deep, deep love of Jesus, vast, unmeasured, boundless free."[11]

Filled with all the Fullness of God

And then Paul prays the prayer that blows the circuit boards! I ask that, according to the riches of His glory, "You be filled up to all the fullness of God" (3:19b).

"Be filled" is in the passive tense, meaning that we do not do the filling. We try to do so in all kinds of ways, but "be filled" is in the so-called "Divine passive," because only God does it. Only God fills us.

"Fill them," Father. This literally means, "completely fill." Fill them up to full capacity, right up to the rim. Yes, please!

And what is the measure of this filling? "To all the fullness of

---

[11] "O the Deep, Deep Love of Jesus," words by Samuel Trevor Francis.

God." Paul takes our hearts into his hands, lifts them up to the Living God, and asks that they be filled so completely that the filling can only be measured by "all the fullness of God."

What is this "fullness of God"? One scholar gets about as close to the meaning as we can get when he writes that "the fullness of God" "means the sum total of the divine attributes."[12] "The fullness of God" is the sum total of God's wisdom, power, truth, beauty, holiness, justice, love. "The fullness of God," like "glory," is all that makes God be God.

Oh my goodness! Kneeling in a jail cell, Paul prays that we—broken, imperfect, empty people—be filled up to the extent that the filling can only be measured by the sum total of the attributes of the Living God.

With what does God fill us so that the filling is measured by "the fullness of God"? The fullness of God! God fills us with the fullness of God so that the filling can only be measured by the fullness of God.

In his letter to the Colossians (a companion to the letter to Ephesus), Paul says that the fullness of God dwells in Christ: "It was the Father's good pleasure for all the fullness to dwell in Him" (Colossians 1:19). Then in Colossians 2:10, Paul says that in Christ we have been made complete, we have been filled. In relationship with Jesus Christ, we participate in all that is in Jesus Christ. If we are *in* Him, we are in His fullness, which is the fullness of God.

See why Paul's prayer has been called the boldest of all prayers? Paul is asking the Father of Jesus to fill the disciples of Jesus

---

[12] Charles Gore, *St. Paul's Epistle to the Ephesians: A Practical Exposition* (London: John Murray, 1898), 80.

Christ with and to the measure of all that makes the Living God the Living God.

Can you handle this? Of course not! We rightly feel overwhelmed with the thought! Paul is not praying for a little spiritual "pick-me-up." Paul is not just praying for a change in perspective that helps us cope with the stresses of our lives. Paul is not praying for a little shot-in-the-arm to help us go on living our self-empowered, self-directed lives. Paul is praying that the God and Father of the Lord Jesus Christ fill us with Himself! He is asking that the Living God fill us so full that the filling can only be measured by the fullness of God Himself!

Because this prayer is so bold, it is important to point out that Paul does not then suggest that because of this filling we somehow become God, or gods. The filling makes us godly, but not God. When we fill a glass with water, the glass does not become water. When we fill a balloon with helium, the balloon does not become helium. When God fills human beings with God, human beings do not become God.

Quite the contrary! To be filled up to the fullness of God finally makes us human. We finally become what we were created to be. It was when God breathed His breath into the lifeless humanoid that Adam became a living being. So for everyone descended from Adam, when the Triune God fills us with all that makes the Triune God be God, we finally become all we were meant to be.

What a compliment this pays us humans! Paul's prayer says we were made in such a way that nothing but God can finally satisfy our hearts. They were made by God, for God. The only thing that finally fills us is God: Father, Son, and Holy Spirit!

The Walk of Being Alive "In Christ"

EPHESIANS 4:1–6:24

EPHESIANS 4:1-6

¹ Therefore I, the prisoner of the Lord, implore you to walk in a manner worthy of the calling with which you have been called, ² with all humility and gentleness, with patience, showing tolerance for one another in love, ³ being diligent to preserve the unity of the Spirit in the bond of peace. ⁴ There is one body and one Spirit, just as also you were called in one hope of your calling; ⁵ one Lord, one faith, one baptism, ⁶ one God and Father of all who is over all and through all and in all.

CHAPTER 12

Walking in Unity

EPHESIANS 4:1-6

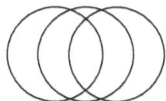

The great turning point in the apostle Paul's carefully and exquisitely crafted letter to the believers in the first century city of Ephesus comes at the start of chapter four:

"Therefore, I, the prisoner of the Lord, implore you to walk in a manner worthy of the calling with which you have been called" (4:1).

The fact is, this "therefore" has actually been there implicitly, right from the beginning of the letter:

- "Blessed be the God and Father of our Lord Jesus Christ, who has blessed us with every spiritual blessing in the heavenly places in Christ" (1:3). Therefore...
- "He chose us in Him before the foundation of the world... He predestined us to adoption..."(1:4-5). Therefore...
- "In Him we have redemption through His blood, the forgiveness of our trespasses" (1:7). Therefore...

- "He made known to us the mystery of His will" (1:9). Therefore...
- "We have obtained an inheritance" (1:11), our future is secure. Therefore...
- We "were sealed in Him with the Holy Spirit... a pledge of our inheritance" (1:13-14). Therefore...
- God is making known to us "the surpassing greatness of His power toward us who believe," power that He exercised in Christ "when He raised Him from the dead and seated Him at His right hand in the heavenly places" (1:19-20). Therefore...
- We were dead in our transgressions and sins, and He "made us alive together with Christ" (2:1, 5). Therefore...
- "And raised us up with Him [Christ]" (2:6). Therefore...
- "And seated us with Him in the heavenly places" (2:6). Therefore...
- Christ, who "is our peace" has "made both groups [Jews and Gentiles] into one," making "the two into one new man" (2:14-15). Therefore...
- "Through Him we both have our access in one Spirit to the Father" (2:18). Therefore...
- We are "growing into a holy temple in the Lord," "being built together into a dwelling of God in the Spirit" (2:21-22). Therefore...
- We are being "strengthened with power through His Spirit in the inner man" (3:16). Therefore...
- Christ has come to dwell in our hearts through faith (3:17). Therefore...
- We are being made strong "to comprehend with all

the saints what is the breadth and length and height and depth" (3:18-19) of the love of God in Jesus Christ. Therefore...
- We are being "filled up to all the fullness of God" (3:19)! Therefore.
- God is "able to do far more abundantly beyond all that we ask or think" (3:20). "Therefore I... implore you"

Therefore...

Again we note that Paul's letter to the Ephesians is written in two halves, nearly equal in length: Chapters 1-3 and chapters 4-6.

- In chapters 1-3, Paul develops the glory of the gospel of Jesus Christ.
- In chapters 4-6, Paul develops the everyday implications of the gospel of Jesus Christ.
- In chapters 1-3, Paul takes us into an alternative reading of reality.
- In chapters 4-6, Paul takes us into the everyday dynamics of this alternative reading.
- In chapters 1-3, Paul celebrates the wonder of being "in Christ." In chapters 4-6, Paul calls us to the walk of being "in Christ."
- Chapters 1-3: the calling.
- Chapters 4-6: walking in a manner worthy of the calling.

Many commentators on Ephesians come to chapter four, verse one, and write something like, "Now Paul is going to apply the gospel to our lives." The word "apply" troubles me because it suggests that what Paul develops in chapters 1-3, a vision of reality shaped by the death, resurrection, and ascension of Jesus, is out of touch and does not "apply" to real life!

The phrase also troubles me because it puts the weight on us to make something happen, to "apply the gospel to our lives." It implies that we will now make the gospel relevant, that we will now make the gospel real to the world.[1]

The phrase mostly troubles me because it makes our lives the issue. In chapters 1-3 Paul has made the Living God the issue. Paul has opened up for us what the Living God has done, is doing, and will do for the world in Jesus Christ. To say that in chapters 4-6 Paul is going to help us "apply the gospel to our lives" now makes our lives the issue.

For three chapters Paul has been helping us see that things have changed in the universe. Because of the life, death, resurrection, and ascension of Jesus, things have changed. We are now living with a new reading of reality. Indeed, we are now living in a new reality. And the point of the 'therefore' is to live in the new reality.

Paul is saying, "Realize what has taken place. Realize that you are now living in a new reality that changes your old reality. Enter in. Get with the program." We now have a new address: in Christ, in the heavenly places. We now live in a new neighbourhood: adopted in the family of God, where redemption and forgiveness reign. We now live in a new country: where the dead in sin are made alive with Christ, raised up with Christ, seated with Christ. We now live in a new universe: where His Spirit

---

[1] I wrestle with "apply" more fully in my *The Glory of Preaching: Participating in God's Transformation of the World*, 158-171.

is at work, coming into the very center of our being to make it possible for Christ to live here; where the love of God is present and working in every dimension of our existence; where we are being filled... so full it can only be measured by all that makes God be God.

Therefore... enter in! Start to move around in the new reality.

Walk Worthy

"Walk," he exhorts us. Not merely "live," as some version have it. "Walk." Paul is using the language of Biblical spirituality. From the beginning, life with the Living God, relationship with the Living God, has been thought of as a "walk." Biblical spirituality is, if you will, peripatetic. Walk, walk, walk.[2]

So Paul calls us to walk into the new world, into Christ, into the life of the Trinity. We have been walking in worlds we have shaped, and worlds our cultures have shaped. Another world, shaped by the gospel, has invaded, and is overtaking all the old worlds. Not that the old worlds are all bad, not at all. It is just that the old worlds do not know the gospel. To paraphrase Paul, "come now and live in the world brought into being by the gospel of Jesus Christ. I will help you navigate your way through the new world."

"Walk." Move out of "our lives." The true "application" of the gospel to "our lives" is to move out of "our lives" into the life of the Triune God. Somehow we get the idea that we can be blessed with every spiritual blessing of the heavenly places in Christ, that

---

[2] For a fuller development of this idea see *Mark Buchanan's God Walk: Moving At The Speed of Your Soul* (Zondervan: Grand Rapids, 2020).

we can be made alive in Christ, raised up with Christ, seated with Christ in the heavenly places; that we can be filled up to all the fullness of God... and keep living the way we were living. How could that possibly be the case? Walk a new walk! Realize the new reality into which you have been called... and move in it.

"Therefore I, the prisoner of the Lord, implore you to walk in a manner worthy of the calling to which you have been called." This could be the heading for the whole of the second half of Ephesians—Walk Worthy.

Here we need to be careful. When we hear "walk worthy," many of us begin to feel weighed down. Worthy? I will never be worthy! I will never measure up! And we begin to feel that way because we have misunderstood Paul's word. The word "worthy" is not about measuring up or achieving some kind of spiritual capacity. The word worthy means, "'bringing up the other beam of the scales,' 'bringing into equilibrium.'"[3] It is about "balance," or better, "suitability."

Something is "worthy" because it fits. "Walk in a manner worthy of the calling" means "walk in a way that fits the calling," "walk in a way that is congruous with your calling," "walk in equilibrium with, in balance with, the call." "Worthy" is not about measuring up; it is about fitting in. It is about fitting into that for which we have been created and redeemed.

It is not that we have to measure up to the new configuration. Rather it is that we need only wake up to it, realize what has happened, and walk in equilibrium with it all.

---

[3] Harold W. Hoehner, *Ephesians: An Exegetical Commentary* (Grand Rapids: Baker Academic, 2002), 504.

In Unity

The first "worthy of the calling" that Paul calls us to is unity.

- "One body and one Spirit,... one hope of your calling; one Lord, one faith, one baptism, one God and Father of all who is over all and through all and in all" (v. 4-6).
- "Until we all attain to the unity of the faith and of the knowledge of the Son of God" (v. 13).
- And "being diligent to preserve the unity of the Spirit in the bond of peace" (v. 3).
- To walk in balance with the new reality is to walk in unity.

But of course! Chapters 1-3 are all about God unifying creation, unifying the world, unifying hearts, unifying the church around and in Jesus Christ. Chapter one gives what could be seen as the theme verse of the whole letter: God "made known to us the mystery of His will... the summing up of all things in Christ, things in the heavens and things on the earth" (Ephesians 1:9-10).

"Summing up all things in Christ." An amazing claim! The cosmos, and humanity within the cosmos, has been running around with its head off, and God's will is to put the head back on! Praise His name! And the Head is Jesus of Nazareth, the One who gave His life for the life of the world.

Then, in chapter 2, Paul develops what he calls "the mystery of Christ" further. The first instalment on God's great plan is bringing Jews and Gentiles together in the new people of God, breaking down all the barriers that used to divide, overcoming all the enmity, and making one new humanity, which constitutes a new society and God's new dwelling place in the world.

"Walk in a manner worthy of the calling... being diligent to preserve the unity of the Spirit in the bond of peace." "Being diligent," is too mild a translation for the word Paul uses. "Be eager" is better, but "be zealous" is even better.

Here again, we need to be careful. Paul's "therefore" comes before "create the unity." For one thing, we cannot create unity, for we are too self-preoccupied. For another, we need not create the unity, for it is already Christ-given. The unity of the Spirit has already been created, so be diligent to maintain it. Be zealous to maintain the unity that the Spirit has already created.

Look at verses 4-6 again: "There is one body and one Spirit, just as also you were called in one hope of your calling; one Lord, one faith, one baptism, one God and Father of all who is over all and through all and in all." Can we find a more concise summary of the unity already created? (Some people think Paul may be quoting an early Christian creed or hymn here.)

One body, the church of Jesus Christ. There is only one body. Oh, there are many different expressions of "church," but the reality is there is finally only one body of Christ. All who belong to Jesus Christ together constitute His body. We may not agree with everyone who belongs to Christ; we may not like everyone who belongs to Christ. Be that as it may, the reality is Christ has only one body. And walking worthy of being included in His body means being zealous to maintain the unity of His one body.

This explains why Paul speaks of "all humility and gentleness, with patience, showing tolerance for one another in love" (4:2). It takes great humility, much gentleness, lots of patience, and long tolerance to live the unity of the one church! And these are virtues inherent in the new reality brought into being by Jesus Christ. He Himself is humility, gentleness, patience, forbearance, and love incarnate, which is why Paul can speak of these virtues in his letter to the Galatians as the "fruit of the Spirit" (5:22-23), the natural consequences of the Spirit of Jesus dwelling with and in us.

Paul does not exhort us to "be humble and gentle" or to "work up humility and gentleness." Paul is saying that humility and gentleness are the natural relational dynamics of the new reality where the Spirit of Jesus is at work. When we lack humility or gentleness or patience, we are not to try to make them happen. When the fruit are not at work in our lives, it simply means that, at that moment, we have not moved far enough into the new reality where such virtues are the norm.

What helps is **one Spirit**, the Holy Spirit. There are many "spirits" at work in the world. The apostle John urged believers to "test the spirits" (1 John 4:1), because there is only one Spirit of God, the Spirit whose passion is to help people know Jesus Christ.

One hope, the hope that Paul has developed in Ephesians 1-3, the hope of the universe recapitulated in Jesus.

One Lord, Jesus Christ. I have pointed out that the word Paul uses is *Kurios*, a loaded term! In the Greek and Roman world, *Kurios* meant "sovereign one." All citizens of the empire were required to say the words "Kaiser Kurios!" "Caesar is sovereign!" In the Jewish world, *Kurios* was the equivalent of Yahweh, the sacred name of God. "One Lord," says Paul. Only One is Sovereign, Yahweh to the rescue, Y'Shua, Jesus of Nazareth. This is how everything gets recapitulated in Him. Who else could be the Head?

One faith. Paul could be referring to the one faith affirmed by all who belong to the one Lord. Paul could be referring to the content of the faith, the story the gospel tells. Jude uses the phrase "the faith once for all handed down to the saints" (Jude 3). Or Paul could be referring to the fact that faith is faith in the one Lord; there is one faith because there is one Lord to have faith in.

I want to suggest that the "one faith" is the faith of the one Lord. The "one faith" is Jesus' faith. In Ephesians 4:13, Paul says we are to be built up "until we all attain to the unity of the faith, and of the knowledge of the Son of God." We are to grow up into the faith the Son of God has. Yes, we are to grow in faith in the Son of God. But what Paul explains is growing up into the faith the Son of God has.

That, I trust, is the one faith that binds us together. Jesus is the one great Believer. In the second chapter of Hebrews, the author has Jesus the Son say to His Father:

- "I will proclaim Your name to my brethren" (2:12); Jesus is the great preacher.
- "In the midst of the congregation I will sing Your praise" (2:12); Jesus is the great worshiper.
- "I will put My trust in Him" (2:13); Jesus is the great believer—who believes for all of us.

The "one faith" is Jesus' faith in the one Father. That is what binds us together—not my faith, or your faith, or all of our faith put together. What binds us in unity is the one faith of the one Lord.

One baptism. Paul could be referring to our baptism into the one Lord, one Spirit, one Father. I suggest, however, following what I said about the one faith, that the one baptism is Jesus' baptism, the baptism of the Lord, both His baptism in the Jordan River, and His baptizing us in and with the Holy Spirit. This is the one baptism that really matters.

At the Jordan River, John the Baptist takes Jesus through the waters of baptism. That was the public moment when Jesus declared His full solidarity with the human race. He, the eternal Son of God, had become fully human, so fully human that He fully identified with our sin. As one of us, as sinful humanity, He goes into the waters for us, repents for us, believes for us.

And now, as John the Baptist announced, Jesus baptizes us in and with the Holy Spirit. Jesus inundates us with and immerses us in the very life of God. That is one baptism that matters, the one baptism that bonds us together.

One God and Father, the Father Jesus knows, and loves, and trusts. The one God and Father whom the one Spirit of the one Lord helps us address as "Abba."

- "Over all," sovereign over everyone.
- "Through all," active in everyone.
- "In all" seeking intimacy with everyone.

As Eugene Peterson renders it in The Message: "One God and Father of all, who rules over all, works through all, and is present in all."

That is the unity that was created which those alive in the new reality are zealous to maintain. One body, one Spirit, one hope, one Lord, one faith, one baptism, one God and Father.

Unity with Diversity

This comprehensive unity came alive for me while I served as pastor of Union Church of Manila from 1985 to 1989. Union Church was formed in 1914 to serve the growing influx of foreigners into the Philippines. It began as a union of Methodists, Presbyterians, Episcopalians, and some Baptists. By the time I became pastor in 1985 there were people in the church from thirty-six different countries of the world, representing thirty-one different Christian denominations! I was regularly in trouble with someone for not "doing it right!" Here was a setting with a great need for the gospel virtues of humility, gentleness, patience, and long suffering.

For example, I had to make sure we served the Lord's Supper to accommodate as wide a practice as possible. So we served using trays passed along the pews, but I had to make sure there was both wine and grape juice available (wine in the cups in the first two rings, grape juice in the other rings). I had to have stations set up for those who wanted to get up out of their pews and come forward, and take from a piece of bread and dip in a cup. I also had to make sure one of the pastors was prepared to place a wafer on the tongue of those who were used to that form of communion. And it worked! A wonderful diversity, thriving within a wonderful unity.

I grew to feel in my guts that what binds us together in the new reality is infinitely greater than anything that threatens to divide us. We have Jesus Christ in common! What can possibly be so important that it could separate us?

The problem is churches, branches of the one body, tend to major on the minors and minor on the majors. At Union Church we had to learn to major on the majors and minor on the minors. Had we majored on the way to do Communion... oh, mercy! Or had we majored on the kinds of songs to sing... oh, mercy! Or on the form of governance... mercy, mercy, mercy! We were forced to major on the majors and minor on the minors. And we found that the majors that bind us are infinitely greater than any of the minors that could divide us.

On my way to church one day, I remembered what my friend Earl Palmer once said to me: none of what tends to divide the one body would have ever won us to Christ in the first place! None of the minor issues that separate the visible church have ever won anyone to the Saviour. Who ever found the Saviour in a debate about the structure of ministry? Who was ever filled with the Holy Spirit in a debate about what kinds of songs to sing? What won us was the love of Jesus Christ. What won us was Jesus Christ Himself. And if we have Him in common, nothing else finally matters.

A fan of the Vancouver Canucks who belongs to Jesus Christ and a fan of the Boston Bruins who belongs to Jesus Christ have infinitely more in common than any two Canucks fans or two Bruins fans who do not yet belong to Christ. A Republican who belongs to Jesus Christ and a Democrat who belongs to Jesus Christ have infinitely more in common than any two Republicans or any two Democrats who do not yet belong to Christ. A Canadian who loves Jesus Christ and an American who loves Jesus Christ have infinitely more in common than any two Canadians or any two Americans who have no interest in Christ. On it goes! A Baptist who loves Jesus Christ and a Pentecostal who loves Jesus Christ and a Roman Catholic who loves Jesus Christ have infinitely more in common than all that sets them apart. One body, One Spirit, one hope, one Lord, one faith, one baptism, one God and Father of all.

Jesus calls us into a radically re-structured reality; an alternative reality. Therefore, walk worthy of the calling to which you have been called... walk in unity.

EPHESIANS 4:7-16

⁷ But to each one of us grace was given according to the measure of Christ's gift. ⁸ Therefore it says,

> "When He ascended on high,
> He led captive a host of captives,
> And He gave gifts to men."

⁹ (Now this expression, "He ascended," what does it mean except that He also had descended into the lower parts of the earth? ¹⁰ He who descended is Himself also He who ascended far above all the heavens, so that He might fill all things.) ¹¹ And He gave some as apostles, and some as prophets, and some as evangelists, and some as pastors and teachers, ¹² for the equipping of the saints for the work of service, to the building up of the body of Christ; ¹³ until we all attain to the unity of the faith, and of the knowledge of the Son of God, to a mature man, to the measure of the stature which belongs to the fullness of Christ. ¹⁴ As a result, we are no longer to be children, tossed here and there by waves and carried about by every wind of doctrine, by the trickery of men, by craftiness in deceitful scheming; ¹⁵ but speaking the truth in love, we are to grow up in all aspects into Him who is the head, even Christ, ¹⁶ from whom the whole body, being fitted and held together by what every joint supplies, according to the proper working of each individual part, causes the growth of the body for the building up of itself in love.

CHAPTER 13

Walking into Maturity

EPHESIANS 4:7–16

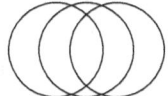

As we have seen, walking worthy of the calling to which we have been called in Jesus Christ means being zealous to live in and nurture the unity that already is. Walking worthy of the calling to which the Triune God calls us means being passionate about living in the unity of the Trinity.

However, the unity created by the Holy Spirit is not about uniformity. Within the unity, there is a God-given diversity! Paul brings this out clearly by following the seven-fold unity of Ephesians 4:1-6 ("one body and one Spirit,... one hope of your calling; one Lord, one faith, one baptism, one God and Father of all who is over all and through all and in all") with a listing in verses 7-16 of the diverse gifts that are given "to each one of us."

Given

Notice the verb "give." Paul uses it three times in these verses:

- "But to each one of us grace was given" (v. 7)
- "and He gave gifts to men" (v. 8)
- "and He gave some" (v. 11)

Jesus Christ so wants us to live in the unity already created that He gives gifts to us to make it all work—a variety of gifts to bring about a creative diversity within the created unity.

"But to each one of us grace was given according to the measure of Christ's gift" (Ephesians 4:7). Each and every one of us whom Jesus has called to Himself has been given grace to function in and contribute to the new society Jesus is bringing about in the world. We all have been graced by Jesus Christ to be full partners with Him in the kingdom of God.

To substantiate this amazing claim, Paul quotes from Scripture, which he often does. This time, he quotes from Psalm 68:18. Paul writes,

> Therefore it says,
> 'When He ascended on high,
> He led captive a host of captives,
> and He gave gifts to men.' (4:8)

If you open your Bible to Psalm 68, you discover that King David wrote:

> You have ascended on high,
> You have led captive Your captives;
> You have received gifts among men.

Paul has changed David's wording. First by changing the pronouns from "You" to "He." And second, and more significantly, by changing the verb from "received" to "gave." So "You have received gifts" becomes "He gave gifts."

What is going on here? Paul loves the Scriptures. He would never play fast and loose with the text of God's Word. Why then the changes? Was Paul lazy that day when he was dictating the letter? Was Tychichus who was taking dictation not careful? Was it that Paul did not have the actual text with him in jail, and he was doing his best to remember what David wrote? Was he so wanting to make a point that he did what many of us do unintentionally, and made the Psalm text say what he wanted it to say?

Better minds than I have wrestled with this and not come to a definitive resolution. Here is how I see it. This psalm was one of the texts read on Pentecost day, the spring harvest festival that was held forty days after Passover. It is both a call for help and a celebration of victory. King David recalls God's saving actions on behalf of the people of Israel, especially when God led them through the wilderness to the Promised Land, and then cries out to God to again preserve His people.

In Psalm 68, verse 18, David uses vivid imagery to recall God's conquest of His enemies and God's ascension to His holy mountain. "You have ascended on high, You have led captive Your captives; You have received gifts among men." As was the pattern in those days, when a king would win a victory in some part of the world he would return to the seat of his government, "ascending" his throne, bringing in his train those whom he had defeated and who were now held captive. And then the king would receive gifts from the captives; he would receive the booty, the spoils of victory.

Part of the reason Paul's mind would go to Psalm 68 is his conviction that Jesus Christ, the great King, has won a great victory over what Paul calls "the rulers," "the powers," "the world forces of this darkness," and "the spiritual forces of wickedness in the heavenly places" (Ephesians 6:12). As victor, Jesus has ascended "far above all the heavens" (4:10) and is seated "far above all rule and authority and power and dominion, and every name that is named, not only in this age but in the one to come" (Ephesians 1:21).

Jesus Christ descended: from the realm of heaven, "across all worlds" down into our humanity, all the way down into the depths of the earth, into our grave.[1] And in the process, Jesus won the great victory over all that stands against the kingdom of the Living God. Jesus has now returned from battle, bringing in His train those He has defeated, disarmed, and dethroned (Colossians 2:15).

What better text for Paul to quote than Psalm 68:18? But why the change from "receive gifts from humans" to "gave gifts to humans"?

I think Paul is drawing out the inherent implication of the affirmations of Psalm 68. What conquering kings took as spoil from their enemies, they often then gave to their own people (see Genesis 14; 1 Samuel 30:26-31; Isaiah 53:12). The triumphant conqueror both received and gave gifts. In his letter to the Ephesians, Paul is drawing this out in light of the victory won in and by Jesus Christ. The risen and ascended Christ receives gifts when He is seated on His throne. But true to His nature, He then gives gifts.

---

[1] I owe the phrase "across all worlds" to C. Baxter Kruger, *Across All Worlds: Jesus Inside Our Darkness* (Vancouver, BC: Regent College Publishing, 2007).

Thus, on the Day of Pentecost, when Jesus poured out the Holy Spirit upon His church, the apostle Peter says in the first Christian sermon: "Therefore having been exalted to the right hand of God, and having received from the Father the presence of the Holy Spirit, He has poured forth this which you both see and hear" (Acts 2:33). The risen and ascended One, who has descended to the depths of the earth, now pours out His very life on His people. Jesus Christ is the conqueror who gives and gives and gives and gives.

"To each of us grace was given according to the measure of Christ's gift." Into the already existing unity—one body, one Spirit, one Lord, one God and Father of all—the victorious Jesus gives a kaleidoscopic diversity of gifts. "To each one," for every person who walks with Jesus Christ is given gifts of grace in order to walk in the fullness of grace.

The Gifts

To make it all work, Jesus gives "support gifts" to the one body. Ephesians 4:11 literally says, "And He gave some apostles, and some prophets..." It is not as it is often translated, "some *as* apostles, and some *as* prophets..." The "as" suggests roles and functions, but in Ephesians Paul is not thinking about roles and functions. He is thinking about persons. The gifts Jesus gives to the one body to help it all work are persons. Yes, they are persons who are uniquely gifted for particular forms of ministry, but the focus here is the persons. "And He gave some apostles, and some prophets, and some evangelists, and some pastors and teachers, for the equipping of the saints."

"Some prophets." Prophets are those to whom Jesus speaks further specific revelation. Like the prophets of old, such people are taken into the counsel of God; they hear and see "a word," which they are then commanded to speak. Prophets emerge from the presence of God able to say, "Thus says the Lord..." Such prophets were at work as the church was emerging in the world: people like Paul and Agabus, and the daughters of Philip (see Acts 11:27-30, 21:9-11).

The work of the apostles was to lay the theological ground for churches, and the work of the prophets was to bring fresh revelation for each new challenge the new churches were facing. You can see then why earlier in his letter Paul speaks of the new society, the new temple, being built in Jesus, as being "built on the foundation of the apostles and prophets, Christ Jesus Himself being the corner stone" (Ephesians 2:20). The apostles and prophets are still serving us through their words in the New Testament!

"Some evangelists," "good-news-bringers." These are people uniquely gifted to move among people who have never heard the gospel. They speak the message given to us by apostles and prophets in the language and thought-forms of the people. Evangelists are uniquely wired to be willing to travel from place to place with the gospel. They live with a "holy restlessness," until every people group and every nation hears the good news.

And "some pastors and teachers." There is some debate about whether Paul is referring to one person, a "pastor-teacher," or two persons, "pastors" and "teachers." I take the second view. Paul is referring to two different persons, pastors and teachers. Apostles, prophets, evangelists, pastors, and teachers all work in the word, but all do it in different modes. Although all pastors teach in one way or another, not all teachers pastor.

The word "pastor" is the word rendered elsewhere as "shepherd." Have you ever thought about the work of a shepherd—beyond the romanticized picture of the shepherd playing her flute at night for gentle, cooperative sheep? A shepherd is running a business! She has not only to guide her sheep from hill to hill, she has to make sure that the next hill has food resources and water. She also has to serve as a veterinarian, checking for wounds and diseases, and as a guard, watching for and warding off wolves and other predators. She has to arrange for shearing of the wool, and find buyers for the wool. On it goes. The shepherd's role is highly administrative, not leaving much time for teaching!

The teacher's job is to keep bringing the one body back to the truth of the gospel as given by the apostles and prophets. The teacher has to spend time poring over and dwelling in the words of the apostles and prophets. Then, the teacher helps members of the body understand the gospel and learn to live in the gospel. This doesn't leave much time for shepherding (pastoring).

The Purpose of the Gifts

Now look carefully at verse 12 of the text. Why has Jesus given some people to the one body? "For the equipping of the saints for the work of service, to the building up of the body of Christ." Many books have been written on this text, and it has been at the heart of renewal movements within the church for the past 40 years or so. And rightly so!

The text has been read in two ways. One is to read it as saying the ascended Jesus has given apostles, prophets, evangelists, pastors, and teachers "for the equipping of the saints," *comma*, "for the work of service," *comma*, "to the building up of the body of Christ." That is, Jesus has given some apostles, prophets, evangelists, pastors, and teachers to do three things:

(1) equip the saints;
The "saints" then do two things:
(2) do the work of ministry; and
(3) build up the body of Christ.

This is the way the church in the Western world read it for centuries, leading to the creation of highly professional pastor-centered, professional pastor-dependent congregations. "The minister"—who is thought to be a combination of apostle, prophet, evangelist, pastor, teacher, priest, therapist, and CEO—equips the saints, does the work of ministry, and builds up the body of Christ.

The other way to read the text is that the ascended Jesus has given some apostles, prophets, evangelists, pastors, and teachers "for the equipping of the saints" *no comma* "for the work of service." That is, they equip the saints so that the saints do the work of ministry, "to the building up of the body of Christ." The ascended Jesus has given some apostles, prophets, evangelists, pastors, and teachers to do one thing:

(1) equip the saints.
The "saints" then do two things:
(1) they do the work of ministry; and
(2) they build up the body of Christ.

Oh, apostles, prophets, evangelists, pastors, and teachers also do the work of ministry and build up the body; for they are also "saints." But they are given by Jesus to do one major thing: equip the saints. And they equip the saints so that the saints can do the work of ministry and the work of building up the body.

The three clauses of Ephesians 4:12 are introduced with different prepositions:

"For the equipping..." *Pros.*

"For the work of ministry..." *Eis.*

"To the building up of the body..." *Eis.*

Pros, eis, eis. "For," "unto," "unto." For equipping the saints unto the work of ministry unto the building up of the body. The ascended Jesus gives apostles, prophets, evangelists, pastors, and teachers to help equip all of God's people for the work of ministry and the up-building of the community of believers.

To make the point more simply: every one who walks with Jesus Christ is a minister. Some ministers are apostles. Some ministers are prophets. Some ministers are evangelists. Some ministers are pastors. Some ministers are teachers. But all believers are ministers.

"To each one," says Paul, "grace was given" (4:7). "According to the proper working of each individual part," says Paul (4:16). Every one of us who walks in the new reality brought into being by Jesus Christ is a minister. The whole thing works as each of us plays our part. The body will not grow as Jesus wants it to grow unless *I* exercise the gifts He has given me. And the body will not grow as Jesus wants it to grow unless *you* exercise the gifts He has given you. More to the point: *You* will not grow unless I exercise the gifts He has given me and *I* will not grow unless you exercise the gifts He has given you.

"For the equipping of the saints." Equipping. The word was used in Paul's day in all kinds of vocational realms. It was used of doctors setting a broken bone. It was used of hoteliers "outfitting" guest rooms. It was used of preparing materials to weave a garment.[2] It was used of fishermen preparing their nets. The ascended Jesus gives, and gives, and gives. He gives gifts to His one body to equip all members of the body to be joyfully active with Him in His ministry in the world, each of us doing our part to build up the new community centered in Him.

The Result of the Gifts

And where is it all going? That is the key question. Another series of clauses: "Until we all attain to the unity of the faith, and of the knowledge of the Son of God, to a mature man, to the measure of the stature which belongs to the fullness of Christ" (Ephesians 4:13).

What a vision of the church! What a vision of what all this gifting and ministry is finally all about! It is all moving toward maturity. It is all moving toward becoming a mature human. The word translated "mature" is *teleios*. It means complete, whole, perfect. It is related to the word *telos*, which means inherent end or destiny. It is all moving toward our becoming what we were intended to be, *teleios* humans, like the one complete human Himself, Jesus Christ. It is all moving toward our being built up in stature; a stature that can finally only be measured by Jesus Christ Himself; indeed, by the fullness of Jesus Christ Himself!

That is why the ascended Jesus gives gifts to each of us. As each of us exercises those gifts on behalf of one another, we all

---

[2] Frank Thielman, *Ephesians* [Baker Exegetical Commentary on the New Testament] (Grand Rapids: Baker Academic, 2010), 279.

slowly but surely grow up into the only true human who ever lived!

And what does that look like? "Until we all attain to the unity of the faith and the knowledge of the Son of God" (Ephesians 4:13). We tend to read the verse as "... attaining to the unity of faith *in* the Son of God," "... attaining to the unity of *knowing* the Son of God." And such a goal is part of what equipping the saints involves: greater and greater faith in Jesus the Son; deeper and deeper knowing of Jesus the Son.

But that is not what Paul is emphasizing in this text. He is saying that the goal of equipping the saints is arriving at the unity of the faith of the Son of God, the faith the Son of God Himself has. Paul is saying that the goal of equipping the saints is arriving at the unity of the knowledge the Son of God Himself has. My goodness! Can it really be? To grow up into the knowledge the Son of God has?

Jesus says, "No one knows the Son except the Father; nor does anyone know the Father except the Son" (Matthew 11:27). No one. Sobering, but true. No human being knows God the Father fully except Jesus the Son of the Father. No human being knows humanity fully either except Jesus the Son in our flesh. No human being knows creation fully except Jesus the Son.

Do you see what Paul is saying? Jesus the Son chooses to share what He knows! More than chooses, Jesus delights to share what He knows! Jesus the Son wants us to know God as He knows God.

Re-read the four Gospels in light of Paul's letter (especially the Gospel according to John) and you see that Jesus' whole life and ministry is about His Father. In every deed He is showing us who the Father is. In every story He is telling us who the Father is. He wants us to know the Father as He knows the Father. That is the goal of equipping the saints!

Jesus wants us to arrive at the true unity of the faith He has, the faith He has in the Father. Can it really be? That we grow up to believe as Jesus believes? To trust as Jesus trusts? To then experience the freedom, poise, and joy Jesus experiences because He so fully knows and trusts His Father?

That is what it finally means to be human: To know God as the one true human knows God, and to trust God as the one true human trusts God.

And that is why the victorious Christ, the risen and ascended Jesus, gives gifts to His church. He gives gifts so that, as we all exercise the gifts together, we are built up as His body and begin to walk further and further into His maturity. As each of the ministers does the ministry each is called to do, we all grow up into knowing God as the Son of God knows God so that we trust God as the Son of God trusts God.

Even so Lord, make it so!

EPHESIANS 4:17-24

¹⁷ So this I say, and affirm together with the Lord, that you walk no longer just as the Gentiles also walk, in the futility of their mind, ¹⁸ being darkened in their understanding, excluded from the life of God because of the ignorance that is in them, because of the hardness of their heart; ¹⁹ and they, having become callous, have given themselves over to sensuality for the practice of every kind of impurity with greediness. ²⁰ But you did not learn Christ in this way, ²¹ if indeed you have heard Him and have been taught in Him, just as truth is in Jesus, ²² that, in reference to your former manner of life, you lay aside the old self, which is being corrupted in accordance with the lusts of deceit, ²³ and that you be renewed in the spirit of your mind, ²⁴ and put on the new self, which in the likeness of God has been created in righteousness and holiness of the truth.

CHAPTER 14

Walking as New Humans

EPHESIANS 4:17-24

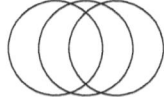

Ephesians 4:17-24 is a dense text, which does not flow as easily as other texts in Apostle Paul's letter to the Ephesians we have already considered. So, before diving in to study this text, let me lift up what I think is Paul's major burden in this part of the epistle.

The Apostle of Jesus Christ wants us to walk as new humans. He wants us to live as the new humans we are becoming in relationship with Jesus Christ, the one True Human. In this text, Paul is continuing the exhortation he began at the turning point in his letter: "Therefore I, the prisoner of the Lord, implore you to walk in a manner worthy of the calling with which you have been called" (Ephesians 4:1). Paul is calling us to live in a way that is congruent with the alternative reality brought into being through the life, death, resurrection, and ascension of Jesus Christ.

"So this I say" (4:17) is literally, "This I say therefore." This is the second "therefore" in a series of "therefores" in the second half of Paul's letter. "And affirm together with the Lord" shows that Paul is not just giving us his own personal advice, but is speaking with the authority of the Lord Himself. "This I say therefore... that you walk no longer just as the Gentiles also walk..." (4:17).

Why put it that way? The letter is written to Gentiles: "Therefore remember that formerly you, the Gentiles in the flesh..." (Ephesians 2:11). Why then say, "Walk no longer just as the Gentiles also walk"? Paul is here using the word "Gentiles" not to refer to non-Jews, but to all people who have not yet encountered Jesus Christ. "Gentiles" here mean those not yet brought into the alternative reality shaped by the gospel of Jesus Christ; those not yet grabbed by the grace of God in Jesus Christ. "Walk no longer as those not yet walking in the new reality centered in, and filled with, Jesus Christ." Rather, walk in the new reality as new humans alive in the new reality.

Moving in a Reality

Imagine a room, such as a restaurant, an office, a library, or a church sanctuary. When you move into a room you discover that there is a way of being inherent to the room. What you cannot experience in other rooms you can in this room. What you did in other rooms you cannot do in this room. It would be hard to play a round of golf in a church sanctuary. You could get hurt trying to play tennis in a restaurant. It would be out of place, "unworthy," to throw Frisbees in a library. Each of these rooms calls for different behaviours, because they evoke different attitudes and invite us into different realities.

Or imagine moving into a new home. When you do this, you have to learn a new way of living. Oh, we bring with us the same fundamental values which shaped our living in our old home, but in the new home things are arranged differently. When Sharon and I last moved, we downsized and got rid of a lot of things we once thought we needed. The new home called for some different values. We were required to learn to live in a way that was congruent with the new space into which the Lord had called us.

Or imagine moving to a new country, with a whole new culture, as Sharon and I did when we lived in Manila, the Philippines. In order to function in a new culture, one is forced to learn to live in all kinds of different ways! In Manila there are different ways of relating, such as not confronting a person directly, but going through a third party, or not touching your face while speaking to another (which suggests you are hiding something). In Manila, you must learn to walk differently—literally so. If I walk in Manila the way I walk in Vancouver, I would be soaking with sweat within the first block! In Manila one has to learn—in order to survive—"the Manila stride": slow, smooth, easy steps, graciously moving through the humidity.

Living in a different reality requires a different mind-set and requires assuming different values and behaviours. That is what Paul is getting at in this section of his letter to the Ephesians.

As we have seen, his letter is written in two halves.[1] In chapters 1-3, Paul opens up for us the new room, home, and country brought into being by the life, death, resurrection, and ascension of Jesus Christ. This new reality invades and encompasses all other realities. Then, in chapters 4-6, through many exhortations,

---

[1] One of the dynamics of oral communication – preaching – is repetition. I think it was Billy Graham who after being asked about the keys to effective preaching said, "There are three: 1. Repeat. 2. Repeat. 3. Repeat."

Paul helps us navigate the new reality. We miss Paul's intention if we turn his exhortations into new rules and regulations by which we must now abide. Through his many exhortations he is simply describing the way of being inherent to the new reality.

"Therefore walk." Walk worthy. Walk in unity. Walk toward maturity. And "walk no longer just as the Gentiles also walk…" Leave behind the way of life you knew before you came to know Jesus Christ and learn to live the new way inherent to the room, house, and world where Jesus Christ is Head.

Learn Christ

Notice the phrase right in the middle of this dense text: "But you did not learn Christ in this way" (Ephesians 4:20). At the center of the reality encompassing all reality is Christ. And we live in this reality by "learning Christ."

Where did Paul get this phrase? From Jesus Himself! "Come to me," He says, "all who are weary and heavy-laden [who have over-burdened yourselves], and I will give you rest. Take my yoke upon you, and learn from Me" (Matthew 11:28-29). The key to living congruent with the new reality shaped by and centered in Christ is to "learn Christ."

An interesting way to put it, is it not? "Learn Christ." We speak of "learning piano," or "learning physics," or "learning hockey." But "learn a person"? Yes! "Get inside Jesus Christ and learn what makes Him tick."

Thus Paul can also say, "you heard Him," (v. 21), not just "heard of Him." You got close enough to hear Him open His heart and mind to you. "You were taught in Him," says Paul (v. 21). In relationship with Him you were taught by Christ! Through those gifted to teach Him, and through His words recorded for us in the gospels, you were taught by Christ.

"Just as truth is in Jesus," says Paul (v. 21). The word "truth" Paul uses means "more than true" as opposed to false. The word means genuine, authentic, the real deal. In Jesus we discover the genuine, the authentic, the real deal. He knows what makes creation tick. He knows what makes the world tick, what makes chemistry tick, what makes economies tick, what makes superconductors tick. He knows what makes humanity tick: psychologically, intellectually, sexually. And he knows what makes God tick! Learn Him. The truth about everything and everyone is in Him!

Putting Aside and Putting On

Then Paul summarizes what he assumes the Ephesians learned as they learned Christ:

> In reference to your former manner of life, you lay aside the old self [literally "the old human"], which is being corrupted in accordance with the lusts of deceit, and that you be renewed in the spirit of your mind, and put on the new self [literally "the new human"], which in the likeness of God has been created in righteousness and holiness of the truth.
>
> Ephesians 4:22-24

When we learn Jesus Christ we are taught to "lay aside," "be renewed," and "put on." He teaches us to lay aside the old human we were before we met Him. He teaches us to be renewed in the spirit of our minds, so we operate from a very different mind-set.

And He teaches us to put on the new human we are becoming since meeting Him, the new human who, like its Creator, is holy and who knows how to make relationships work.

Lay aside the old, put on the new. Change your clothes. It makes sense, does it not? Different spaces call for different sets of clothing. We have been called into a new world encompassing all other worlds. So lay aside the old human you were and put on the new human you are becoming. Paul also speaks this way in his letter to the Colossians (3:8-12) and in his letter to the Romans:

> The night is almost gone, and the day is near. Therefore let us lay aside the deeds of darkness and put on the armour of light. Let us behave properly as in the day, not in carousing and drunkenness, not in sexual promiscuity and sensuality, not in strife and jealousy. But put on the Lord Jesus Christ... (13:12-14a)

When we "learn Christ," we learn to lay aside all that is not in sync with Him and His desires; and we learn to put on all that *is* in sync with Him and His agenda for the world. We have been called into a new reality. It only makes sense that we want to change our clothes.

The Futility of Their Mind

Here is the major emphasis of Paul's dense text: It all happens through the renewing of our minds. Notice that between the "lay aside the old self" (v. 22) and the "put on the new self" (v. 24) there is "be renewed in the spirit of your mind" (v. 23). The changing of clothes happens through the renewing of the spirit of our minds. I think Paul's phrase, "the spirit of your mind," means "what makes your mind tick." Be renewed in Christ in what makes your mind tick. "Learn Christ" so that your mind ticks as His mind ticks.

"Be renewed" is in the present tense, emphasizing continuous action. "Be continuously renewed." Why? Because there is a lot of renewing that needs to take place! In verse 17, Paul has encouraged us to walk no longer as the old humanity does "in the futility of their mind." This is what we are up against as we work to "lay aside" the old and "put on" the new and seek to live as new humans in the new reality shaped by the gospel.

What is Paul getting at? What does he want us to know? Or, more precisely, what is it that he believes Jesus teaches us? What truth is Jesus wanting us to know as we seek to live as new humans?

He wants us to realize that the Fall has affected our minds.[2] When the first humans chose to go it without God, when they chose to disobey God's one command not to try to be their own god, their disobedience affected the human mind. Clearly the Fall affects our bodies: we all die. And clearly the Fall affects the created order: it all decays. And clearly the Fall affects our relationships: we all experience some sort of alienation. What Paul wants us to realize, what He believes Jesus teaches us when we "learn Christ," is that the Fall also affects our brains. Our brains are not able to function as they were intended to function.

Paul is not saying that the mind of the old humanity is dumb. Hardly! Look at what our minds can do! By "futility of mind" Paul is meaning that the old-humanity mind cannot by itself,

---

[2] Read Genesis 2-3.

on its own, arrive at the truth, at the genuine, at the authentic, at the "real deal."

The old-humanity mind begins its reasoning process from un-truth. The old-humanity mind begins with the un-truth that there is no God. Or if the mind believes there is a God, it begins with its own image of God. But because the mind is finite, it will never correctly imagine the infinite God. If we start with a faulty presupposition, our reasoning—however otherwise brilliant—will slowly, but surely, move from faulty toward futility. So Eugene Peterson paraphrases Paul in 4:17 in this way: "They have refused for so long to deal with God that they've lost touch not only with God but with reality itself."

Paul lays out the trajectory of futility, the downward spiral:

- "Being darkened in their understanding." A frightening fact about the mind: exclude from our thinking the light of the world and our thinking goes dark, we no longer see clearly.
- "Excluded from the life of God." Leave the Living God out of the picture and we end up out of touch with life itself, grasping at anything that promises life.
- "Because of the ignorance that is in them." Again, it is not that our old humanity is stupid, it is just that when we leave a crucial factor out of the equation, we can not expect to understand ourselves and the world.
- "Because of the hardness of their heart." The willful choice to ignore the heart of reality makes the heart hard to reality.
- "Having become callous,", numb to Holy Reality.
- "Have given themselves over to sensuality for the

practice of every kind of impurity with greediness." As J.B. Phillips paraphrases Paul: "They have stifled their consciences and then surrendered themselves to sensuality, practising any form of impurity which lust can suggest."

This trajectory leads to an awful fact of life: "being corrupted in accordance with the lusts of deceit," says Paul, desires born out of un-truth, fueled by the deceiver himself, the father of lies.

Lay it all aside, is the call. Jesus teaches us to lay it all aside, all the un-truth, the deceit that awakens desires that only lead to degradation and violence. Lay aside the un-truth made appealing by the promises of pleasure "the spirits" of the fallen world make, leading to destructive behaviour.[3]

Walk no longer as the old-humanity-mind does "in the futility of the mind." Be renewed in the spirit of your mind.

Be Renewed

"Be renewed" is in the passive tense, meaning we cannot renew the mind! The futile mind cannot renew itself. It has to be renewed from outside itself.

This is what Jesus Christ comes to do! He enters into the world ruined by the choices of the futility of the mind, and He heals the human mind. He takes hold of our minds, and rewires them, helping us think clearly.

---

[3] Paraphrasing Ibid., 305. Frank Thielman, *Ephesians* [Baker Exegetical Commentary on the New Testament] (Grand Rapids: Baker Academic, 2010), 305.

Only Jesus can heal the mind because only He really knows what makes us tick. Only He can straighten out all the twisted thinking. "The truth is in Jesus," says Paul. The truth is Jesus. He says, "You will know the truth, and the truth will make you free" (John 8:32). He takes us into the furnace of His holy truth and love, melts our hardened hearts, and remakes our minds to tick as His mind ticks. And, as He does, we change clothes and begin to walk as new humans, becoming more and more like the only True Human who ever lived.

As I have worked through the apostle Paul's dense text, a story in *The Chronicles of Narnia* kept coming to mind. Narnia is another world, created out of the "being-renewed mind" of C.S. Lewis. In many ways, Narnia feels more real than the reality we think we know with our eyes and ears and hands. The lead character in *The Chronicles* is a lion named Aslan. It is hard not to fall in love with Aslan!

The story that kept coming to mind is about Eustace Clarence Scrubb; a precocious and obnoxious young boy, whom other children in the story, like Lucy and Edmund, find quite irritating. In fact, the first line of the book *The Voyage of the Dawn Treader* is: "There was a boy called Eustace Clarence Scrubb, and he almost deserved it."[4]

Eustace wanders off by himself and stumbles upon a dragon's cave. The cave is filled with piles of golden treasure. Lust is awakened and he covers himself with gold jewelry. After some time, he falls asleep on a pile of gold with a gold bracelet on his arm. When he wakes up, he discovers to his horror that he has

---

[4] C.S. Lewis, *The Voyage of the Dawn Treader* (New York: Harper Collins, 1952), 3.

become a dragon! We become like what we lust after.

One week later, he meets Edmund. We pick up the story as Eustace is sharing his experience:

> "I looked up and saw the very last thing I expected: a huge lion coming slowly towards me. And one queer thing was that there was no moon last night, but there was moonlight where the lion was. So it came nearer and nearer. I was terribly afraid of it. You may think that, being a dragon, I could have knocked any lion out easily enough. But it wasn't that kind of fear. I wasn't afraid of it eating me, I was just afraid of *it*—if you can understand. Well, it came closer up to me and looked straight into my eyes. And I shut my eyes tight. But that wasn't any good because it told me to follow it."[5]

The lion brings him to a well, which was

> "like a very big, round bath with marble steps going down into it. The water was as clear as anything and I thought if I could get in there and bathe it would ease the pain in my leg. But the lion told me I must undress first.
>
> "I was just going to say that I couldn't undress because I hadn't any clothes on when I suddenly thought that dragons are snaky sort of things and snakes can cast their skins. Oh, of course, thought I, that's what the lion means. So I started scratching myself and my scales began coming off all over the place. And then I scratched a little deeper, and instead of just scales coming off here and there, my whole skin started peeling

---

5 Ibid., 106-107.

off beautifully, like it does after an illness, or as if I was a banana. In a minute or two I just stepped out of it. I could see it lying there beside me, looking rather nasty. It was a most lovely feeling. So I started to go down into the well for my bathe."[6]

But he discovers he is still covered with scales. He removes another layer, but finds he has more underneath.

"Then the lion said—but I don't know if it spoke—You will have to let me undress you. I was afraid of his claws, I can tell you, but I was pretty near desperate now. So I just lay flat down on my back to let him do it.

"The very first tear he made was so deep that I thought it had gone right into my heart. And when he began pulling the skin off, it hurt worse than anything I've ever felt. The only thing that made me able to bear it was just the pleasure of feeling the stuff peel off. You know—if you've ever picked the scab of a sore place. It hurts like billy-oh but it *is* such fun to see it coming away,"

"I know exactly what you mean," said Edmund.

"Well, he peeled the beastly stuff right off—just as I thought I'd done it myself the other three times, only they hadn't hurt—and there it was lying on the grass: only ever so much thicker, and darker, and more knobbly looking than the others had been. And there I was as smooth and soft as a peeled switch and smaller than I had been. Then he caught hold of me—I didn't like that much for I was very tender underneath now that I'd no skin on—and threw me into the water. It smarted like

---

[6] Ibid., 107-108.

anything but only for a moment. After that it became perfectly delicious and as soon as I started swimming and splashing I found that all the pain had gone from my arm. And then I saw why. I'd turned into a boy again."[7]

The lion clothes Eustace, and he finds himself back with the other children. He then wonders if it was all a dream.

"No. It wasn't a dream," said Edmund.
 "Why not?"
 "Well, there are the clothes, for one thing. And you have been—well, un-dragoned for another."
 "What do you think it was, then?" asked Eustace.
 "I think you've seen Aslan," said Edmund.[8]

You have seen Jesus Christ. You have heard Jesus Christ. You have learned Jesus Christ. He is renewing your mind. Freeing you to lay aside the old human and put on the new.

A few pages later, Lewis writes:

It would be nice, and fairly true, to say that "from that time forth Eustace was a different boy." To be strictly accurate, he began to be a different boy. He had relapses. There were still many days when he could be very tiresome. But most of those I shall not notice. The cure had begun.[9]

---

[7] Ibid., 108-109.
[8] Ibid., 110.
[9] Ibid., 112.

EPHESIANS 4:25-32

²⁵ Therefore, laying aside falsehood, speak truth each one of you with his neighbor, for we are members of one another. ²⁶ Be angry, and yet do not sin; do not let the sun go down on your anger, ²⁷ and do not give the devil an opportunity. ²⁸ He who steals must steal no longer; but rather he must labor, performing with his own hands what is good, so that he will have something to share with one who has need. ²⁹ Let no unwholesome word proceed from your mouth, but only such a word as is good for edification according to the need of the moment, so that it will give grace to those who hear. ³⁰ Do not grieve the Holy Spirit of God, by whom you were sealed for the day of redemption. ³¹ Let all bitterness and wrath and anger and clamor and slander be put away from you, along with all malice. ³² Be kind to one another, tender-hearted, forgiving each other, just as God in Christ also has forgiven you.

CHAPTER 15

Walking in Step with the Spirit

EPHESIANS 4:25-32

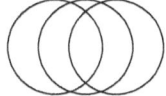

In the paragraph of his letter to the Ephesians before us, Paul shifts gears. In this paragraph, as many have put it, Paul finally brings the plane down out of the clouds and lands it where we live our daily lives.

In the section of his letter right before this text, Paul calls us to walk as the new humans that we are becoming because of, and in relationship with, Jesus Christ. We have been called to let Jesus renew our minds so that we can lay aside the old humans we were before meeting Him, and put on the new humans we are becoming since meeting Him. Paul now puts arms and legs on the call, providing specific concrete examples of what laying aside and putting on look like.

I am reminded of the story of a preacher, early last century, who was preaching against the besetting sins of that time. (I do not like the phrase "preached against," for preaching is not about denouncing, but announcing the gospel.) This preacher had preached against racism and violence and injustice. From the back pew, one of the elderly pillars of the church yelled out: "Preach it pastor!" He then started getting more concrete—as Paul does in this text. He preached against gambling: "Preach it pastor!" He preached against the use of tobacco: "Preach it pastor!" He preached against the misuse of alcohol: "Preach it pastor!" Then he preached against gossiping. He paused, waiting for the elderly parishioner to respond. Nothing. Finally, he heard a quiet voice say, "Now you've gone from preaching to meddling!"

The Structure of the Text

In this section, Paul is developing the call to "lay aside the old, put on the new," by giving five sets of opposites, five sets of "not... but." "Not this... but this." This is similar to much of the book of Proverbs, and to much of what Jesus does in His famous Sermon on the Mount: "You have heard it was said... but I say to you." As people in process of becoming new humans, "not this... but this." Lay aside the old—"not." Put on the new—"but" (sometimes, "rather").

I think you can also see that at the heart of the five sets of opposites are two fundamental exhortations: "Do not grieve the Holy Spirit of God" (v. 30) and "do not give the devil an opportunity" (v. 27). These two exhortations are interrelated. When we give the devil a launching pad for his diabolical work, it grieves the Holy Spirit. And when we grieve the Holy Spirit, the accuser is sure to try to take advantage, and begin to mess with our hearts and minds.

Now, whatever else we learn from the text, these two exhortations help us realize that we do not live in a neutral universe. Besides us humans, there are two "spirits" at work in every dimension of our existence, especially in any relational context. One is finite, the other (thank God!) is infinite, but both are at work.

Paul writes the exhortation regarding the devil after the second set: "Be angry, and yet do not sin... do not give the devil an opportunity" (v. 26-27). And Paul writes the exhortation regarding the Holy Spirit after the fourth set: "Let no unwholesome word proceed from your mouth, but only such a word as is good for building up... do not grieve the Holy Spirit of God" (v. 29-30). Because the two exhortations are so fundamental for our living as new humans in the new reality, I suggest that Paul intends the two to be read with each of five sets.

So,

- "laying aside falsehood, speak truth each one of you with his neighbour" (v. 25)... do not grieve the Holy Spirit, do not give the devil a place from which to work.
- "Be angry, and yet do not sin, do not let the sun go down on your anger" (v. 26)... do not grieve the Holy Spirit, do not give the devil a launching pad for his destructive plans.
- "He who steals must steal no longer; but rather he must labor, performing with his hands what is good" (v. 28)... do not grieve the Holy Spirit, do not give the devil an opportunity.
- "Let no unwholesome word proceed from your mouth, but only such a word as is good for edification according to the need of the moment" (v. 29)... do not grieve the Holy Spirit, do not give the devil a platform.

- "Let all bitterness... and slander be put away from you, along with all malice. Be kind to one another, tender-hearted, forgiving each other, just as God in Christ also has forgiven you" (v. 31-32)... do not grieve the Holy Spirit, do not give the devil space to work.

Now Paul's gone from preaching to meddling!

Why put these commands in the negative, especially the exhortation relative to the Holy Spirit? Why "do not grieve" and not "do what pleases" the Holy Spirit? Is that not a more inviting way to put it? Paul could certainly say it that way, so why put it in the negative?

Sadly the negative gets our attention in a way the positive does not. To "do what pleases the Holy Spirit," we would say, "of course... yes." And we would likely move on our merry ways. But "do not grieve the Holy Spirit" arrests us. It makes us stop and think. The Spirit of God can be grieved? Mere human beings can bring sorrow to the Spirit who created the world, who animated the life of Jesus of Nazareth, who gives us our breath? We can sadden the Spirit? We can cause pain for the Spirit? Paul expresses it in the negative to get our attention.

I think, however, that Paul wants to get us to the positive. That is, after facing the fact that we can grieve the most Intimate Friend anyone can ever have, we will *want* to please Him. We will want to co-operate with Him. We will want to bring Him joy.

So, I suggest that we best capture Paul's deeper concern in Ephesians 4:25-32, by saying with each of the five sets of opposites, "walk in step with the Spirit." Paul uses the word "walk" in the texts before this text, and in the texts after this text. So I suggest that his deeper call in this "not... but" text is "walk in step with the Spirit."

Even the negative exhortation regarding the devil can be rendered in a positive form: "Stay ahead of the devil." Walk in step with the Holy Spirit and there will be no space in which the devil can get a foothold!

- "Laying aside falsehood , speak truth each one of you with his neighbour." Walk in step with the Spirit, and "the father of lies" has no place to operate.
- "Be angry, [but] do not let the sun go down on your anger." Walk in step with the Spirit, and the divider has no junk with which to work.
- No longer steal, but work with our hands so we can bless others. Walk in step with the Creator Spirit, and the evil one has no place in the workshop.
- Let no unwholesome word proceed out of our mouths, but let us speak only words that build people up in the faith. Walk in step with the Spirit of the Word-made-flesh, and the distorter of words has nothing to play games with.
- Put away all bitterness and slander, and extend compassion and grace to one another. And as we do so we find ourselves dancing with the Holy One and the one who hates Jesus has no handle on the soul of the community.

Grieving the Holy Spirit of God

This is the only place in all of the New Testament where this full title ("the Holy Spirit of God") is used. Elsewhere He (not it, the Spirit is a person) is called the Spirit, the Holy Spirit, the Spirit of God, the Spirit of Christ (Romans 8:9, 1 Peter 1:11), the Spirit of Him-who-raised-Jesus-from-the-dead (Romans 8:11), the breath [Spirit] of Life (Revelation 11:11), the Spirit of life in Christ Jesus (Romans 8:2), the Spirit of glory and of God (1 Peter 4:14), the Spirit of adoption (Romans 8:15), and the Spirit of holiness (Romans 1:4). But here He is given His full title, "The Holy Spirit of God."

As I noted earlier in this book, many people bristle at the word "holy." In one sense, we ought to, for none of us is holy yet. The wonder of the gospel is that we are declared "holy" by the blood of Christ, but none of us is in fact fully holy. So we rightly bristle at the word.

But we need not do so. Holy is what the Spirit of God is. And holy is what the Spirit of God wants us to be. To be holy is to be pure, clean, full of light. Who does not want to be clean? To be holy is to be whole. Who does not want to be whole? The passion of the Holy Spirit of the Holy God is that we know the Holy One Himself, Jesus Christ, and that we become like the Holy One Himself. Oh, to become pure like Jesus. Please!

The good news is that the Holy Spirit of God works in all kinds of ways to make this so. As Margaret Clarkson puts it in her hymn, the Spirit "woos us, subdues us, and seals us His own."[1] From the earliest days of our childhood, He began to woo us to Jesus. He slowly broke down our fear and resistance. He slowly overcame our stubbornness and rebellion. He slowly captured our hearts, filling our hearts with His life! He slowly renews our

---

[1] Margaret Clarkson, "Sing Praise to the Father," Hope Publishing Company, 1966.

minds, helping us understand Jesus better and better, slowly drawing us deeper into the intimacy He enjoys with Jesus and the Father. Blessed Holy Spirit of God!

Paul is opening up a very tender dimension to the new reality into which we have been called. The Source of Life in the new reality can be saddened. When we think or speak or act in ways that are not congruent with the character of Jesus, the Spirit is deeply grieved, and the unclean spirit is given an opportunity to work his uncleanness.

The Holy Spirit grieves (Greek, lupeo, grieve, experience pain, be distressed) because thoughts, words, and behaviours out of sync with the character of Jesus are eventually self-destructive. Festering anger, bitterness, foul language, and laziness that leeches off others, all eat away at the centre of our personhood. And the Spirit grieves.

The Spirit grieves because thoughts, words, and behaviours out of sync with the character of Jesus give the destroyer a place from which to try to undo the work of Jesus. We find ourselves beginning to play the game on the devil's terms—lies, deception, slander, malice—and we cannot beat him at his game. We will lose. And the Spirit grieves.

And the Holy Spirit grieves because when we adopt ways of thinking, speaking, and acting out of sync with Jesus, it means we are not trusting Him. It means we do not think Jesus is who the Spirit says He is. It means we think "our way"—or, God forbid, the devil's way—is the way to get along in the world. And the Spirit is grieved.

This is why we too eventually begin to grieve, not only because we feel sorry for what is happening to us, but because we are experiencing the grief of the only One who can give us life. We are experiencing His sadness and displeasure.

You have experienced this, have you not? I know I have. I do something that displeases Him, and it feels like the Spirit leaves me. Thank God, He does not actually leave. But, there is a relational strain—it feels like He left. And it is awful! It is similar to marriage, or other close relationships, when one partner offends the other and the other withdraws. The marriage is not over, the relationship is not ended, but there is deep sadness.

So too with the Spirit of life. The relationship is not over. The Spirit does not walk away. As Paul says, the Spirit is the One "by whom you were sealed for the day of redemption" (v. 30). He owns us. He is the down-payment on our future in Jesus Christ (1:14). He does not dump us. But there is real, objective grief and a consequent loss of clarity, or loss of zeal, or loss of peace, or loss of joy.

On the Day of Pentecost, when the risen and exalted Jesus poured out the Holy Spirit upon the first community following Jesus with a heart for the city, we are told there was what seemed like wind and fire. Refreshing, cleansing, invigorating wind and purifying fire igniting passion for Jesus as Lord. Paul is here telling us that it is possible to think or speak or act in ways that make it feel like the wind has gone out of the sails, that the fire is dying down, or even, dying out.

And just as we can go through such times as individuals, so too can congregations. There is no wind. There is no fire. Because somehow the Holy Spirit of God has been grieved.

Not... But

Let us walk through the five sets of opposites one more time.

"Lay aside falsehood." The word is *pseudo*. Why does falsehood grieve the Spirit? Because He is, as Jesus calls Him, "the Spirit of Truth" (John 14:17, 15:26, 16:13). In the section before this "meddling" text, Paul says that in Jesus Christ, who is the Truth, we are being freed from the futility of our minds and being renewed into truth. To speak falsehood is to go back into futility. To speak falsehood is to enter into the deceiver's playland, where *pseudo* leads to more *pseudo* leading to more *pseudo*.

Get in step with the Spirit: speak the truth. Each one to their neighbours, especially to our neighbours who belong to the community shaped by, and centered in, the truth. "For we are members of one another," says Paul. The word he uses is never used for members of an organization, but is always used for members of an organism. We are members of the body of Christ, organically bound to each other, and the body works when truth is spoken "in love" (as Paul adds).

"Be angry, and yet do not sin." There are times when it is right to be angry. On a number of occasions Jesus, the Man of compassion, got very angry. The trick is to be angry for the right reason at the right time in the right way. In the Ephesians text Paul uses the word "angry" twice, but uses different Greek words. The first time ("be angry") the word is *thumos*. It refers to a sudden flare up of anger that soon subsides. The second time ("do not let the sun go down on your anger") the word is *orge*. It refers to anger that does not subside, but has settled, because it is not dealt with, and just sits there, festering.

Get in step with the Spirit: be angry. There are many reasons to be angry. But do not let the sun go down on the anger, for festering anger grieves the Spirit and gives the enemy a major foothold. The devil loves to fan the flames of festering anger and to get us to a place of hardened anger.

A number of years ago I was serving a church in California. Over a period of months I sensed something blocking the work of the Spirit in the congregation. On Sunday mornings I sensed something "off" in the right hand front section of the second service. Whereas there was much joy and gratitude being manifested in the singing in other sections of the sanctuary, this section felt "sour," even dead. As I prayed about this, I became aware that two men in the section were angry with each other—and had been for twenty years! They would not talk to each other. I spoke to them about it, pleading with them to let some of us help them resolve the anger. They would not budge. So I went from preaching to meddling, and told them they were missing out on the new work of the Spirit and that their festering anger was affecting others.

"He who steals must steal no longer." Possibly some of the believers in Ephesus had lost their jobs—maybe because of their allegiance to Jesus as Lord—and in needing to take care of their families, had given in to the temptation to steal. Possibly some of the believers were shopkeepers in Ephesus and were cheating their customers. Either scenario grieves the Spirit. Stealing violates the other person; it is saying that my needs or desires are greater than the other's needs, desires, or dignity. And, stealing implicitly says, "Sorry, Lord, You can't be trusted to help me; I have to take life into my own hands." Such a move of the heart delights the devil, for it gives him the opportunity to nurture further idolatry in our hearts.

"But work with your hands." Get in step with the Spirit, the Creative Spirit, who delights to enable us to make a contribution to our common life. Even if we do not get paid for it, we find dignity in being able to work in a way that blesses other people!

"Let no unwholesome word proceed from your mouth." The word Paul uses here is too politely rendered "unwholesome." It is used of rotten wood, and withered flowers.[2] Jesus uses it of worthless fruit (Matthew 7:17-18) and rancid fish (Matthew 13:48). Unprofitable would be a better translation; putrid or foul is better still.

Why do such words grieve the Spirit? Because they hurt those to whom they are addressed. And because they reveal the condition of the heart from which they emerge. The unclean spirit loves to work with such uncleanness, and the Holy Spirit who dwells within us wants to wash away all such filth.

Speak words that edify, says Paul. Get in step with the Spirit: use words the way He uses words, to build people up, to bring grace to people's lives.

"Let all bitterness and wrath and anger and clamour and slander be put away from you." It all gives the malicious slanderer a heyday. He loves such a cesspool. And it grieves the Spirit because it is all so contrary to His character. It is what Jesus Christ came to rescue us out of.

Instead, get in step with the Spirit: be kind to one another. This word *chrestos* is related to the word *christos*, Christ. Be like Christ, who is *chrestos*, kind, gentle.

And be tender-hearted. This deeply visceral word, *splangkna*

---

[2] Harold W. Hoehner, *Ephesians: An Exegetical Commentary* (Grand Rapids: Baker Academic, 2002), 628.

(guts, bowels) is often used of Jesus. Jesus sees the crowds wandering like sheep without a shepherd... and He is moved in His guts. Jesus sees the lepers and He's moved to want to heal. Jesus sees the widow whose son has just died and His heart breaks for her. Get in step with the Spirit: let your guts get ripped up and care for others.

"And forgive each other." The word Paul uses here (*charizomenoi*) is not his normal word for "forgiveness," but literally means "bestow grace." Go around gracing one another, says Paul, just as God in Christ goes around heaping grace onto you.

Justice is giving others what they deserve.
Mercy is *not* giving others what they deserve.
Grace is giving others what they *do not* deserve.

Grace one another, says Paul. There is a time for justice. There comes a time for mercy. But it is always time for grace, for grace is unmerited, undeserved. There is never a time when any of us merit God's favour; there is never a time when any of us deserves God's blessings. Go around giving one another what we have not earned... just as God in Christ goes around giving you what you have not earned.

Walk in step with the Holy Spirit of God.

EPHESIANS 5:1-2

¹ Therefore be imitators of God, as beloved children; ² and walk in love, just as Christ also loved you and gave Himself up for us, an offering and a sacrifice to God as a fragrant aroma.

CHAPTER 16

Walk as Imitators of God... Really?

EPHESIANS 5:1-2

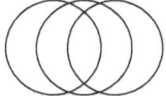

"Therefore, be imitators of God" (Ephesians 5:1). Really? The word the apostle Paul uses is *mimetes* from which we get the English word "mimic." "Therefore, mimic God." Really?

Before focusing on the main exhortation of the passage ("Be imitators of God"), let me call your attention to a number of features of the text that help us keep the focus on the main exhortation.

Therefore...

First, "therefore." Many of you know that when you are reading the Bible and come across the word "therefore," it is always good to ask "What is the 'therefore' there for?" As we have worked our way through Paul's letter to the Ephesians, we have come to see that he composed it in two halves:

- Chapters 1-3: an alternative reading of reality;
- Chapters 4-6: living the alternative reading of reality.

Or, as New Testament scholar, Timothy Gombis suggests:

- Chapters 1-3: the drama of God's triumph in Christ;
- Chapters 4-6: the roles we have been assigned to play in the unfolding drama.[1]

Chapter 1 begins with a blessing: "Blessed be the God and Father of our Lord Jesus Christ, who has blessed us with every spiritual blessing in the heavenly places in Christ" (Ephesians 1:3). Paul then goes on to open up some of the blessings (for there are more blessings than Paul names in his letter!).

In Christ we:

- were chosen from the foundation of the world;
- are adopted into the God's family;
- have been redeemed by the blood of Christ;
- have had our sins forgiven;
- have been clued in on the mystery of history;
- have obtained an inheritance;
- have been sealed with the Holy Spirit, who is the guarantee of our inheritance;
- have been made alive with Christ;
- have been raised up with Christ;
- have been seated with Christ where Christ is seated;
- are God's "poem," created for good works in the world;
- have been brought so near to God that we now constitute God's temple in the world;

---

[1] Timothy G. Gombis, *The Drama of Ephesians: Participating in the Triumph of God* (Downers Grove: IVP Academic, 2010), 134-135.

- now have direct access into God's Holy Presence, through Christ, in the Spirit;
- have been strengthened by the Spirit with power in our inner being;
- have Christ dwelling in our hearts,;
- are learning to grasp how broad and long and high and deep is the love of Christ;
- are being filled up to all the fullness of God!

Blessings indeed!

Chapters 1-3 end with a benediction: "Now to Him who is able to do far more abundantly beyond all that we ask or think, according to the power that works within us, to Him be the glory in the church and in Christ Jesus to all generations forever and ever. Amen" (Ephesians 3:20-21). Amen indeed!

And then: "Therefore" (Ephesians 4:1). Of course! Realizing what Paul develops in chapters 1 to 3, there has to be a "therefore." In fact, there has to be a series of "therefores":

- "Therefore I, the prisoner of the Lord, implore you to walk in a manner worthy of the calling to which you have been called" (Ephesians 4:1).
- "So this I say [Therefore]... walk no longer" as those who walk in the futility of their minds (Ephesians 4:17).
- "Therefore, laying aside falsehood, speak truth" (Ephesians 4:25).
- "Therefore, be imitators of God" (Ephesians 5:1).
- "Therefore be careful how you walk" (Ephesians 5:15).

Walk

A second feature of the text: "walk." Some translations render Paul's word simply as "live." As I said in chapter 12, I prefer "walk," for it emphasizes the Biblical vision of the spiritual life: we are not only made to simply live, but to "move out," to be active, to take a new road, to walk.

- "Walk in a manner worthy of the calling with which you have been called" (Ephesians 4:1).
- "Walk no longer as" those who walk in the futility of their minds (Ephesians 4:17).
- "Walk in love" (Ephesians 5:2).
- "Walk as children of Light" (Ephesians 5:8).
- "Be careful how you walk" (Ephesians 5:15).

Just As

The third feature, crucial to hold before us: "just as." Imitate God. How? Walk in love. What does that look like? "Just as Christ also loved you."

Paul uses this phrase ("just as") a number of times in the letter, and indeed, in all of his letters.

- "Just as He chose us in Him [Christ]" (Ephesians 1:4).
- "Forgiving each other, just as God in Christ also has forgiven you" (Ephesians 4:32).
- "Husbands, love your wives, just as Christ also loved the church and gave Himself up for her." (Ephesians 5:25).

The Main Exhortation

Let us now focus on the main exhortation: "be imitators of God." It is a seemingly impossible challenge. Can you think of anything more challenging? In every realm of life: family, work, sports, politics, economics, academics..."mimic God." Really?

This is the only place in the Bible where the challenge is put this way, but the challenge is found all over the place. In the Old Testament:

- "You shall be holy, for I the Lord your God am holy" (Leviticus 19:2).
- "Show your love for the alien [stranger], for you were aliens in the land of Egypt," and the Lord showed His love to you (Deuteronomy 10:19).
- God's people are to free servants every seven years, for "you were a slave in the land of Egypt, and the Lord your God redeemed you" (Deuteronomy 15:12-15).

Over and over again: Because I am who I am, you be; because I have done for you, so you do.

Jesus speaks the challenge, especially in His Sermon on the Mount.

> "Love your enemies, and pray for those who persecute you, so that you may be sons of your Father who is in heaven; for He causes His sun to rise on the evil and the good, and sends rain on the righteous and the unrighteous."
>
> Matthew 5:44-45

> "Therefore, you are to be perfect, as your heavenly Father is perfect."
>
> Matthew 5:48

Yikes!

Now, as you read the unfolding story the Bible tells, imitating God slowly and rightly becomes imitating Jesus, God in our flesh. "Follow Me," He says, and we soon discover that He is following God His Father. When Jesus calls us to imitate God, He is calling us to do what He does. We imitate God by imitating Jesus, God in our skin. So the apostle Peter can say, "For you have been called for this purpose, since Christ also suffered for you, leaving you an example for you to follow in His steps" (1 Peter 2:21). We imitate the God we cannot see by walking in the steps of the God we can see.

You may know that this language led to a tradition within the church of calling people to an almost literal imitation of Jesus, most powerfully so in the book *The Imitation of Christ*, written by Thomas à Kempis in the early fifteenth century.[2] Many significant players in Western history have sought to live out à Kempis' vision. One many will know was Dag Hammerskjöld, the Swedish statesman of the twentieth century, who in fearfully turbulent times served as Secretary-General of the United Nations. Hammerskjöld lived in the book, keeping a copy by his bedside.

This tradition also came to the fore in the early twentieth century in a book called *In His Steps* by Charles Sheldon, a

---

[2] Thomas à Kempis, *The Imitation of Christ* (Garden City, NY: Doubleday, 1955).

powerful story of a fictitious community seeking to follow in the steps of Jesus.[3] It was this book that posed the question that comes around every so often, which is now found on posters and wrist-bands: WWJD? The thought is that when facing choices, one is to ask "What Would Jesus Do?"

John Stackhouse in his helpful book, *Making the Best Of It: Following Christ in the Real World*, argues that the question is finally not all that helpful, for it is the wrong question. We are not and never will be Jesus. He makes us like Him, but we will never actually be Him. And for another, Jesus is doing a unique work: He is bringing to fulfillment the promises to Israel, inaugurating the kingdom of God, and confronting and defeating the enemies of life (sin, evil and death). This work is something that none of the rest of us can do.[4]

Still, the challenge of challenges is there in the text: "Be imitators of God." As I wrestle with the challenge of the Ephesians text, three questions come to mind that can help us: Where? What? How?

Question one: Where can I see God as God really is, so I know what I am to imitate?

Question two: Clearly, I cannot imitate everything about God; I cannot imitate any of the "omni-s": God's omnipresence, omnipotence, or omniscience. So what about God does He specifically want me to imitate?

---

[3] Charles M. Sheldon, *In His Steps* (Old Tappan, NJ: Fleming H. Revell, [1897]).
[4] John G. Stackhouse Jr., *Making the Best of It: Following Christ in the Real World* (Oxford: Oxford University Press, 2008), 189-191. A better question is "what IS Jesus doing?" The call is then to co-operate with what Jesus is doing, to participate in His work.

Question three: How in the world can I, a mere human being, and a sinful human being at that, possibly imitate anything Divine?

Where Can I See What to Imitate?

Where can I see God as God really is so I know what I am to imitate? All over the place! God has revealed Himself all over the place.

God has revealed Himself in creation: "The heavens are telling of the glory of God; and their expanse is declaring the work of His hands" sings the Psalmist (Psalm 19:1). Through creation God tells us who He is and what He is like.

And He reveals Himself in historical acts like the exodus. For the people of the Old Testament, God clearly revealed His nature and character when He rescued them from Egypt. In the face of injustice and oppression, God met Moses at the burning bush, and declared: "I have surely seen the affliction of My people... I have given heed to their cry because of their taskmasters, for I am aware of their suffering [I feel their sufferings]. So I have come down to deliver them" (Exodus 3:7-8). For centuries the Jews have hung on to that fundamental revelation of the true God.

We also see God in His good Law, especially in the Ten Commandments, which do not begin with "you shall not," but with "I am the Lord your God". The Jews loved the Law because in it they saw the character and passions of the Living God. Interestingly, on either side of his exhortation in Ephesians 5:1, Paul seems to be giving a Christianized re-working of the Commandments.

And we see God in the incarnation, in God's coming to live as one of us in Jesus of Nazareth. How often did Jesus say things like, "He who sees Me sees the One who sent Me" (John 12:45)? How often did Jesus say things like, "whatever the Father does, these things the Son also does in like manner" (John 5:19)? As we watch Jesus act, as we see Him relate to children and women and outcasts and the elite, we are watching God at work.

What Am I to Imitate about God?

But what of all that God has revealed about Himself does He want me to imitate?

Are we to imitate His works in creating the world? No way! God did it all "out of nothing." I cannot do that. You cannot do that. But we can co-operate with and participate in God's creative works. We can join in God's passion for order, beauty, and bounty. And we can resist, even reject, work that brings chaos, that devalues the human person, or that deprives anyone of God's abundance.

Can we imitate the God of the Exodus? No way. That was a work no one can mimic. God overcame, "from outside," entrenched oppression and an economic system that needed the poor to remain poor. People are trying to do this work, but we cannot finally do it ourselves. God must break in from outside the unjust systems. And He does, and He will. We can co-operate with and participate in His work, resisting and rejecting all work that goes against His work.

Should we imitate the God of the Law? Here the answer is not "no way." The Law emerges out of the Creator's very being. The commandments emerge out of the heart and mind of the One who made us. They tell us who God is.

- Do not lie, because I, God, do not lie.
- Do not steal, because I, God, do not steal.
- Do not bear false witness, because I, God, do not do it.
- Do not commit adultery, because I, God, am faithful to you My Bride.

And the commandments tell us who we are. The commandments are not just spun out of thin air. They are not an imposition on humanity; they are an exposition of who we are constituted to be. We are "hard-wired" for integrity and fidelity and generosity. We are "hard-wired" for keeping the Sabbath. This is why as individuals and as societies we suffer when we violate the good Commandments. When we violate the good Law we violate ourselves.

Are we to imitate the incarnation, and do all that we see Jesus doing? No, not all. We cannot do the work Jesus uniquely came to do. And certainly not all the "omni-s"! I am freshly struck by the fact that Jesus Himself did not do all the "omni-s". He could not copy His Father's omni-presence. If Jesus was in Jericho He could not be in Bethany. He did not copy His Father's omniscience. Jesus had to ask, "Who touched Me?" when crowds pressed around Him (Mark 5:30). He says He does not know the day of His return (Mark 13:32). So even God-in-the-flesh did not imitate everything about God!

What Jesus does imitate, and what we are called to mimic, is God's love. As we watch Jesus relate to all kinds of different people, we are watching the love of His Father in action. "Like father, like son," they say. In nearly every conceivable human interaction we watch the visible-God copy the love of the invisible-God.

And Jesus then turns to us and says, "A new commandment I give to you, that you love one another, even as I have loved you" (John 13:34). He had already re-iterated the two great commandments: love God with all your being, and love your neighbour as yourself. You always make sure you have food and shelter and work, now make sure your neighbour has food and shelter and work. A radical command. But not as radical as Jesus' new commandment: Love one another the way I love you. Love the way the God I am copying loves you.

Thus in our text, Paul says, "Therefore be imitators of God, as beloved children; and walk in love, just as Christ also loved you and gave Himself up for us" (Ephesians 5:1-2). "Gave Himself up for us"—that is what His love does. That is what love does.

Jesus says, "I am the Good Shepherd... and I lay down My life for the sheep" (John 10:14-15). Jesus lays down all He is for us, He gives up all He is for us. No one takes His life from Him, He gives it freely. When Jesus dies He is not a victim. Evil is not taking His life; He is giving Himself up for us. And of all that God reveals about Himself, this is what we are called to mimic.

This is what the apostle Paul makes so clear in the hymn he records in his letter to the Philippians (Philippians 2:5-11): "Have this attitude in yourselves which was also in Christ Jesus." Think this way, come at life this way, copy this way: "Have this attitude in yourselves which was also in Christ Jesus, who *because* He existed in the form of God" (my translation). Paul is not saying something about God-in-the-flesh contradicting the way of God in heaven ("who *although* He existed in the form of God"). Not although... but because. Because He existed in the form of God He empties Himself. Jesus thinks that the best way to be God is to empty Himself, to give Himself away. He takes the form of a servant. Because He existed as God, He thinks the best way to be God is to be a servant! He gets down on His knees and washes feet!

And in that act, He is imitating God. He learned it from His Father. It is what the Father does. "Because" Jesus is God He washes feet. "Because" He is God He gives Himself up for us, and goes to the cross. He is only doing what He sees His Father doing. Jesus is imitating God when He gives Himself up on the cross.

I often imagine myself standing near the cross, asking, "Why are You doing this? You are God, why are You doing this?" Or I imagine myself in the Upper Room where Jesus is washing His disciples feet. I get down close to Jesus, and I ask, "Why are You, God-in-the-flesh, doing this? This is beneath divine dignity."

And He looks up at me, and says, "You do not get it yet, do you? I only do what I see My Father doing. I am imitating the true and Living God." It is *because* Jesus is God that He lives as a Servant. There is no other God but the God who gives Himself for the life of the world.

How Am I to Imitate God?

So, how in the world am I, a mere human being, to imitate such a God?

Look at the text. It is full of gospel! Notice how Paul puts it: "Therefore be imitators of God, as beloved children" (Ephesians 5:1). He used the term "beloved" in the opening paragraph of the letter: "... to the praise of the glory of His grace, which He freely bestowed on us in the Beloved" (Ephesians 1:6). In the first chapter, the term refers to Jesus Christ—He is the Beloved. And in relationship with Him we too are the beloved. Paul is saying that we can love because we are being loved. We can wash feet because our feet are being washed.

And Paul says, we are "beloved children." We have been adopted into God's family. The Father has adopted us, and is treating us the way He treats His only-begotten Son. The Father is loving us the way He loves Jesus the Son. "Like father, like son." "Like father, like daughter." Like Jesus, we too are growing to the place where we say, "I only do what I see my Father doing."

And in this relationship we are being re-created. We were originally created in the image of God. We sinned, we fell, and the image was distorted. But God is re-creating us in the image of Jesus Christ, who is the image of God: "... and put on the new self, which in the likeness of God has been created" (Ephesians 4:24). We are being created in the image of the God who thinks being God means giving Himself up for the life of the world.

What Paul is saying to us today is that the people of our city are to look at us and be able to say, "So... that is what God is like." The waiter at the restaurant where we eat is to say as we leave, "So, that is what the God of love looks like!" Our fellow-workers at the office are to say as we interact with them, "Huh. That's what the God of the cross looks like."

The fact is, we all automatically mimic the god in whom we really believe. We can sing all the hymns and recite all the creeds, but what we really believe comes out in the way we treat people. We all copy the god we really believe in.

The good news is that we can copy the True and Living God, for we are being re-created in the image of this God. Our DNA is being altered. It is now in our DNA to give ourselves up for others. Miserable people are miserable because they do not yet get it. Miserable people are turned in on themselves and are violating who they were created to be.

Be still before this God and ask Him to show you just one way today and this week you can imitate THIS God and give yourself up for someone else.

EPHESIANS 5:3-14

³ But immorality or any impurity or greed must not even be named among you, as is proper among saints; ⁴ and there must be no filthiness and silly talk, or coarse jesting, which are not fitting, but rather giving of thanks. ⁵ For this you know with certainty, that no immoral or impure person or covetous man, who is an idolater, has an inheritance in the kingdom of Christ and God.

⁶ Let no one deceive you with empty words, for because of these things the wrath of God comes upon the sons of disobedience. ⁷ Therefore do not be partakers with them; ⁸ for you were formerly darkness, but now you are Light in the Lord; walk as children of Light ⁹ (for the fruit of the Light consists in all goodness and righteousness and truth), ¹⁰ trying to learn what is pleasing to the Lord. ¹¹ Do not participate in the unfruitful deeds of darkness, but instead even expose them; ¹² for it is disgraceful even to speak of the things which are done by them in secret. ¹³ But all things become visible when they are exposed by the light, for everything that becomes visible is light. ¹⁴ For this reason it says,

> "Awake, sleeper,
> And arise from the dead,
> And Christ will shine on you."

CHAPTER 17

When Christ Shines on You

EPHESIANS 5:3-14

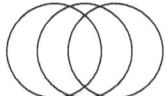

We have been walking through the letter the "apostle of grace" wrote to disciples of Jesus living in the first century city of Ephesus. As we get to the section in front of us in this chapter, there are many possible initial reactions we could have:

- Some of us will say, "Oh man, I get enough negative noise from others... I do not need this today."
- Others of us could say, "No wonder people do not like reading the Bible anymore!"
- Still others might respond with, "It is about time someone said some hard things . . . this is exactly why our world is going down the tubes."
- Still others will think, "I already know I am not living the kind of life I ought to... and this just makes me feel worse."

- Others of us may react with, "Wow, this is getting much too close; this text is invading private places of my life, and I am going to tune out right now."

I understand all those initial reactions! But I submit to you that if you will let this text do what the apostle Paul wrote it to do, you will discover that it is wonderfully liberating. The text is full of good news.

The text is illustrating what happens when Jesus Christ shines on us. The portion of Ephesians in front of us demonstrates what occurs when the Light of the world shines on you and on me. In verse 14, Paul writes, "For this reason it says, 'Awake, sleeper, and arise from the dead, and Christ will shine on you.'"

"For this reason" is Paul's way of undergirding what he has developed before it. What Paul addresses in the text before this are the kinds of things from which sleepers awake, and from which the dead arise when Messiah shines on sleepy, dead human beings.

Early Christian Hymns

"For this reason it says." What says? Most of the time when the writers of the New Testament use the phrase "it says," they are quoting Scripture, which for them at that moment in history was only the Old Testament. But there is no Old Testament text that says, "Awake, sleeper, and arise from the dead, and Christ will shine on you."

Many Biblical scholars suggest that what we have in Ephesians 5:14 is an early Christian worship song. In the New Testament we have a number of such hymns. For example, Philippians 2:5-11, with which we worked in the last chapter:

> Have this attitude in yourselves which was also in Christ Jesus,
> who, although [because] He existed in the form of God,
> did not regard equality with God a thing to be grasped,
> but emptied Himself,
> taking the form of a bond-servant,
> and being made in the likeness of men.
> Being found in appearance as a man,
> He humbled Himself
> by becoming obedient to the point of death,
> even death on a cross.
> For this reason also,
> God highly exalted Him,
> and bestowed on Him
> the name that is above every name,
> so that at the name of Jesus,
> every knee will bow,
> of those who are in heaven,
> and on earth and under the earth,
> and that every tongue will confess
> that Jesus Christ is Lord,
> to the glory of God the Father.

I have often wondered what tune the church used to sing that song!

There is the hymn in Colossians 1:15-18, which got a hold on me when I was in University in 1968 studying Theoretical Physics and Mathematics:

> He [Jesus Christ] is the image of the invisible God,
> the firstborn of all creation.
> For by Him all things were created,
> both in the heavens and on earth,
> visible and invisible,
> whether thrones or dominions
> or rulers or authorities—
> all things have been created
> through Him and for Him.
> He is before all things,
> and in Him all things hold together.
> He is also head of the body, the church;
> and He is the beginning, the firstborn from the dead,
> so that He Himself will come to have first place in everything.

And on it goes! Oh, to know what that song sounded like when sung in the cities of the Roman Empire.

There is the hymn in 1 Timothy 3:16, what Paul calls "the mystery of godliness":

> He who was revealed in the flesh,
> Was vindicated in the Spirit,
> Seen by angels,
> Proclaimed among the nations,
> Believed on in the world,
> Taken up in glory.

All these examples of early Christian hymns have worked their way into congregational worship throughout Church history.

And there is the hymn, or more accurately, the chorus, in the letter to the Ephesians, which was likely sung when someone was baptized. It could have been sung at other times as well, but it is especially appropriate to sing over believers as they emerge from the waters of baptism:

> Awake, sleeper,
> and arise from the dead,
> and Christ will shine on you.

I would love to know how that was sung in the church in Ephesus!

Now, even though Paul is not directly quoting a Biblical text when he says, "For this reason it says," he is likely incorporating a number of different Old Testament texts. Like Isaiah 9:2:

> The people who walk in darkness will see a great light;
> those who live in a dark land, the light will shine on them.

And Isaiah 60:1-2:

> Arise, shine; for your light has come,
> and the glory of the Lord has risen upon you.
> For behold, darkness will cover the earth,
> and deep darkness the peoples;
> But the Lord will rise upon you,
> and His glory will appear upon you.
> (See also Isaiah 26:19; 51:17; 52:1; and 60:19-20.)

This was the expectation of Zacharias, the father of John

the Baptist, who, when his son was born, sang of another Son, Mary's Son, saying:

> the Sunrise from on high will visit us,
> to shine upon those who sit in darkness and the shadow
>   of death,
> to guide our feet into the way of peace [Shalom, wholeness].
>
> Luke 1:78-79

All of this is taken up in the chorus Paul cites in his letter. And the big point I want to make about this hymn is that it undergirds all that comes in Ephesians before Paul recites it. From 5:3-13, Paul is simply opening up for us what happens when Christ wakes us from mental and spiritual sleep, when Christ raises us from mental and spiritual death—when Christ shines on us.

When Christ Shines on Us

When He does shine, says Paul, "all things become visible when they are exposed by the light" (v.13). We begin to see things clearly. I love it when new believers, fresh from a saving encounter with Jesus, say things like, "Where have I been all my life? I see things I never saw before." As a nineteenth century hymn sings, "Something lives in every hue Christless eyes have never seen."[1] When Christ shines on us, we begin to see the world clearly, which brings both joy and sorrow. We begin to see

---

[1] "Loved with everlasting love" ("I am His, and He is Mine"), text by George W. Robinson.

ourselves clearly, which also brings both joy and sorrow. We begin to see the actions of governments and corporations clearly, which, depending on whether those in leadership see, either discourages or encourages us. And we begin to see God clearly. This brings us a whole host of emotions!

> *"Awake, sleeper, and arise from the dead,*
> *and Christ will shine on you."*

When He does, says Paul, we become light. Amazing! "For you were formerly darkness, but now you are light in the Lord" (v. 8). Not, "for you formerly lived in darkness, but now you live in light," though that would be a true thing to say. But, "you *were* darkness, but now you *are* light." Again, amazing!

I am not sure of all the apostle has in mind in this claim. But I have witnessed it, again and again. When a person comes to Christ or, I should say, when Christ comes to a person, the light radiates out of them, in their eyes and on their skin. You have seen it, have you not? People say to the new believer, "There is something different about you. I can see it on you. You are different." In union with the Light, in intimacy with the Light of the world, we become, in some sense, light. The fact is, we slowly become like that to which we are constantly exposed. Be exposed to the very Light of Life and there is a sense in which we become light.

> *"Awake, sleeper, and arise from the dead,*
> *and Christ will shine on you."*

When He does, says Paul, we want to be clean, like He is clean. "But immorality or any impurity or greed must not even be named among you, as is proper among saints" (v. 3). In the verse right before this one, Paul calls us to "walk in love." The opposite of love is immorality, impurity, and greed.

The word he uses which we translate "immorality" is *porneia* which comes into the English language in words like "pornography," one of the biggest industries in our time, funded by corporations you would be shocked to have named. Pornography is eating away at the soul of our world, causing many people to go to sleep mentally and spiritually, and causing so much relational death. The Light of Life breaks the spell. Thanks be to Him! He breaks through the darkness, grabs hold of our souls, and leads us into freedom.

Jesus breaks the spell of greed. The same word is translated in other places as "covetousness." A lot of money fuels greed and coveting. But when Christ shines, things begin to change. We discover, sometimes to our horror, that Paul is right: coveting is idolatry (v. 5). We make a god out of that which we covet. We "have to have" the thing or person, and all of life revolves around getting that thing or person. Please Lord, shine! Radiate through all our idolatry; we do not want to be living for false gods.

"Awake, sleeper, and arise from the dead,
and Christ will shine on you."

When He does, says Paul, the way we speak begins to change. "There must be no filthiness and silly talk, or coarse jesting, which are not fitting, but rather giving of thanks" (v. 4). He is referring to humour that is used to put other people down, as well as to obscenity and vulgarity, all of which are out of sync with love. John Stott put it so well:

> The reason why Christians should dislike and avoid vulgarity is not because we have a warped view of sex, and are either ashamed or afraid of it, but because we have a high and holy view of it as being in its right place God's good gift, which we do not want to see cheapened.[2]

Interestingly, Paul sees the giving of thanks as an antidote to foul and mean speech. Giving thanks for other people makes us realize again that they are God's creation; giving thanks makes us treat them as His gifts. No one in the light wants to denigrate something God has made.

"Awake, sleeper, and arise from the dead,
and Christ will shine on you."

When He does, says Paul, the kingdom of God becomes more real to us, and we want to live consistent with the kingdom. "For this you know with certainty, that no immoral or impure person or covetous man, who is an idolater, has an inheritance in the kingdom of Christ and God" (v. 5).

Paul is not referring to momentary lapses; he is referring to deliberate, intentionally repeated, settled choices.

Why no inheritance in the kingdom? Because, thank God, the kingdom is all about wholeness, righteousness, goodness,

---

[2] John R.W. Stott, *God's New Society: The Message of Ephesians* [The Bible Speaks Today] (Downers Grove: InterVarsity Press, 1979), 193.

and truth. The further Jesus draws us into the kingdom, the more we realize how good it is and the more we find everything incongruous with the kingdom odious and want it taken away.

This partly explains why, when we get serious about following Jesus into the kingdom of God, things begin to be uncomfortable. The kingdom values are coming up against the values nurtured by greed and lust and fear, and our worlds are being turned up-side-down which, thankfully, means our worlds are being turned right-side up again!

The Wrath of God

"Awake, sleeper, and arise from the dead,
and Christ will shine on you."

When He does, says Paul, we understand one of the reasons for so much of the turmoil in our world today: the wrath of God. "Let no one deceive you with empty words, for because of these things the wrath of God comes upon the sons of disobedience" (v.6).

The wrath of God is not what so many think it is. It is not God throwing lightning bolts at human beings whom He finds disgusting. No, the wrath of God is, as Australian scholar Leon Morris puts it, God's settled opposition to all that is incongruous with His love and holiness.[3]

And the wrath of God is expressed in letting us have our way. It is awful—I would rather get lightning bolts! The wrath of God

---

[3] Leon Morris, *The Apostolic Preaching of the Cross* (Grand Rapids: Wm. B. Eerdman Publishing, 1965), 180.

is God giving us the full implications of not wanting Him and His ways. When God sees that a person or nation has finally chosen not to choose Him and His ways, He lets the person or nation have their way.

Christ shines on us to help us realize just how critical what we do with Him is. Choose other gods—like pornography, violence, or racism—and we become like them. That is wrath. And the God of grace shines the Light of life into the darkness so we realize how consequential human decisions really are.

> *"Awake, sleeper, and arise from the dead,*
> *and Christ will shine on you."*

When He does, says Paul, our ambitions change, and we simply want to please Him. "Walk as children of Light,... trying to learn what is pleasing to the Lord" (v. 8-10). Of course! When the Light goes on we want to live in sync with Him. In every realm of life—"Lord, what pleases You?" In our work, in our relationships, in our entertainment and sports, in the books we read and the movies we choose to watch, and in the way we spend His money. When the Light goes on we want, as never before, to live in full harmony with Him.

Being Light to Others

> *"Awake, sleeper, and arise from the dead,*
> *and Christ will shine on you."*

When He does shine, says Paul, the world around you is affected. How can it be otherwise? "Therefore do not be partakers with them" (v. 7) and "do not participate in the unfruitful deeds of darkness, but instead even expose them" (v. 11).

Paul does not say what some have made him out to say; he does not say, "do not associate with them." That is neither possible nor pleasing to the Lord. How will people know the love of God if those who know Him remain in holy huddles?

"Do not partake," and "even expose." Not the persons, but the deeds. A big distinction! The Light shines not to expose people but to expose the deeds that are ruining people.

As those who "walk in the light" walk in dark places, dark deeds and attitudes and schemes are exposed, sometimes by "children of the light" speaking into the dark deeds, as the churches in our city and world may need to do soon regarding the horrific problem of sex-trafficking. I cannot begin to imagine the pain little girls suffer: being abducted from their homelands, sold to strangers, used by grown men. And I cannot begin to imagine how dark must be the souls of those who do it. Expose the practice, Jesus! Burn Your Light into such inhumanity. And use us if You need to.

But the exposure happens mostly by "children of the light" simply showing up; their mere presence brings conviction about the deeds of darkness. I still remember one of the last times I went skiing—1995. My sons had gotten onto the chair lift and I was in the one that followed, sitting with a young woman I did not know. All the way up the mountain she was going on and on about the party she was going to that night. She spoke enthusiastically about all the drinking that would take place, and about the "good sex" she was hoping to have. I just listened and prayed! On and on she went, celebrating all this non-kingdom stuff. Then just before we reached the top, she asked what I do for a living. And I thought, "OK Lord, here it comes."

"I am a Christian pastor," I said, gently. She flipped out! "Oh my God!" she started saying. I asked the Lord to credit her words as a prayer. "Oh, my God! If I had known, I would not have said everything I have just said." She was in misery, or better, in "severe mercy." She could hardly wait till we reached the top. As she readied herself to leave the chair and ski down the hill, I said, "He knows, you know." Off she flew—really fast. I look forward to meeting her again in the fully realized kingdom; for the deep sense of conviction that came upon her had to finally lead her to the Saviour.

> *"Awake, sleeper, and arise from the dead,*
> *and Christ will shine on you."*

When He does, we experience a desperate need for God. We realize that we cannot be alive and whole without God. Paul does not say so in the text. But all he says leads us there. There is no way we can live free and clean without God: without the Father, without the Lord Jesus, without the Holy Spirit.

Douglas Coupland is a creative Canadian novelist, who first introduced terms like "McJob" and "Generation X." Towards the end of a collection of essays entitled *Life After God*, Coupland, who at the time did not claim to be a Christian, writes:

> Now—here is my secret: I tell it to you with an openness of heart that I doubt I shall ever achieve again, so I pray that you are in a quiet room as you hear these words. My secret is that I need God—that I am sick and can no longer make it alone. I need God to help me give, because I no longer seem to be capable

of giving; to help me be kind, as I no longer seem capable of kindness; to help me love, as I seem beyond being able to love.[4]

Yes! Yes! Yes!

The Light is shining! Jesus Christ the Light is shining! A sleeper is waking up! A human being is rising from the dead! It is the spiritually and mentally asleep who see no need for God. The dead feel no need for God. It is when the Light breaks through that a human being is finally human—desperately needing and wanting God.

"Blessed are the poor in spirit... for theirs and only theirs is the kingdom."

---

[4] Douglas Coupland, *Life After God* (New York: Simon & Schuster, 1994), 359.

EPHESIANS 5:15-21

[15] Therefore be careful how you walk, not as unwise men but as wise, [16] making the most of your time, because the days are evil. [17] So then do not be foolish, but understand what the will of the Lord is. [18] And do not get drunk with wine, for that is dissipation, but be filled with the Spirit, [19] speaking to one another in psalms and hymns and spiritual songs, singing and making melody with your heart to the Lord; [20] always giving thanks for all things in the name of our Lord Jesus Christ to God, even the Father; [21] and be subject to one another in the fear of Christ.

CHAPTER 18

Walk Filled with the Very Life of God

EPHESIANS 5:15-21

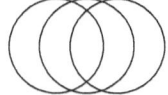

Be filled with the Spirit.
Be filled with the Spirit of God.
Be filled with the Holy Spirit.
Be filled with the Breath of God.
Be filled with the Wind of God.
Be filled with the River of God.
Be filled with the Source of Living Water.
Be filled with the Spirit.

This is not the last exhortation in Paul's letter to Ephesian believers. That distinction belongs to: "Finally, be strong in the Lord and in the strength of His might. Put on the full armour of God" (6:10-11). But, "be filled" is the last "therefore" in a series of "therefores" in the letter. And this is the "therefore" that makes all the other "therefores" possible.

To help us *feel* what the apostle of Jesus Christ is after in the text, it helps to read all the other "therefores" in his letter, and immediately follow each with the last "therefore," "be filled with the Spirit."

- "Therefore I, the prisoner of the Lord, implore you to walk in a manner worthy of the calling with which you have been called"(4:1). "Be filled with the Spirit."
- "So [therefore] this I say, and affirm together with the Lord, that you walk no longer just as the Gentiles also walk, in the futility of their mind" (4:17). "Be filled with the Spirit."
- "Therefore, laying aside falsehood, speak truth each of you with his neighbour... be angry, and yet do not sin..." (4:25-26). "Be filled with the Spirit."
- "Therefore be imitators of God, as beloved children; and walk in love" (5:1-2). "Be filled with the Spirit."
- "Therefore... you were formerly darkness, but now you are Light in the Lord; walk as children of Light" (5:7-8). "Be filled with the Spirit."
- "Therefore be careful how you walk, not as unwise men but as wise" (5:15). "Be filled with the Spirit."
- "So then [therefore] do not be foolish, but understand what the will of the Lord is" (5:17). "Be filled with the Spirit."

It is being filled with the Spirit of God that makes it possible for us to live all the other life-enriching exhortations that Paul gives us in his letter—including the last one: "Finally, be strong in the Lord" (6:10).

Do Not Get Drunk with Wine

"Do not get drunk with wine,... but be filled with the Spirit." Paul speaks this way not because he is a teetotaler or because he thinks drinking wine is evil. "The days are evil," he says (v. 16). And therefore, the days are fraught with all kinds of potential pitfalls; overdrinking wine and other spirits is but one of them.

Paul does not speak this way because he is an up-tight moralist. He speaks this way because people in Ephesus were abusing wine. And, as in our day, they were abusing food and work and entertainment and religion.

Life in Ephesus revolved around the goddess Diana (also called Artemis). By the time Paul writes his letter, the temple of Diana in Ephesus was known for its "worship events" that involved "ritual drunkenness and frenzied behaviour."[1] Worshipers would come under the control of Diana by coming under the control of wine.

Paul says "the days are evil," because people were being so incredibly foolish. They thought they could find the fullness of life in unrestrained sexual activity and by being caught up in euphoria induced by drunkenness. "Dissipation," Paul calls it. "Wasted," as we say in our day. Wasted, with nothing to show for it except a lot of brokenness and gnawing emptiness.

Paul tells us "do not get drunk with wine" because something very fundamental to our wholeness is at stake. What we seek to fill the emptiness gets a hold on us and begins to drive us. What we seek to ease the emotional pain, what we look to for "a little

---

[1] Frank Thielman, *Ephesians* [Baker Exegetical Commentary on the New Testament] (Grand Rapids: Baker Academic, 2010), 357.

boost" to keep us going, slowly but surely, begins to master us.

Overdrinking is but one example. Overeating is another, as is over-working, too much television, too much Internet, too much social media, or too much coffee. Too much of anything other than the Spirit of God eventually leads to dissipation, to waste.

"But be filled with the Spirit." The only filling that finally fills.

Every human being is a disciple of someone or of some ideology. So the question is never, "Will I be a disciple?"; the question is always, "Whose disciple will I be?" If not Jesus', then whose? The question is never, "Will I be impacted by a spirit?" for everyone is impacted by a spirit of some sort. The question is always, "Of all the spirits at work in the world and around me, to which will I respond? To which will I yield?"

So, let us focus on the last "therefore" in Paul's letter, the "therefore" that makes all the other "therefores" in the letter to the Ephesians possible:

> Therefore, be careful how you walk, not as unwise men but as wise, making the most of your time, because the days are evil. So then do not be foolish, but understand what the will of the Lord is. And do not get drunk with wine [or with food or work or toys] for that is dissipation, but be filled with the Spirit. (5:15-18)

Walk the wonder of being alive "in Christ" by being filled with the very life of God!

The Structure of This Section

Let us step back and look at the larger specific context in which Paul gives this exhortation, Ephesians 5:15-6:9. This section is very carefully crafted as one unit.

There is first a series of three "not-buts": "not this, but this."
Then there is a series of manifestations of living the "not-but."
> Thus, this...
> And this...
> And this...
> And this...

Then the last "this" is worked out in three spheres of life.
> This sphere.
> And this sphere.
> And this sphere.

More concretely, the three "not-buts":

- Not walk as unwise,... but as wise.
- Not be foolish,... but understand what the will of the Lord is.
- Not get drunk with wine,... but be filled with the Spirit.

Then four manifestations, or results, of the "be filled," all given in participles:

- Speaking to one another in psalms and hymns and spiritual songs.
- Singing and making melody with your heart to the Lord.
- Always giving thanks for all things in the name of our Lord Jesus Christ to God, even the Father;
- Being subject to one another in the fear of Christ.

A number of translations render all of these as commands: speak to one another, be subject to one another. But they are not commands; they are the results of obeying the big command to "be filled with the Spirit."

And then the last manifestation, or result, of being filled - "being subject to one another in the fear of Christ" - is worked out in three relational spheres: wife and husband, children and fathers, and servants and masters.

- Wives being subject to husbands;
  AND husbands being subject to wives.
- Children being subject to parents;
  AND parents being subject to children.
- Servants being subject to masters;
  AND masters being subject to servants.

These new relationships bring into being a whole new kind of humanity, a new society, as John Stott puts it.[2] And the one major exhortation that makes it all happen is "be filled with the Spirit."

Be Filled with a Person

Earlier in the letter Paul spoke of being "sealed with the Holy Spirit":

---

[2] John R.W. Stott, *God's New Society: The Message of Ephesians* [The Bible Speaks Today] (Downers Grove: InterVarsity Press, 1979).

> In Him [in Christ], you also, after listening to the message of truth, the gospel of your salvation—having also believed, you were sealed in Him [in Christ] with the Holy Spirit of promise, who is given as a pledge of our inheritance, with a view to the redemption of God's own possession, to the praise of His glory. (1:13-14)

When anyone believes in Jesus Christ as Saviour and Lord, He stamps us as His own with His seal of ownership: He gives us His Spirit, the same Spirit who rests upon and lives in Him, the same Spirit who animates His obedience to His Father. Jesus gives the Spirit as a seal of ownership and as a down-payment on all His promises. Wonderful!

Earlier in the letter Paul spoke of being "indwelled" by the Spirit: "In whom [in Christ] you also are being built together into a dwelling of God in the Spirit" (2:22). Paul prays that we would be strengthened with power "through His Spirit in the inner man" (3:16).

When anyone believes in Jesus Christ as Saviour and Lord, He comes to take up residence in our lives through His Spirit. This is what makes a person a Christian, a Christ-in-one. His life now dwells in us.

But although we are sealed with the Spirit, and although the Spirit comes to live in us, He may or may not be filling us. I think all of us who are believers can testify to this fact.

Think of being a house. (We worked with the image earlier in the book). The Spirit comes to seal the house as belonging to Christ. The Spirit comes to live in the house. But He may or may not actually fill all the rooms of the house. That is not hard to imagine! Thus the exhortation, "be filled with the Spirit."

The verb Paul uses means to "completely fill," to bring something "to completion." Paul is saying to us: you are sealed with the Spirit and the Spirit has moved into your hearts and souls. Now be filled, be completely filled. Let the sealing and the indwelling have its full effect—be filled up.

Be filled with a Person. I want to stress this. The Spirit is not just a force or an influence. This is why the New Testament never speaks of the Spirit as "it," but always as "He" or "Him." The Spirit is as personal as Jesus in whose name He comes, and as personal as the Father from whom He comes. Be filled with a Person, who thinks, acts, feels, and has an agenda! (Read the book of Acts!).

Be filled with a Person who is fully God. Be filled with the third person of the Trinity. Be filled with a very creative Person, who in the beginning hovered over the chaos and darkness, and brought the world into being. Who "in the fullness of time" overshadowed the womb of the virgin Mary, and brought the God-Man into being. Who then animated the body of Jesus of Nazareth, enabling Him to do all He did for the world. Be filled with that Person; be filled with that God!

Do you see what a huge compliment Paul is paying us? The compliment he pays us when he prays his second prayer (Ephesians 3:19). He is saying that we humans are so wonderfully made that only the Living God can fill us! No other spirit can do it. However good, no other spirit can fill us, for we are too grand a creature. The only reality that can finally fill us is the very life of God Himself!

A Passive Command

The command is given in the passive voice—"Be filled with the Spirit." The active voice would be "I fill," while the passive voice is "I am filled." Paul is talking about something we cannot make happen. We cannot make ourselves filled with the Spirit.

The most essential factor for living the Christian life (indeed, for living life at all) is something we cannot make happen. We cannot fill ourselves with the Spirit. Paul puts it in the passive to help us realize our utter dependence on God. I cannot make it happen for you; you cannot make it happen for me. No religious gimmicks or spiritual gymnastics can make it happen. Only God can fill us with God.

And Paul puts it in the passive voice because we cannot control what happens when He does fill us. We have no control over the Holy Spirit. Much "religion" is finally all about controlling the Divine, trying to fit the Divine into our rituals, programs, and strategic plans. That is why "religion" can be so lifeless; the Spirit will not co-operate with our attempt to control Him. The passive tense reminds us that we have no control. We are, after all, talking about the Wind of God, the mighty *Ruach Adonai*. We are talking about the Fire of God, the untamable River of glory.

A Continuous Command

Note also that the command is in the present tense. In the Greek language, tense has more to do with the kind of action than the time of the action. The present tense emphasizes continuous action. So the command is, literally, "Keep on being filled."

The implication is that being filled by and with the Spirit is an on-going phenomenon.

This is partly because as we grow and learn and become new creations there is more to fill! As we move out in ministry, we need more of the filling. In the book of Acts we read of the same persons and groups being filled a number of times:

- On the day of Pentecost, the 120 disciples were together in the Upper Room, and they were filled with the Spirit (2:4).
- The infant church comes under persecution, and as they meet to pray they are filled again (4:31).
- Stephen is chosen as one of the first deacons because he is obviously filled with the Spirit (6:3). And then later, after preaching a powerful sermon before the Jewish Sanhedrin, he is filled again (7:55).
- Peter goes to the house of the Roman soldier Cornelius and preaches the gospel to Gentiles. And they are all filled with the Spirit (10:44).

On and on it goes through the book of Acts. We are not filled just once. The filling is too dynamic for any "once-for-all-ness." We are filled again, and again, and again as we move forward in discipleship.

And the filling is continual because we often stymie the filling. Earlier in the letter Paul told his readers, "Do not grieve the Spirit of God, by whom you were sealed for the day of redemption" (4:30). In his first letter to the believers in Thessalonica, Paul wrote, "Do not quench the Spirit" (5:19).

We, mere humans, can grieve and quench the Spirit of the

Living God by our attitudes, by the way we speak to and about one another, by holding grudges, by refusing to forgive one another, by hanging onto bitterness, by playing games with the truth, by toying with the things of the darkness. Doing such things causes the Holy Spirit to back off. You who have walked with Jesus Christ for some time have experienced it a number of times, have you not? I have.

We do something offensive to the Spirit, and it feels as though "the air goes out of the room." Well, it does. The Wind of God stops blowing. He quits breathing His refreshing breath. He does not leave... thanks be to His grace! But He does let us experience something of the implications of our anti-kingdom attitudes and speech. It is painful when it happens. He seems to "hold back" His vitality.

Not that the Spirit is touchy, or an easily wounded narcissist! It is just that He takes us seriously. He takes our attitudes and speech seriously. If we do not want the way of the Holy Spirit, He backs off and we experience again the emptiness and lostness and dis-orientation of unholiness. So, because we can grieve and quench Him, we need to "continually be filled." And in His mercy He loves to do it... again and again and again.

An Invitation

While "Be filled..." is passive, continuous, it is also in the imperative mood, meaning that somehow we have a role to play. We cannot control or manipulate the Spirit of God, but we do have a role to play or we would not be commanded. "Be filled..." is not just friendly advice. Paul does not just provide encouragement for the spiritually weak and empty; he gives a command.

What is our role in the "continually be filled with the Spirit"?

Decide. Decide we want to be filled—mysterious as it all may be. Desire to be filled. Confess anything we think might be in the way of being filled. And confess our fear that we might be taken where we had not planned to go. The fact is, the Spirit will take us to new places spiritually. So part of our role is to confess our fear and let go of our need to control our destinies. Decide you want to be filled, and drink.

Yes, drink. Take a big drink! Could not Paul say it that way given his reference to being drunk with wine? Instead of trying to ease the pain by filling our souls with wine, drink the Water of Life, the Very Life of God.

This is what Jesus invites us to do at the Jewish Feast of Tabernacles, or Sukkoth, held in early October.[3] It was at this feast when the people of God celebrated God as Light, that Jesus made His great claim, "I am the Light of the world; he who follows Me will not walk in darkness, but will have the Light of life" (John 8:12).

And it was at that feast that the people of God celebrated God as the giver of water. They remembered with gratitude and joy that out in the desert God made water to flow from the rock. They remember with great anticipation God's promise to one day pour out what He called "living water" on parched and thirsty human souls.

On the great day of the feast, while the people are singing from the prophet Isaiah, "you will joyously draw water from the

---

[3] I have described what this Feast is all about in chapter 5 ("The Light of the World") of my book, *Who Is Jesus?* (Vancouver: Regent College Publishing, 2011).

springs of salvation" (12:3), Jesus stands up, and cries out, "If anyone is thirsty,"...and who is not? Look at the long lines outside our city's pubs, people waiting hours to get inside to drink something to make life "life." Jesus knows why we stand in such lines; He knows what we are thirsty for. "If anyone is thirsty, let him come to Me and drink." And when you do, says Jesus, "From his innermost being will flow rivers of living water." This, says the apostle John who remembered Jesus' invitation, Jesus "spoke of the Spirit, whom those who believed in Him were to receive" (John 7:37-39).

When was the last time you had a good drink? When was the last time you drank Living Water? Why not do it today? Take a big, long drink. And then drink again tomorrow morning, and every morning for the rest of your life. Wake up, and say to the Living Lord, "I am thirsty, let me drink again."

Or, breathe. That too Paul would say to us. With your whole being breathe in deeply the Breath of Life. When was the last time you took a deep breath of God? Why not do it today? And then tomorrow morning, and every morning for the rest of your life.

The word for Spirit in the Greek is *pneuma,* which also means breath. It is from this word that we get the English word "pneumatic." Live pneumatically: Wake up, everyday and say to the Living Lord, "As I breathe in the air around me, Lord, let me breathe in Your Life."

> Breathe on me, breath of God, fill me with life anew;
> that I may love whatever You love, and do what you would do.
>
> Breathe on me, breath of God, until my heart is pure,
> until with You I will one will, to do and to endure.

> Breathe on me, breath of God, so that Your will is mine,
> until this earthly part of me glows with You fire divine.[4]

And when He does, when He breathes on us, when He gives us a drink, when He fills us again with Himself, we find ourselves speaking to one another differently—"with psalms, hymns and spiritual songs;" we find ourselves singing and making melody to the Lord; we find ourselves giving thanks even in the crummiest of circumstances; and we find ourselves being subject to one another in the fear of Christ.

Be filled with the very life of God!

And watch what starts taking place...

---

[4] "Breathe on me, Breath of God," written by Edwin Hatch (1835-1889).

EPHESIANS 5:21

²¹ and be subject to one another in the fear of Christ.

CHAPTER 19

Spirit-Filled Relationships

EPHESIANS 5:21

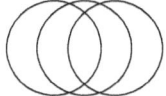

What starts to happen is a revolution! The revolution Paul opens up in the revolutionary text that is 5:18-6:9. It was revolutionary when it was read in first century Ephesus, and it is still revolutionary in the twenty-first century cities of our world. Although the text has now been read for nearly 2,000 years, and has worked redemptive changes in many cultures around the globe, no culture has yet to work out its full implications.

As we saw in the last chapter, at the heart of this revolutionary text is one basic exhortation: "Be filled with the Spirit" (Ephesians 5:18). Quit trying to fill your soul with what finally does not fill. You were created in such a way that what finally fills you is the Spirit of God, the third Person of the Trinity.

Everything else Paul develops in Ephesians 5:15 to 6:9 flows from that filling. Indeed, what Paul develops in the text is *impossible to live without the filling.*

We saw in the last chapter, that what we are looking at is a series of consequences, or results, of the filling with the Holy Spirit of God:

- Speaking to one another in psalms and hymns and spiritual songs.
- Singing and making melody in your hearts to the Lord.
- Giving thanks always for everything in the name of the Lord Jesus Christ to God, even the Father.
- And being subject to one another in the fear of Christ.

Notice that the consequences are all given as participles, not imperatives, as some translations render them. They are all the results of the one big imperative, "Be filled."

The final participle ("being subject") should not be translated "be subject," as too many translations have it. It is not in the imperative; it is a participle in a series of participles.[1] And it is not a new sentence, as too many translations have it. And certainly not a new paragraph, as some have it. As a friend of mine in the Philippines, Bong Manayon, wisely observes, to make it a command and a new sentence or paragraph "may inadvertently communicate something that was never there."[2]

"Being subject" is a result of "being filled." The participle the result of obeying the imperative.

And then Paul gives us a series of human relationships in which the "being subject" is worked out: Wives and husbands,

---

[1] This is one of reasons I like working with the NASB translation of the Bible. It honours such grammatical constructions with greater care.
[2] Bong Manayon, *In the Same Way: Philemon & The Ephesian Household Code* (Manila: Alethinos Media, 2007), 39.

children and fathers, servants and masters.

This is why I say we are dealing with a "radical" and "revolutionary" text. Being filled with the Spirit of God goes to the root of relational dynamics and turns things upside-down—so that our relationships can be right-side-up.

Because of our sin, and because of what Paul calls "the principalities and powers" in the last part of his letter, human relationships have been twisted, changed from what God had originally willed for humanity. Jesus Christ comes into the world and, through His Holy Spirit, begins to untwist and untangle, restoring relationships to God's original design.

Household Codes

Now, in this section of his letter to the Ephesians, Paul is working with what many call a "household code." Every society has codes of conduct, expectations of persons in various relational spheres. All the household codes in all first century societies involved three sets of relationships: husband-wife, father-child, master-servant.

In most cases the husband, father, and master was the same person. For most people the home was also the place of work. People lived and worked in the same space, in one building, or in a small cluster of small buildings. This is the case even today all over the world. The husband-wife, father-child, and master-servant relationships are all being lived out under one roof. And Paul dares to say that, when the Holy Spirit comes, when He fills human beings with His life, the dynamics in those relationships change. There is a new household code.

There has to be a new code. In the first century, women, children, and servants were virtually treated as objects to be used by husbands, fathers, and masters for their own ends. I am sure there were exceptions; I am sure there were husbands, fathers, and masters who recognized and honoured the image of God in women, children, and servants. But for all practical purposes women, children, and servants were pawns on the chessboard, moved around at the whim of husbands, fathers, and masters.

In the first century the household was the basic building block of society. It was argued that if the household ran well, the larger society would then run well. The great political-philosopher Aristotle, for instance, thought much about life within the household. Major sections of his work *Politics* is given to household management. Aristotle maintained that if husband-wife, father-children, and master-servant relationships work then the larger political realm would work. Thus the codes.

And thus, the need for a new code. In most first century political visions, the husband-father-master, the patriarch, was the only one who was viewed as truly human.[3] For instance, Aristotle did not think women had the same rational capacity as men, and therefore needed to be ruled by their husbands. He writes: "Hence there are by nature various classes of rulers and ruled. For the free rules the slave, the male the female, and the man the child in a different way."[4] That is just the way it was.

William Barclay summarizes the situation:

---

3 Timothy G. Gombis, *The Drama of Ephesians: Participating in the Triumph of God* (Downers Grove: IVP Academic, 2010), 177.
4 Aristotle, *Politics*, 1260a, 9-14, as quoted in Ibid., 177.

> The Jews had a low view of women. In his morning prayer there was a sentence in which a Jewish man every morning gave thanks that God had not made him 'a Gentile, a slave or a woman.' In Jewish law a woman was not a person, but a thing. She had no legal rights whatsoever; she was absolutely her husband's possession to do with as he willed.... The situation was worse in the Greek world.... companionship and fellowship in marriage was impossible.... The Greek expected his wife to run his home, to care for his legitimate children, but he found his pleasure and his companionship elsewhere.... Home and family were near to being extinct, and fidelity was completely non-existent. In Rome the matter was still worse.[5]

Again, there were, by God's mercy, exceptions. But the "code" was wives subjugated to husbands, children subjugated to fathers, and servants subjugated to masters. That is just the way it was.

Then Jesus Christ entered the picture. Then the Spirit of Jesus Christ began to fill people of the Jewish and Greek and Roman worlds. And "just the way it is" was turned upside-down.

The Radical Foundation

In this chapter, we will look more closely at the radical foundation for the new household code by examining the result of being filled with the Spirit that gets worked out in all these relationships: being "subject to one another in the fear of Christ" (5:21).

---

[5] William Barclay, *The Letters to the Galatians and Ephesians*, Revised Edition (Philadelphia: Westminster Press, 1976), 168-170.

Before we do, you may be wondering about verse 22. Though I have been saying that Paul gives us a series of results (participles) of the one commandment ("be filled with the Spirit"), it looks like verse 22 gives another command: "Wives, be subject to your own husbands, as to the Lord."

However, when you look at the text carefully, you will notice that the verb ("be subject") is not in the original text. In the New American Standard Bible, "be subject" is italicized, not for emphasis but to tell us that it has been added. Paul did not write the words, "be subject." They were inserted by translators who wanted the text to read more smoothly. But it is not what Paul was originally getting at, as we will see more clearly in a moment.

It is only as we are filled with the Spirit that we find ourselves being "subject to one another in the fear of Christ." Without the filling of the Spirit it is impossible to be subject to another human being. The Spirit comes and works a revolution in the human heart. And we find ourselves living a new "household code."

Being "subject to one another in the fear of Christ." Why does Paul add the clause "in the fear of Christ"? It is not that we are to live "afraid of Christ"! The word Paul uses means "awe," or "reverence for," or "respect of." We are to live in awe of Christ, in reverence of Him. I think we can paraphrase Paul like this:

> Being subject to one another, out of deep respect for Christ, for Who He is, for how He lives, for His very different way of being Lord.

"Being subject to one another, in light of the kind of Lord Jesus is."

Standing Under

"Being subject" literally means "standing under." *Hupostasso is* the word Paul uses. It is made up of two words: *hupo*, under; and *stasso*, stand. When we are filled with the Spirit, we find ourselves "standing under." Under Jesus Christ—"in the fear of Christ." And under one another:

Wives standing under husband.
And husbands standing under wives.

Children standing under parents.
And parents standing under children.

Servants standing under masters.
And masters standing under servants.

Under. Not over, but under.

I think Paul is here working with a text in the Gospel according to Mark, a critical text for understanding Jesus and His kingdom (Mark 10:35-45). Two of the first disciples, James and John, come to Jesus and say, "Teacher, we want You to do for us whatever we ask of You." Slightly presumptuous! And arrogant. Jesus replies—graciously so! —"What do you want Me to do for you?" They reply, "Grant that we may sit, one on Your right and one on Your left, in Your glory."

They just put it out there: "In the kingdom You have come to establish, we want to sit with You on the throne, one on the right, one on the left." When the other disciples hear the conversation, they are indignant.

So Jesus calls the whole group to Himself and says: "You know that those who are recognized as rulers of the Gentiles lord it over them; and their great men exercise authority over them." That is the instinct of our non-kingdom-ized humanity: over them. That is the instinct of our not-filled-with-the-Spirit humanity: over them.

Then Jesus says, "But it is not this way among you." Not so in the kingdom I am bringing into the world. "Whoever wishes to become great among you shall be your servant; and whoever wishes to be first among you shall be slave of all." Jesus is not putting down the quest to be great. He wants us to be great. But it is not by going over... it is by being under. The greatest, the first, is the servant.

Linger with these two words over and under.

Old humanity reading of reality: over.
New humanity reading of reality: under.

Old humanity without the Holy Spirit: climbing over.
New humanity with the Holy Spirit: standing under.

In Greek, the word over is *huper* and the word under, is *hupo*. From *huper* we get the English word "hyper." From *hupo* we get the English prefix "hypo-," as in hypodermic (under the skin). The Latin of *huper* is *super;* of *hypo* it is *subo/sub*, as in submarine (under water) and subterranean (under the earth).

The instinct/drive of the old humanity:
huper, hyper, super, over.

The instinct/drive of the new humanity:
hupo, hypo, sub, under.

"Being subject to one another," living is submission to one another, standing under one another, implies that I can really only "understand" this text if I "stand-under." I can only understand Jesus Christ if I stand under Jesus Christ. I can only understand Sharon, my wife, if I stand under Sharon. I can only understand you if I stand under you.

Go back to the event in Mark's Gospel. Jesus says, "it is not this way among you, but whoever wishes to become great among you shall be your servant; and whoever wishes to be first among you shall be slave of all" (Mark 10:43-44). Then verse 45 blows the circuit boards of our understanding of relationships: "For even the Son of Man did not come to be served, but to serve, and to give His life a ransom for many."

"Son of Man" was Jesus' favourite self-designation. It turns out there is no higher title that anyone can have. Found in the book of Daniel, it refers to the Ruler over all rulers, to the King over all kings, to the Prime Minister over all prime ministers, to the President over all presidents. But Jesus tells us that not even the ruler over all rulers exerts His "over-ness." Even the King over all kings goes under and lives as a servant.

So when the Spirit of the Son of Man comes and fills us, we find ourselves moving from over to under.

Wives standing under their husbands.
And husbands standing under their wives.

Children standing under their parents.
And parents standing under their children.

Servants and employees, standing under their masters and CEOs.
And masters and CEOs standing under their servants and employees.

In the kingdom of God, when the Spirit of the great King comes, a revolution takes place: we live in mutual submission. All have equal dignity. All have equal value. Different roles, yes. Different responsibilities, yes. But all are equal before Christ. And all are in submission to Christ.

A Lived Example

All are also in submission to one another. "For even the Son of Man did not come to be served, but to serve, and to give His life…" (Mark 10:45). This gets fleshed out on the cross, when Jesus gave His life for the life of the world. This is why Paul says to husbands, "love your wives, as Christ also loved the church and gave Himself up for her" (Ephesians 5:25).

All of this is lived out most clearly in the Upper Room when Jesus washed His disciples feet (John 13:1-17). Jesus rises from the table, lays aside His outer garments, grabs a water basin and a towel, gets down on His knees, and washes His disciples' feet. He then gets up, puts the garments back on, takes His place at the table, and says, "Do you know what I have done to you?"

Of course they do—He has washed their feet! But do they really know what He has done? "You call Me Teacher and Lord;

and you are right, for so I am. If I then, the Lord and the Teacher, washed your feet, you also ought to wash My feet." Right? No. This is what the disciples, and we, expect Jesus to say. "I have washed your feet... now wash Mine." No one that night had bothered with this servant task, no one had extended normal hospitality to Jesus.

If Jesus had said this, the disciples would have climbed all over each other to be the first to grab a washbasin and towel and express their love, gratitude, and respect by getting down on their knees to wash the Master's feet. But He does not say, "I washed your feet... now wash Mine." He says, "If I have washed your feet, you also ought to wash one another's feet." I wash His feet by washing yours.

So Lesslie Newbigin, a twentieth century British Anglican missionary to India can say:

> This is something which subverts and replaces all normal patterns of authority. It would be impossible to draw a "management chart" in which A is subject to B and B is subject to A. Yet this is what is called for. The disciples are to be—literally—"servants of one another" (Gal. 5:13). This is a kind of equality, but it must not be confused with the egalitarianism which is based on the doctrine of the "rights of man." That, in the end, makes every man a monad fighting for his rights, because it is of the essence of our human situation that each of us tends to estimate his own rights more highly than those of his neighbour. This is a different kind of egalitarianism which is based upon the fact that the one who alone is master has proved himself the slave to us all equally. He has laid aside his life for us all. And the debt which we owe to him [Jesus] is to be

discharged by our subjection to our neighbour in loving service. Our neighbour is the appointed agent authorized to receive what we owe to the master.[6]

That is what Paul is saying in his letter to the Ephesians. That is why I choose to use the words "radical" and "revolutionary" of this text. Think of the people in your life. They are appointed agents authorized to receive the love you want to pour on Jesus.

We will see this more clearly in the next chapter:

Wives: your husbands are the appointed agent
authorized to receive the love you want to pour on Jesus.

Husbands: your wives are the appointed agent
authorized to receive the love you want to pour on Jesus.

Children: your parents are the appointed agent
authorized to receive the love you want to pour on Jesus.

Parents: your children are the appointed agent
authorized to receive the love you want to pour on Jesus.

Employees: your bosses are the appointed agent
authorized to receive the love you want to pour on Jesus.

Bosses: your employees are the appointed agent
authorized to receive the love you want to pour on Jesus.

---

[6] Lesslie Newbigin, *The Light Has Come: An Exposition of the Fourth Gospel* (Grand Rapids: William B. Eerdmans, 1982), 170-171.

This is why we need the filling of the Spirit. This alternative reading of reality is so revolutionary only the Spirit of the Servant-Lord can affect such a miracle!

EPHESIANS 5:22-33

²² Wives, be subject to your own husbands, as to the Lord. ²³ For the husband is the head of the wife, as Christ also is the head of the church, He Himself being the Savior of the body. ²⁴ But as the church is subject to Christ, so also the wives ought to be to their husbands in everything.

²⁵ Husbands, love your wives, just as Christ also loved the church and gave Himself up for her, ²⁶ so that He might sanctify her, having cleansed her by the washing of water with the word, ²⁷ that He might present to Himself the church in all her glory, having no spot or wrinkle or any such thing; but that she would be holy and blameless. ²⁸ So husbands ought also to love their own wives as their own bodies. He who loves his own wife loves himself; ²⁹ for no one ever hated his own flesh, but nourishes and cherishes it, just as Christ also does the church, ³⁰ because we are members of His body. ³¹ For this reason a man shall leave his father and mother and shall be joined to his wife, and the two shall become one flesh. ³² This mystery is great; but I am speaking with reference to Christ and the church. ³³ Nevertheless, each individual among you also is to love his own wife even as himself, and the wife must see to it that she respects her husband.

CHAPTER 20

First Example of Spirit-Filled Relationships

EPHESIANS 5:22-33

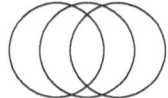

A number of years ago *Christianity Today* ran a cartoon about the apostle Paul and the women of the first century city of Ephesus. Paul has just arrived at the city gates, carrying a bed-roll and some scrolls. He is greeted by women whose faces suggest they are angry, and they are carrying placards reading things like "Women of Ephesus Unite," and "Paul is a Male Chauvinist Pig!" Under Paul's feet, the caption reads: "Oh... I see you got my letter."

The cartoon got it wrong. If anyone in Ephesus would have staged a protest against Paul it would have been the men. For what Paul writes in his letter, especially in the section we are looking at in this chapter, turns first-century understanding of relationships on its head. It would be the men who would have gotten in Paul's face saying, "What are you doing Paul? You are upsetting the established order of things!"

In fact, what Paul develops in this section of his letter

(Ephesians 5:15-6:9) is so revolutionary that even after 2,000 years the church has yet to work out the full implications.

A Note for Singles

Before we begin to focus on the revolution taking place in the relationship between wives and husbands, and husbands and wives, I am aware that not everyone reading this book is married. Many of you are single. Some of you are wanting to be married, but have not yet found the "right partner." Some of you are called to the single life in order to be fully engaged in particular kingdom ministries. Some of you have lost your spouse, either through death or divorce, each excruciatingly painful. I want to say to those not married that this text nevertheless speaks to you in three ways.

First, what the Spirit who inspired Paul says about the marriage relationship relates to every relationship. Yes, Paul emphasizes the unique bond between wife and husband: "the two shall become one flesh." But what he says to wives and husbands works in every other relationship as well, as I trust you will see.

Second, the section on marriage speaks to those who are not married because of the way the text flows from verse 21 to 22. Look carefully at how Paul puts it: "Being subject to one another in the fear of Christ, wives to your own husbands, as to the Lord" (my translation).

As we saw in the last chapter, the "be subject" usually found in verse 22 ("wives be subject to your own husbands") is not in the original text, but was inserted by translators who wanted the text to read more smoothly. The "ought to be" in verse 24 ("so also the wives ought to be to their husbands...") has also been inserted by translators. So why no verb ("be subject") in verse 22, and why no "ought" in verse 24?

My scholar friend in Manila, Bong Manayon, whom I quoted earlier, asks, "Could it be that Paul had something else in mind?" He suggests that given the social reality, wives were already submitting to their husbands, and that to say "be subject," would be redundant. He writes,

> Considering the bigger picture of where Paul is coming from, the greatest in the kingdom of God is the servant—could it be that he is actually upholding the wives as *the model* of servanthood to their husbands?[1]

In verse 22, Paul is not telling wives to be subject. He does not need to! They already get it, as do children and servants. In speaking of wives directly on the heels of "being subject to one another," Paul is telling us what Spirit-filled relating to one another looks like in all the relational spheres. So the New Testament scholar, Markus Barth, argues that there is an implied "e.g." ("for example") in verse 22. "E.g., wives to your own husbands." Writes Barth:

> Stylistic and material reasons recommend the addition of "e.g." in the English translation. "E.g." communicates exactly what is indicated by the structure of the Greek sentence: the subordination of wives is an example of the same mutual subordination which is also shown by the husband's love, the children's

---

[1] Bong Manayon, *In the Same Way: Philemon & The Ephesian Household Code* (Manila: Alethinos Media, 2007), 48; italics his.

obedience, the parents' responsibility for their offspring, the slaves' and masters' attitude toward one another.[2]

So we could render the flow from verses 21 to 22 this way: "Being subject to one another out of reverence for Christ, just as wives to their husbands." Wives have been living the "underness" of the kingdom for centuries.

Now, because of the coming of Jesus Christ and the filling with His Spirit, husbands finally *get to catch up.* So do fathers, and so do masters. All three of the parties who held the power also get to live the way of the kingdom. "The great ones exercise authority over... it is not so among you." Wives have understood this for centuries. And Paul holds them up as models of what "being subject to one another" looks like in all relational spheres.

Third, what Paul says of the marriage relationship speaks to all relationships because what he says points to the relationship between Christ and the church. Christ is a husband to all of us! All of us, female and male, are His bride. You may not be married right now, but if you believe in Jesus Christ as your Saviour and Lord, you are married to Him!

Jesus often speaks of His relationship with us in terms of bride and Groom. In the Upper Room, on the night before going to the cross, He says to the first band of disciples, mostly male: "Do not let your heart be troubled.... In My Father's house are many dwelling places;... If I go and prepare a place for you, I will come again and receive you to Myself, that where I am, there you may be also" (John 14:1-3).

---

[2] Markus Barth, *Ephesians: Translation and Commentary on Chapters 4-6* [Anchor Bible] (Garden City, NY: Doubleday, 1974), 610.

Jesus is echoing the words of the Jewish Betrothal service. The engaged man would take a cup of wine, and over it, say to the engaged woman: "I go to prepare a place for you in my father's house. When I have prepared the place, I will come again, and take you to myself, that where I am, you may be also."[3]

In the last book of the Bible, Jesus says to the church in Laodicea: "Behold, I stand at the door and knock; if anyone hears My voice and opens the door, I will come in to him and will dine with him, and he with Me" (Revelation 3:20). Jesus is echoing words from the great love poem, the Song of Solomon: "A voice! My beloved was knocking: 'Open to me, my sister, my darling, my dove, my perfect one!" (Song of Solomon 5:2). All of us, together, married and non-married, are His bride.

This means that when Paul speaks to wives he is speaking to women who were already wives before they married. And, when he speaks to husbands he speaks to men who were already wives before they married! So, although Paul is speaking in Ephesians 5:22-33 to the wife-husband, husband-wife relationship, what he develops speaks to all of us in any relationship.

Now, there are a number of ways we can proceed at this point. We could simply listen to what Paul says to wives, and then listen to what Paul says to husbands. I think a more helpful way is to lift up the dynamics of the revolution being worked out in the wife-husband, husband-wife relationship. Paul is turning the relationship on its head, and I see four dynamics of the revolution at work.

---

[3] "How Might Yeshua Fulfill the Fall Feasts?" Copyright 1994-2014 by Burke Magee and Glenna Cox; PO Box 581; Carnation, WA: 98014. www.returntogod.com/Hebrew/Fall.htm (accessed July 16, 2014).

Relational Revolution: Speaking to the Powerless

First, Paul speaks directly to those who were powerless in the first century. He speaks directly to women, children, and servants. It is unheard of! Why speak directly to wives, children, and servants, when they had no status in the society?

In the first century (and in many parts of the world today), one spoke to the wife *through* the husband; one spoke to the children *through* the father; one spoke to the servants *through* the master. The "proper" way for Paul to speak would be:

"Now husbands, tell your wives to be subject to you."

"Fathers, tell your children to obey you."

"Masters, tell your servants to be subject to you."

But, no, Paul speaks directly to the powerless! That simple act was revolutionary. It elevated wives, children, and servants to genuine personhood! Indeed, it elevated the powerless to equal status!

Relational Revolution: The Primary Relationship

The second dynamic of the revolution: Paul can speak directly because each party of the wife-husband, husband-wife relationship has a relationship that precedes and supersedes the wife-husband, husband-wife relationship. Each party of the relationship has a relationship with Jesus Christ, and that relationship informs and shapes all other relationships.

Notice the phrase in verse 22, "as to the Lord." "Wives, to your own husbands, as to the Lord." Is Paul saying the husband functions as Lord? No. No one is Lord in any relationship but Jesus the Lord. Is Paul saying the wife should treat her husband as if he were Jesus? No. The husband is not Jesus in any way.

Paul is saying that wives are to "stand under" their husbands because they have a relationship with the Lord who understands His Lordship in terms of servanthood. "As to the Lord," means, I think, "because you belong to a different kind of Lord." Paul says the same thing to servants: "With good will render service, as to the Lord, and not to men" (Ephesians 6:7). We serve one another because we belong to the Lord who is the Great Servant.

Thus when I performed wedding services, I would say to the couple, "Remember: before you belong to one another, you belong to Christ." To the groom: "Before she is yours, she is His." To the bride: "Before he is yours, he is His." And "being His" shapes the way husband and wife relate.

A wife "stands under" her husband, not because her husband is inherently worthy of it, nor because his status as husband deserves it, but because her Lord calls her to do so. And, so too, the husband "stands under" his wife because his Lord calls him to do so.

Both wives and husbands have a relationship that precedes and supersedes the marriage relationship. And that relationship calls her and frees her, and calls him and frees him, to live the way of the kingdom of God, serving as the great Servant serves.

Relational Revolution: The Model

Thus, the third dynamic of the revolution: the model for the wife-husband, husband-wife relationship is the Christ-church, church-Christ relationship, a relationship that transcends all cultural understanding of marriage.

No culture at any time in history has got it fully right. It is what Paul calls "a mystery," "a great mystery," "a mega-mystery" (Ephesians 5:32). It is something we never would have figured out on our own, something that God must reveal to us.

Wives—"as the church to Christ."

Husbands—"as Christ to the church."

Wives, relate to your husbands as the church relates to Christ, in submission to Him as the Head. As you may know, there is much debate about what Paul means by "head." It seems to me that he tells us in the text: "Christ also is the head of the church, He Himself being the Saviour of the body" (Ephesians 5:23). This is in line with what Jesus Himself says in Mark 10:45: "For even the Son of Man did not come to be served, but to serve, and to give His life a ransom for many."

For Jesus, "being Lord" means "being servant." For Jesus, "being Head" means "being Saviour." Who would not want to submit to One who understands headship as saviour-ship? Oh mercy me! Love my wife as Christ loves the church? That is what the apostle says in verse 25: "Husbands, love your wives, just as Christ also loved the church and gave Himself up for her." He goes to the cross for her! He lays down His life for us. He gives His all!

While serving in Manila, I had a weekly Bible class. One day we were working through this text, and a woman stood up and angrily said, "This is crazy! Why are wives told to submit, when husbands are told only to love?" My response was, "Only love?" If wives are called to do "an under," husbands are called to "a double under."

Husbands, stand under your wives by loving them the way Christ loves the church. Christ gave Himself up for the church. "So that He might sanctify her," says Paul, that He might make

FIRST EXAMPLE OF SPIRIT-FILLED RELATIONSHIPS

us holy and, therefore, whole. "Having cleansed her by the washing of water with the word," says Paul, "that He might present to Himself the church in all her glory, having no spot or wrinkle or any such thing; but that she would be holy and blameless" (v. 26-27).

That is how I am to love my wife Sharon! That is how I am to live out "being filled with the Spirit," "being subject to one another"! Paul is working with first century marriage customs. The bride and groom would "cleanse" themselves, sometimes taking semi-sacred baths. They would go to great lengths to present themselves in festive, elegant attire. So Christ does with us, His bride. He goes to great lengths to make us all He intends us to be.

"Holy and blameless." These are the same words that we met in the opening paragraph of Ephesians, where Paul blesses God for choosing us before the foundation of the world, that we should be "holy and blameless" before Him (Ephesians 1:4). Husbands are called to love their wives by participating in Christ's work in their wives' lives, doing all they can to enable their wives to be all Christ wants them to be.

Paul is also working in this passage with what God said long ago through the prophet Ezekiel. God was speaking to the people of Israel who had drifted off in unfaithfulness, adultery. God, nevertheless, will not give up on Israel. God says:

> I also swore to you and entered into a covenant with you so that you became Mine... Then I bathed you with water... and anointed you... [and] clothed you... [and] adorned you... so you were exceedingly beautiful... for it [your beauty] was perfect because of My splendor which I bestowed on you.
>
> Ezekiel 16:8-14

Paul takes those same words and applies them to Christ and His church. This is how Christ is loving His church. And this is how husbands are called to love their wives. Can you feel how revolutionary this was in the first century? Can you feel how revolutionary it is right now?

"Husbands, love your wives as Christ loves the church." As New Testament scholar Frank Thielman puts it: husbands are to imitate "the self-sacrificial, nurturing, and supporting roles that Christ fills" in relation to all of us.[4] After working through the text along these lines, the woman in the Bible class in Manila said "I would be crazy not to be subject to a husband who gets the text!" Indeed.

"Love as Christ loves." We love because He first loves. Husbands can love their wives because Christ is loving husbands before they seek to love their wives and because Christ is loving their wives before they do.

Thus at weddings I would also say, "Before you love each other, you are already being loved." To the groom: "Before you love her, she is already being loved." To the bride: "Before you love him, he is already being loved." This takes a huge burden off our shoulders. When we cannot, for whatever reason, love the other as Christ loves, we are to look at the other, and, realizing she or he is being loved, join Jesus in His loving.

Relational Revolution: Loving Yourself

One more dynamic of the revolution: "He who loves his own

---

[4] Frank Thielman, *Ephesians* [Baker Exegetical Commentary on the New Testament] (Grand Rapids: Baker Academic, 2010), 379.

wife loves himself." "So husbands ought also to love their own wives as their own bodies. He who loves his own wife loves himself" (Ephesians 5:28). What does Paul mean? What is he getting at? I am not sure. Nowhere else in the Bible do we find it put just this way.

It seems that Paul is working with the second greatest command. The first is "Love the Lord your God" with all your heart. The second is "love your neighbour as yourself" (Leviticus 19:18). Oh, how the world would change is we could just live that second command! Each of us makes sure that we eat well; now make sure your neighbour eats well. Each of us makes sure we have a place to sleep; now make sure your neighbour has a place to sleep. Each of us makes sure we have a job; now make sure your neighbour has a job.

A husband's closest neighbour is his wife; a wife's closest neighbour is her husband. So the second greatest command starts with: "Love your spouse as you love yourself." You make sure you have all you need to be fully human; make sure your spouse has all she or he needs to be fully human. Make sure your spouse has all she or he needs to grow in Christ, to live the kingdom life.

But Paul seems to be pushing it further, or deeper. "He who loves his own wife loves himself." Not just love "as himself" but "loves himself." Somehow the husband's own well-being is tied up in how well he loves his wife! Yes, her well-being is clearly affected by the way he loves her. But so is his. As the husband loves his closest neighbour, somehow he is loving himself.

This is not just because of the "one flesh" reality of marriage, but because in loving his wife as he loves himself, it turns out he ends up loving himself. As the husband loves his wife it turns out that one of the greatest of human needs is being met, the need to love. Yes, we have the need to be loved, but just as great, if not greater, is the need to love.

How often do we hear people say, "Well my spouse no longer meets my needs... I need to move on." When was "meeting my needs" ever part of the deal? Besides, no one human can meet all our needs. Only the one true human, Jesus Christ, can meet all our needs. But more to the point, one of our greatest needs is the need to learn to love. We are not yet truly human until we love. Love another person, especially a person who cannot meet our needs, and we end up loving ourselves into love.

A Lived Relational Revolution

One of my heroes is Robertson McQuilkin. For 30 years he was professor of ethics and hermeneutics and President of Columbia Bible College and Seminary (1960-1990). During the later years of his tenure his wife Muriel developed Alzheimers. At first Dr. McQuilkin tried to care for Muriel and run the College and Seminary. But as the condition worsened he had to make a choice: his ministry or his wife. In his letter of resignation he wrote:

> My dear wife, Muriel, has been in failing mental health for about 12 years. So far I have been able to carry both her ever-growing needs and my leadership responsibilities at Columbia. But recently it has become apparent that Muriel is contented most of the time she is with me and almost none of the time I am away from her. It is not just "discontent." She is filled with fear—even terror—that she has lost me and always goes in

search of me when I leave home. So it is clear to me that she needs me now, full-time.

Perhaps it would help you understand if I shared with you what I shared in chapel at the time of the announcement of my resignation. The decision was made, in a way, 42 years ago when I promised to care for Muriel "in sickness and in health... till death do us part." So, as I told the students and faculty, as a man of my word, integrity has something to do with it. But so does fairness. She has cared for me fully and sacrificially all these years; if I cared for her for the next 40 years I would not be out of her debt. Duty, however, can be grim and stoic. But there is more: I love Muriel. She is a delight to me—her childlike dependence and confidence in me, her warm love, occasional flashes of that wit I used to relish so, her happy spirit and tough resilience in the face of her continual distressing frustration. I don't *have* to care for her, I *get* to! It is a high honor to care for so wonderful a person.[5]

McQuilken was urged by many to search the world over for some kind of cure so he could keep his ministry while caring for his wife. He finally concluded that that was not what he was to do. "We would trust the Lord," he said, "to work a miracle in Muriel if he so desired or work a miracle in me if he didn't."[6]

The Lord chose to do the later—work a miracle in him. He would care for Muriel come what may. It was very hard work. People would say, "But she does not know who she is or who

---

5 Robertson McQuilkin, *A Promise Kept: The Story of an Unforgettable Love* (Carol Stream, IL: Tyndale House, 2006), 21-23.
6 Ibid., 3.

you are." And he would respond, "But I know who she is... and I love her." Then McQuilken writes:

> My imprisonment turned out to be a delightful liberation to love more fully than I had ever known. We found the chains of confining circumstances to be, no instrument of torture, but bonds to hold us closer.
>
> But there was even greater liberation. It has to do with God's love. No one ever needed me like Muriel, and no one ever responded to my efforts as totally as she. It's the nearest thing I've experienced on a human plane to what my relationship with God was designed to be: God's unfailing love poured out in constant care of helpless me.[7]

"He who loves his own wife loves himself." In doing everything he can for his wife, a husband discovers fullness of life. In giving his life away for his wife, a husband finds life. Unheard of in Paul's day! Revolutionary in Paul's day—and in ours. This is what happens when the Spirit of Jesus Christ comes. It is what happens when we are filled with the very life of God.

---

7 Ibid.., 32-33.

EPHESIANS 6:1-9

¹ Children, obey your parents in the Lord, for this is right. ² Honor your father and mother (which is the first commandment with a promise), ³ so that it may be well with you, and that you may live long on the earth.

⁴ Fathers, do not provoke your children to anger, but bring them up in the discipline and instruction of the Lord.

⁵ Slaves, be obedient to those who are your masters according to the flesh, with fear and trembling, in the sincerity of your heart, as to Christ; ⁶ not by way of eyeservice, as men-pleasers, but as slaves of Christ, doing the will of God from the heart. ⁷ With good will render service, as to the Lord, and not to men, ⁸ knowing that whatever good thing each one does, this he will receive back from the Lord, whether slave or free.

⁹ And masters, do the same things to them, and give up threatening, knowing that both their Master and yours is in heaven, and there is no partiality with Him.

CHAPTER 21

Further Examples of Spirit-Filled Relationships

EPHESIANS 6:1-9

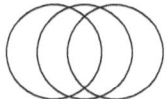

We have been working our way through a very revolutionary text! All of the letter to the Ephesians is a revolutionary text, for it invites us into an alternative reading of reality, and invites us to live in the alternative reality it introduces us to.

But we have also seen that the Apostle Paul's instructions on how we are to relate to one another are truly revolutionary: under, not over. In all your relationships, be filled with the Spirit, being subject to one another. Revolutionary!

In this chapter, we'll examine what this alternative reading of relationships looks like in the context of children-parents and parents-children, and slave-master and master-slave. Equally revolutionary!

Children

We can paraphrase Paul: Children, be filled with the Spirit... being subject to your fathers and mothers. Fathers and mothers, be filled with the Spirit... being subject to your sons and daughters.

You can see in the text that what Paul says to children turns on the word "honor." For children, being subject involves honouring. In speaking to the children, Paul goes back to the fifth of the ten commandments: "Honor your father and mother."

What does it mean to honor our parents? The Hebrew word in the fifth commandment carries a wide range of meanings, but its basic meaning is "to make heavy" or "to treat as weighty." It is the verb form of the noun "glory." The glory of God is the weightiness of God's self manifestation, His inherent heaviness. To honor our parents means to give weight to them. It means to feel the weightiness of their position. In the book of Leviticus, the word "honor" is replaced by the word "reverence"—"Everyone of you should reverence his mother and his father" (19:3). We are to recognize the load parents carry.

God has entrusted to parents the weighty responsibility of taking care of God's most vulnerable creatures. Parents carry the weight of protecting and feeding and clothing us. Parents carry the weight of forming our self-image, of building the basis of our self-worth. Parents carry the weight of putting the building blocks of our world-view together, of helping us develop the basis of our significance and security. Parents carry the weight of giving us our initial understanding of God! That's a huge burden, and every parent enters this responsibility as a rookie!

So we honor our parents by respecting the weightiness of their role in life. Such respect, however, is not absolute. That is, as children grow older, they are to put their parents' input on the scale, and weigh it against God's input. For sons and daughters are also called to respect the Living God. They are also called to honor God, to obey the first commandment: "You shall have no other gods before Me" (Exodus 20:3). Literally, it is "You shall have no other gods between us"—including parents.

Jesus, who clearly upholds the fifth commandment, can say to us "He who loves father or mother more than Me is not worthy of Me; and he who loves son or daughter more than Me is not worthy of Me" (Matthew 10:37). We honor our parents in the context of honouring Jesus as Lord. As Lord of my life, Jesus has the last word over the decisions I make with my life, over my values, over my goals, over the way I live my life, over my self-perceptions. Absolute respect can only be given to the Lord Himself.

Now, honouring our parents also means obeying them as long as we live at home. So, Paul says, "Children, obey your parents in the Lord, for this is right." This is right because it honours God's ordering of human society. God has placed parents in the place of authority on God's behalf. We subject ourselves to God by subjecting ourselves to our parents. We stand under God by standing under our parents, and we stand under our parents by obeying them.

Yet again, such obedience is not absolute. As children grow toward adulthood, they develop other relationships which also have to be honoured. And there will come a time when the obligations of these other relationships may conflict with the requests of parents.

One such relationship is marriage. When a son or daughter marries, they owe greater allegiance to their spouse than to their parents, and we parents have to embrace this. My son has a greater allegiance to his wife that to Sharon and me. Our daughters have a greater allegiance to their husbands than to Sharon and me. The God who says, "Honour your parents" also says "A man shall leave his father and mother, and be joined to his wife, ad they shall become one flesh" (Genesis 2:24). Marriage calls one to a new loyalty, a loyalty that is stronger than the ties of blood.

And then there is the relationship with the Living God, a relationship that calls for the child's absolute obedience and allegiance. Absolute allegiance can only be given to God in Jesus Christ. The first commandment is always first! "You shall have no other gods between us."

This is lived out when the lawgiver Himself became a human being and lived our life. As a young boy, Jesus submitted to His parents' direction and leadership. When He was about twelve years old, however, they had this large family gathering, and Jesus left and went to the temple to talk with the teachers. His parents looked all over for Him, and when they found Him, His mother said to Him, "Son, why have you treated us this way? Behold, Your father and I have been anxiously looking for You" (Luke 2:48). And then Jesus responded, "Why is it that you were looking for Me? Did you not know that I had to be in My Father's house?" (Luke 2:49) Jesus' relationship with His heavenly Father trumped the relationship with His mother and father, with Mary and Joseph. Yet, we should note that Luke who tells of this incident, also tells that after this, Jesus went and "continued in subjection to them" (v. 51) until the time God the Father called Him to His unique mission.

Now, honouring our parents also means caring for them, accepting the weightiness of their needs. Such care is going to take on different forms at different times of life. While parents are still able to take care of themselves, I think we are to care by protecting their reputation and by covering up their faults.

There's a very touching story in the book of Genesis that illustrates this care (Genesis 9:20-23). The great flood has subsided, and Noah and his family are settled on the land again. One day Noah drinks some of the wine from his new vineyard. He drinks too much and gets drunk. One of Noah's sons finds him laying in the tent, stark naked, and the text tells us that the other two of Noah's sons took a garment, walked backwards into the tent, and covered their father's nakedness. We are to care for our parents by not shaming them, by keeping their faults within the family, unless we need to talk about those faults with someone who can help us process them.

And clearly we care for our parents by providing for their needs when they can no longer care for themselves. Old Testament scholar Brevard Childs points out that God spoke the fifth commandment into a context where parents were kicked out of the house because they could no longer work.[1] Ghastly! And sadly, it happens all over the world.

We honor elderly parents by caring for them when they can no longer care for themselves. Think about how they cared for us when we were totally dependent on them. Think of all the inconvenience we caused our parents—we stifled their lifestyle, big time, with our dirty diapers and messy eating habits, and keeping them up all night! Is it not only fair that we, for a few years, be inconvenienced? Unheard of in Paul's day!

Again, Jesus models this for us. On the cross, even as He is dying, He makes provision for His mother. To the beloved disciple, Jesus said in reference to Mary, "Behold, your mother!" John tells us that "from that hour the disciple took her into his own household" (John 19:26-27).

---

[1] Brevard S. Childs, *The Book of Exodus: A Critical, Theological Commentary* (Philadelphia: Westminster Press, 1974), 418.

Parents

A friend of mine once said to me that we need an eleventh commandment: Parents, honour your sons and daughters. Is this not what the apostle Paul does in this text? After quoting the fifth commandment, he writes, "Fathers, do not provoke your children to anger, but bring them up in the discipline and instruction of the Lord" (Ephesians 6:4). Unheard of in the first century!

Fathers were usually not involved in their children's lives. I mean, why should they be? Children were nobodies. At best they were treated as slaves. Just the fact that Paul speaks to fathers concerning their children was revolutionary! And as Paul calls children to recognize the weightiness of their parents, so he calls parents to recognize the weightiness of their children as persons. Again, this is unheard of in the first century. Children were things to be possessed and manipulated.

Now, the radical thing Paul says to fathers (and I think he also says this to mothers!) is "Do not provoke your children to anger." Apparently, fathers did this in the first century! What is Paul getting at? Fathers treated their sons and daughters as mere things, doing with their children whatever they wanted to do. This rightly evoked anger in the souls of their children. If fathers were involved with their children, they insisted on having their own way. Children must be and become what the parents want them to be and become, which understandably, evokes anger in the soul of a child.

Instead, says Paul, fathers are to bring up their children in the discipline and instruction of the Lord. The little phrase "of the Lord" changes everything. Fathers are to bring up their children to know the Lord Jesus and to know the will of the Lord Jesus, which calls for a great investment of time on the part of fathers and mothers.

This involves getting inside the souls of our children so that we can understand what makes them tick. What makes our children tick is often not what makes us tick. "Train up a child in the way he should go, even when he is old he will not depart from it" (Proverbs 22:6). Many people have taken that to mean shove your child into this certain mold, and even if they rebel against it, one day they will return to it. Now, that attitude crushes the child's spirit and rightly evokes anger in their spirits—even if they don't understand what is evoking the anger.

But the Scriptures tell us that God has made each child unique. God has given each child unique temperaments, gifts, and interests. This is how Proverbs 22:6 literally reads: "Train up a child according to his bent, and when he is old he will not depart."[2] Our job as parents is to discover our children's unique characteristics and train them up in ways consistent with their nature, character, and interests. The promise is that when our children discover the Creator's way and will for them, they will not depart from it.

That, I think, is what Paul means by bringing up a child in the nurture and admonition of the Lord. It means being more concerned about their relationship with Jesus Christ than anything else. It means being more concerned about the quality of

---

2 See Bruce K. Waltke, *The Book of Proverbs: Chapters 15-31 [New International Commentary of the Old Testament]* (Grand Rapids: William B. Eerdmans, 2005), 205. Dr. Waltke's own translation of the verse is "Dedicate a youth according to what his way dictates; even when he becomes old, he will not depart from it" (ibid., 194).

that relationship than about what schools they go to, or what status they have in society.

> Parents should care more for the loyalty of their children to Christ than for anything besides, more for this than for their health, their intellectual vigour and brilliance, their material prosperity, their social position, their exemption from great sorrows and great misfortunes.[3]

We honor our children by seeking their independent dependence on Jesus as Lord.

When I went away to college (September, 1965), my father gave me a little pocket bible, and on the inside cover of the pocket bible he wrote the words, "Here is a story about a man who can do more for you than your dad." My dad honoured me by pointing me to Jesus as Lord. But like many dads, he did not realize the full implications of this! For my dad was running the risk that "the man" might call me to something different than what my dad was calling me to.

I'm the oldest of five sons. In a Swedish household, the oldest son does what father does with his life. That's just the way it is. My dad was a really good physicist. So I grew up in the world of physics and mathematics. It was a given that I would study physics, and I did! And I loved it, especially the philosophical and theoretical parts.

I honoured my dad by listening to his desires for me. And I

---

[3] R. W. Dale in Francis Foulkes, *The Epistle of Paul to the Ephesians: An Introduction and Commentary* [Tyndale New Testament Commentaries] (Grand Rapids: Wm. B. Eerdmans, 1963), 166.

honoured my dad by reading the Bible he gave me about the Man who could do more for me than he could. Early one morning I was reading that Bible, and I came across Colossians 1, where Paul makes the great claim that all things are made by Jesus Christ, for Jesus Christ. Isn't that amazing? Things in heaven and on earth, visible and invisible.

And then I read a line that leapt out and grabbed me. "In Him [Christ] all things hold together" (Colossians 1:17). J.B. Phillips renders this as, Christ is "the upholding principle of the whole scheme of creation." I left from my quiet time to go to the lecture hall. A visiting German physicist was writing this massive equation on the three blackboards in the hall. An exquisitely beautiful equation... I can still see it! And it dawned on me that he was simply describing in quantum mechanical terms how Jesus Christ holds it all together. And something in my spirit leapt. Or, as I should say, a bent in me that had not been acknowledged came alive.

A few weeks later, Martin Luther King Jr. was killed, and as I listened to his sermons being played on the radio that night, what I had secretly felt all my life came to life—I was made to preach Jesus. I told my dad. He was devastated. He was hurt. He was angry. He had dreamed all of his life of me being a physicist. He had just started a new corporation and dreamed of me taking it over. The pain in my dad was so deep we could not speak for three months.

My father finally, reluctantly, accepted that I was on another path. He watched as I came alive studying theology and the Bible at seminary. He watched as I grew as a preacher. And when it came time for me to be ordained he asked if he could speak at the service. This is what my dad said at my ordination: "I believe

Darrell would have had a successful career in physics had not the heavenly Father stepped in and changed my plans for him. On this occasion, I want to say I submit to the Father's plan for my son." And until the day he died, he was one of my greatest fans. He passed my sermons on to all his physics friends. My dad was doing what Paul calls dads to do.

Sharon and I have tried to do the same thing with our children. It's hard work! It's deep work. It involves getting inside their skin, and finding their unique bent. Sharon and I have tried the best we could, and we did it because we made a promise when we dedicated our children: this child is not my own, I will raise him or her to follow Jesus Christ as Lord. We were saying in that moment that Jesus' claim on their lives precedes and supersedes any claim we can make. His word will be the last word.

Servants and Masters

This leads us then to the dynamics of the revolution taking place between servants and masters. "Be filled with the Spirit... being subject to one another in the fear of Christ... servants to masters and masters to servants." You might know that many people think that Paul wimps out here and endorses the institution of slavery. But he does not! And those throughout history who have taken Paul to justify slavery haven't read him carefully enough.

What Paul says to servants is more revolutionary than outright rebellion would have been. Had he tried to overtly overthrow slavery, he would not have gotten anywhere, because he would have been dismissed as a radical troublemaker.

I mentioned earlier that while serving in Manila I had a weekly Bible class, and we were working through Ephesians.

When we came to this section on masters and servants you could feel the temperature in the room begin to rise, because just about everyone in that room had household servants (including Sharon and I, much to Sharon's discomfort).

The class was okay with Paul saying, "Slaves, be obedient to those who are your masters." They were fine with that. Things got a little warmer when Paul said things like, "Not by way of eye-service, as men-pleasers, but as slaves of Christ, doing the will of God from the heart" (6:6). "What do you mean doing the will of God? I thought they were doing my will, not the will of God!" "As to the Lord, and not to men," says Paul (Colossians 3:23). "What do you mean? Serving Jesus and not me, not the master?"

Then the temperature rose very high when we read, "and masters, do the same things to them, and give up threatening" (6:9). One woman blurted out, "If you let this text loose in this part of the world it's going to undo our way of life." Exactly. Slowly, but surely.

"As to the Lord, as to Christ." Christ is the Lord who services. Because you belong to the Lord, your Lord calls you to follow in his serving way. Even the master! It's brilliant, because it means that the servant is no longer a slave of the human Lord. I am no longer a servant of the human who is lording it over me, I am a slave of Jesus Christ, who tells me that my freedom is found in serving.

The human master who thinks that he or she is the master is not the one dictating my behaviour. Jesus Christ dictates my behaviour. I serve the human master because I am copying the true master. "Serve from the heart," says Paul. Serve with grace, with courage, with excellence. Go the extra mile. Do the work to honour Jesus, and one day your master will say, "Hey, I did not order you to serve me in this way!" And you can respond, "I'm not under your orders!"

Then comes the most revolutionary line in the book, the text that captures the drumbeat of this whole passage: "And masters, do the same things to them." The same things servants are doing for their masters, masters are to do for their servants.

I've mentioned my scholar-friend, Bong Manayon, who lives in the Philippines, who likes to be called Peter. He grew up in a household with many household servants, and he and his wife live in a house with many household servants. One day he was working at his desk on this precise text, and he was wondering what it meant. At that very moment, one of the servants came into the room with his favourite lunch, a peanut butter sandwich and a Coke. Peter realized, "I am to treat her the way she treated me—it is as simple as that."[4] And as revolutionary as that!

Because Jesus Christ has come, because the Spirit of Jesus Christ has come, be filled with His Spirit, and you will find yourself living in a different kingdom, following a very different kind of King.

---

4 Bong Manayon, *In the Same Way: Philemon & The Ephesian Household Code* (Manila: Alethinos Media, 2007), 87.

EPHESIANS 6:10-12

¹⁰ Finally, be strong in the Lord and in the strength of His might. ¹¹ Put on the full armor of God, so that you will be able to stand firm against the schemes of the devil. ¹² For our struggle is not against flesh and blood, but against the rulers, against the powers, against the world forces of this darkness, against the spiritual forces of wickedness in the heavenly places.

CHAPTER 22

Stand Firm Against the Powers

EPHESIANS 6:10-12

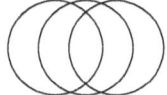

Every culture in every era of history, every people group around the globe, every institution, every organization, every family, and every individual operates out of a "reading of reality." N.T. Wright calls our "readings of reality," the "lenses" through which we look at the world, the grid on which are plotted the experiences of life.[1] To put it more simply: we all wear a set of glasses. We all have deeply ingrained presuppositions about the make-up of the universe and our lives within it. Our set of glasses determines the degree to which we understand what is going on in the world, and it determines how well we function in all that is going on in the world.

The apostle Paul's "reading of reality" was radically transformed by an encounter with Jesus Christ, and in his letter to the

---

[1] N.T. Wright, *The New Testament and the People of God* (Minneapolis: Fortress Press, 1992), 125-126.

Ephesians he develops this new, expansive "reading of reality" centered in, and saturated with, Jesus Christ. This new reading of reality is a revolutionary alternative reading—as we have experienced throughout our journey through the letter!

But nowhere is the phrase "alternative reading of reality" more apropos than for the text before us. "Our struggle," says Paul, and the word refers to an up-close and personal struggle, "is not against flesh and blood, but against the rulers, against the powers, against the world forces of this darkness, against the spiritual forces of wickedness in the heavenly places" (Ephesians 6:12). Our wrestling to live the alternative reality shaped by Jesus Christ and His gospel, is not a battle against other human beings. Oh, it involves human beings! But the struggle is not finally with or against other human beings. What an alternative reading, what a different set of glasses!

While serving as the Secretary General of the United Nations, from 1961 to 1971, Burmese diplomat U Thant expressed his bewilderment over the state of human existence on the planet. Speaking before an audience of some 2,500 people who had gathered to talk about the conditions necessary for world peace, U Thant asked a number of searching questions:

> What element is lacking so that with all our skill and all our knowledge we still find ourselves in the dark valley of discord and enmity? What is it that inhibits us from going forward together to enjoy the fruits of human endeavor and to reap the harvest of human experience? Why is it that, for all our professed ideals, our hopes, and our skills, peace on earth is

still a distant objective seen only dimly through the storms and turmoils of our present difficulties?[2]

The answer depends on what set of glasses you are wearing.

Finally

We have been working our way through Paul's letter to the Ephesians, and as we get to verse 10 of chapter six, we read, "Finally." This is not finally as "in conclusion," or "I have now reached the end of the matter." The word Paul uses is better rendered "henceforth," or even "henceforward," meaning, "from now on" or "this is the way it is going to be for the rest of the journey." We are going to find ourselves in tension, in a struggle, in a battle, the rest of our lives.

John Stott helps us 'feel' the impact of Paul's 'henceforward':

> But now Paul brings us down to earth, and to realities harsher than dreams. He reminds us of the opposition. Beneath surface appearances an unseen spiritual battle is raging. He introduces us to the devil (already mentioned in 2:2 and 4:27) and to certain "principalities and powers" at his command. He supplies us with no biography of the devil, and no account of the origin of the forces of darkness. He assumes their existence as common ground between himself and his readers. In any case, his purpose is not to satisfy our curiosity, but to warn us of their hostility and teach us how to overcome them. Is God's plan to

---

[2] Ray C. Stedman, *Spiritual Warfare: Winning the Daily Battle with Satan* (Portland, OR: Multnomah, 1975), 19.

create a new society? Then they will do their utmost to destroy. Has God through Jesus Christ broken down the walls dividing human beings of different races and cultures from each other? Then the devil through his emissaries will strive to rebuild them. Does God intend his reconciled and redeemed people to live together in harmony and purity? Then the powers of hell will scatter among them the seeds of discord and sin. It is with these powers that we are told to wage war, or—to be more precise—to "wrestle" (v. 12, AV). This metaphor is not necessarily incompatible with that of the armed soldier which Paul goes on to develop, as if he "changed the scenery from that of the battlefield to that of the gymnasium [Hendriksen, p 273]." He is simply wanting to emphasize the reality of our engagement with the powers of evil, and the grim necessity of hand-to-hand combat.[3]

"Therefore," "Henceforward," "Finally," be strong in the Lord, and in the strength of His might." We have no other choice, for we are no match for the true opposition. We are no match for the real enemy of the gospel. Only our Lord is strong enough to stand on His own. "Be strong in the Lord, and in the strength of His might."

The terms Paul uses are the same terms he uses in his first prayer for the Ephesians. There he prays that we might know the surpassing greatness of God's power toward us who believe, "power ... in accordance with the working of the strength of His might" (1:19). This, says Paul, is the power God exercised when He raised Christ from the dead and seated Him at His right

---

[3] John R.W. Stott, *God's New Society: The Message of Ephesians* [The Bible Speaks Today] (Downers Grove: InterVarsity Press, 1979), 261-262.

hand "in the heavenly places, far above all rule and authority and power and dominion" (1:20-21). "Henceforward," be strong in the strength of God's mighty might.

"Be strong in the Lord." More literally, "grow strong in the Lord." How? "Put on the full armour of God," says Paul. "So that," says Paul, "you may be able to stand firm against the schemes of the devil"(6:10-11). We are to clothe ourselves with a different kind of armour because we are battling a different kind of opponent. Alternative reading.

Our Opponents

We realize how important God's armour is when we begin to understand our opponent, or host of opponents as is the case. So let us focus on verse 12 of the text: "For our struggle is not against flesh and blood, but against the rulers, against the powers, against the world forces of this darkness, against the spiritual forces of wickedness in the heavenly places."

To what is Paul referring?[4] He has already used this language earlier in the letter, in his first prayer, where he describes the power that God exercised when He raised Christ from the dead, and when God seated Christ at His right hand, in the heavenly places, "far above all rule and authority and power and dominion" (1:21). And Paul used this language when speaking of one of the roles of the church in the world: "so that the manifold

---

[4] I commend to you a very helpful resource for understanding this dimension of Biblical revelation. *Understanding Spiritual Warfare: Four Views – Walter Wink, David Powlison, Gregory Boyd, C. Peter Wagnes and Rebecca Greenwooe.* Edited by James K. Bailey and Paul Rhodes Eddy (Baker Academic, Grand Rapids, 2012).

wisdom of God might now be made known through the church to the rulers and the authorities in the heavenly places" (3:10).

What does Paul mean by this? The church has grappled with this for centuries! Some argue that Paul is referring to visible, material, human powers and forces. Some argue Paul is referring to the human "structures" that seemingly order the world, structures like tradition, the state, courts, laws and regulations, corporate alliances, political parties, banking policies, even religions. All of it can become very oppressive. All of it can begin to work against God's purposes. And it can "feel" very overwhelming.

Others claim that Paul is referring to invisible, non-material, but still essentially human powers and forces. They argue Paul is referring to the fact that human structures can begin to "take on a life of their own." As we know, a grouping of humans can develop a "spirit," an "ethos," a "force," a "corporate identity." It becomes more than the sum of its parts. That "spirit" or "force" can then begin to influence convictions and behaviours, causing people to believe things in the group they would never believe if not in the group; causing people to act in ways in and with the group they would never adopt if not in the group. IBM takes on a life of its own. Apple Computer takes on a life of its own that goes on even after Steven Jobs. "City Hall" takes on a life of its own. Being "Conservative" takes on a life of its own. Being "Liberal" takes on a life of its own. Churches take on a life of their own. I have served five churches and preached in many more, and each of them has "a life of its own." Some of that life is congruous with the kingdom of God; some of it is not. Some of that life is very liberating and healing. Some of it is oppressive and hurtful.

But it seems to me that Paul is referring to something more and other. It seems Paul is referring to "structures" other than anything humans devise. It seems Paul is referring to a "spirit" other than any human spirit or combination of human spirits. Notice that he explicitly refers to a personal being, whom he calls "the devil" (v. 11), and "the evil one" (v. 16). And note that he refers to the "powers" as "the spiritual forces of wickedness" (v.12), who he says are located "in the heavenly places" (v.12).

It seems that Paul is referring to non-material, non-human, supra-human powers. The powers interact with the material, the human. They influence the human "spirit," "ethos." But the powers are other than the human and the humanly generated. The powers work in the earth, but they are not "earthly." Rulers, powers, forces... "in the heavenly places."

Heavenly Places

We meet this phrase elsewhere in the letter to the Ephesians:

- "Blessed be the God and Father of our Lord Jesus Christ, who has blessed us with every spiritual blessing in the heavenly places in Christ" (1:3).
- Christ is seated "in the heavenly places" (1:20)
- God has raised us up and seated us with Christ "in the heavenly places" (2:6).
- The manifold wisdom of God is "made known through the church to the rulers and the authorities in the heavenly places" (3:10).

"Heavenly places" is another dimension of reality, very close at hand, which interacts with the dimension we can see and hear and touch and smell. It is where Christ is, where we somehow are seated with Christ, and where the opponents of Christ are, and from where they operate. "Alternative reading"—big time!

As we saw in our second chapter, most of us live with a two-dimensional "reading of reality": the human self and the physical environment. But the Biblical reading is at least four-dimensional:

1. The human self, who is more glorious than the two-dimensional reading knows!
2. The physical environment, which is also more glorious than the two-dimensional reading knows!
3. The Living God, who is more glorious than any of us have yet to realize!
4. The heavenly places, where non-material, supra-human powers and forces exist, influencing the material and the human more than we realize.

Paul calls these non-material, supra-human powers rulers (*archai*), powers (*exousiai*), world-forces (*kosmokrators*) and spiritual beings (*pneumatika*). They are created, an important fact to note! Whatever these rulers, powers, and forces are, they are created by God and for God's purposes. Some obey, some rebel, but they are not eternal beings, and they are certainly not God's equal! If they were equal to God, Paul could not say, "Therefore, take up the full armour of God, that you may be able to resist in the evil day... to stand firm."

What is Paul wanting us to know? Here is where C.S. Lewis helps us. He was often asked if he believed in the devil, and would answer:

If by "the Devil" you mean a power opposite to God and, like God, self existent from all eternity, the answer is certainly No. There is no uncreated being except God. God has no opposite.... The proper question is whether I believe in devils. I do. That is to say, I believe in angels, and I believe that some of these, by the abuse of their free will, have become enemies to God... Satan, the leader or dictator of devils, is the opposite, not of God, but of Michael.[5]

Spiritual Powers

Angels were created to work with God. We meet this reading of reality all over the Bible. We read in a number of places of God meeting in a "heavenly assembly," interacting with the angels. Sometimes they are called "gods," sometimes they are called "sons of God," sometimes "the hosts of heaven," or "the heavenly hosts." One of the Living God's names is "Yahweh Sabaoth," "Yahweh of the hosts," "Lord of hosts, Lord Sabaoth." The prophet Zechariah, who especially works with this alternative reading of reality, uses this name throughout his prophecy.

We read of the prophet Micaiah saying, "I saw the Lord sitting on His throne, and all the host of heaven standing by Him on His right and on His left" (1 Kings 22:19). The book of Job opens, "Now there was a day when the sons of God came to present themselves before the Lord, and Satan also came among them" (Job 1:6). The prophet Isaiah tells of the day when, after

---

5 C.S. Lewis, *The Screwtape Letters & Screwtape Proposes a Toast* (New York: MacMillan, 1961), vii. This is taken from the second preface, written in 1960, which is not included in all editions of *Screwtape Letters*.

King Uzziah died, "I saw the Lord sitting on a throne... Seraphim [some kind of exalted being] stood above Him..." At one point in the worship service, the Lord asks: "Whom shall I send, and who will go for Us?" Isaiah says, "Here I am, send me!" (Isaiah 6:1-8). A bold thing to say, because the Lord's question was not addressed to Isaiah; it was not addressed to any human being. It was addressed to the hosts of heaven: "Who will go for Us," the heavenly assembly.

Then there is Psalm 82, tucked in the middle of the Prayer Book, and opening up this alternative understanding of the universe. The Psalmist, Asaph, tells of God taking "His stand in His own congregation." He tells of God then judging "in the midst of the rulers," literally, "in the midst of the gods." Are there other "gods" alongside Yahweh? No. The Psalmist is referring to the spiritual powers and forces around Yahweh. God speaks to the powers and forces: "How long will you judge unjustly and show partiality to the wicked? Vindicate the weak and fatherless; Do justice to the afflicted and destitute. Rescue the weak and needy; Deliver them out of the hand of the wicked" (v. 2-4). That is the role God created the powers for—to make justice happen. Then the Psalmist laments that the "rulers," the "gods," have not done their assigned jobs. And as a result, "All the foundations of the earth are shaken" (v.5). When the heavenly hosts do not do justice, the foundations of the earth are shaken.

We see this alternative reading being lived out in the fifth century before the birth of Jesus in the experience of the prophet Daniel (in chapter 10 of Daniel). Daniel says that during the third year of Cyrus, the human king of Persia, a message was revealed to him after he had been praying and fasting for twenty-one days. The messenger, who turned out to be an angel, told Daniel that

God has been aware of his praying the whole twenty-one days. But the angel could only now come because "the prince of the kingdom of Persia was withstanding me for twenty-one days." The heavenly messenger went on: "then behold, Michael, one of the chief princes, came to help me, for I had been left there with the kings of Persia" (10:13). The kings of Persia are clearly human kings. But the prince of Persia appears to be a non-human force, as does Michael, one of the chief princes. When the heavenly messenger says it is time for him to leave, he explains, "I shall now return to fight against the prince of Persia; so I am going forth, and behold, the prince of Greece is about to come" (10:20).

"Prince." Hence the term "principalities," "powers." There is more to the movements of nations (and institutions) than we realize. History is not just about what humans and human organizations do. History is also about what the Holy God does. And it is about what the "princes," "rulers," "powers," and "forces" do.

What an alternative reading of reality! God has created angelic, spiritual powers and forces to be part of His running of the universe. Some co-operate with Him; some do not. Some do not accept their place before God, and then seek to subvert God's purposes. Some hate God and, therefore, hate Jesus Christ because they know that He came to defeat those who have rebelled, which Jesus did on the cross and through the empty tomb.

Our Struggle

Some of the spiritual powers will not surrender to the very truth they know—Jesus is Lord. They know the gospel, but will not surrender. So they do everything they can to blind human beings to the truth about Jesus, to hinder the progress of God's good news, to lead those Jesus rescues back into slavery to sin; they do everything they can to divide Jesus' followers and to destroy the church, to ruin what Jesus redeems. This is why, although we who follow Jesus Christ are caught up in the battle, we ourselves are not the point of the battle.

Canadian psychiatrist John White put it best in his book *The Fight*:

> His [Satan's] supreme object is to hurt Christ and Christ's cause. You personally are of no interest to him. It is only as you relate to Christ that you assume significance in his eyes. Before you became a Christian he was mainly interested in blinding you to the truth of Christ or perhaps in seducing you further into his terrain. But this was not because of your personal importance. He only used you to get back at God.[6]

Do not take the battle personally! But do take it seriously.

Once more: "Our struggle," says Paul, "is not against flesh and blood." If it were we might be able to stand on our own, and we could fight with human, earthly means. But our fight, as J.B. Phillips translates Paul, "is against organizations and powers that are spiritual. We are up against the unseen power that controls this dark world, and spiritual agents from the very headquarters of evil." And this fight requires a very different posture.

Church historian Richard Lovelace sadly notes that "much of the church's warfare today is fought by blindfolded soldiers who cannot see the forces ranged against them, who are buffeted

---

[6] John White, *The Fight* (Downers Grove, IL: InterVarsity Press, 1978), 78.

by invisible opponents and respond by striking one another."[7]

When we first met this reading of reality in our study of Ephesians, I turned for help to Walter Wink, who has thought and written a lot about it. Although I do not agree with everything he teaches, I think he is on the mark in using a little equation to help us in the battle. P = O + I.

As we saw in chapter 5, Dr. Wink reminds us that the powers (P) are made up of both an outer manifestation (O) and an inner spirituality (I). "The powers, whether benign or satanic, always consist of an outer, visible form (constitutions, judges, armies, leaders, buildings) and an inner, invisible spirit that provides its legitimacy, credibility, and clout.[8] O: King of Persia; I: Prince of Persia.

Wink warns the church that "our incapacity to recognize the spirituality of institutions has left us tinkering with their parts while ignoring their essence," and goes on to say that "the church cannot be content with addressing the material aspects of unjust institutions. It must speak to the spiritual reality of the institution as well."[9]

Thus Paul's "henceforth," "henceforward." Our struggle is not against flesh and blood. Humans are not the enemy. Our struggle is against suprahuman forces. And we struggle with them using very different means. Placards and bull-horns, rocks and fists, handguns and assault rifles, have no long term effect against the real opposition. What finally affects the real

---

[7] Richard F. Lovelace, *Dynamics of Spiritual Life: An Evangelical Theology of Renewal* (Downers Grove: Inter-Varsity Press, 1979), 18.
[8] Walter Wink, "The Powers Behind the Throne: An Election-Year Equation for Discerning the Spirits," *Sojourners* Vol. 13, no. 8 (September 1984), 24.
[9] Ibid.

opposition is buckling truth around our guts, and wearing righteousness and justice across our chests, and putting on the shoes of peace, and holding up the shield of faith, and covering our head with salvation, and speaking the Word of God, and praying at all times in the Spirit of God.

Some Qualifying Statements

Let me make a number of qualifying statements to help us live out the Apostle Paul's exhortation.

First, the powers of darkness and wickedness are not our only enemies. The Bible tells us we also battle sin, the flesh, and the world. We know about sin. We do not take it seriously enough, but we know the struggle. We also know about the flesh, the human self—centered in the self and empowered by the self.

"The world" refers not to God's good creation, but to "human society organizing itself without God." "The world" is where we all live everyday. "The world" has no interest in God and God's purposes. Indeed, "the world" rejects God and God's claim upon creation and civilizations.

So we also battle these enemies. And the devil and his "principalities and powers" then mess with these other enemies. They love to fan the flames of sin, fuel the desires of the flesh, and give energy to the world's quest to live without God.

Second, we humans are responsible for our own choices and actions. Although we come under great pressure from the powers, we are still responsible for our attitudes and behaviours. Some of you may remember the comedian Flip Wilson. He used to perform these routines in which he did something stupid or obnoxious and then squeal, "The devil made me do it!" That is never true. The devil may entice us to do it, the devil may pressure us to do it, but he never makes us do it. We make us do it.

Third, as I emphasized previously, the battle is not between equals. The devil is not God's equal. Martin Luther can say of the devil: "on earth is not his equal," meaning that we are no match for Satan and his powers.[10] But the devil is not God's equal; he and his powers are no match for God. Thank God! Evil is not an equal opposite to good. The devil is not an equal opposite to Jesus Christ.

And fourth, a critical qualifying statement: the outcome of the battle has already been settled. Jesus wins. He already has—on the cross and through the empty tomb. As E. Stanley Jones notes, "I don't work to the victory—I work from the Victory to the victory."[11] This sets the whole tone and posture of the struggle. We know the final outcome.

So Paul simply calls us to "stand." He uses the verb four times:

- "so that you will be able to stand firm…" (v. 11),
- "so that you will be able to resist [a form of the verb stand]…" (v. 13),
- "and having done everything, to stand firm" (v. 13),
- Stand firm therefore…" (v. 14).

The implication is that since Jesus Christ has already won, we are to hold the ground He has already won.[12] The exhortation

---

[10] In his great hymn, "A Mighty Fortress is our God."
[11] E. Stanley Jones, *A Song of Ascents* (Nashville: Abingdon Press, 1968), 22.
[12] Harold W. Hoehner, *Ephesians: An Exegetical Commentary* (Grand Rapids: Baker Academic, 2002), 836.

is not "march on and take the ground," but "stand firm" on the ground already taken by the Saviour and Redeemer.

How We Stand Firm

How? That is the question: How do we stand firm in the nature of our true struggle? How do we resist "in the evil day," as Paul puts it? "Be strong in the Lord" (v.10).

Take careful note: we are not exhorted to "be strong." Paul does not challenge us to "pull up our bootstraps" and get on with the fight. He exhorts us to be strong "in the Lord." A big difference!

We are not strong enough in and of ourselves. We are strong when, in our weakness, we throw ourselves on the strength of the Lord. As Jesus said the night before going to the cross, "Abide in Me, and I in you... for apart from Me you can do nothing" (John 15:4-5). Apart from Him we cannot stand firm against the powers. New Testament scholar William Lane puts it this way: "It is tactical suicide to underestimate the strength of the Enemy."[13] And I would add, it is tactical suicide to overestimate our ability to stand!

But the good news is we do not have to be strong by ourselves. We are called to "be strong—not in yourselves but in the Lord, in the power of his boundless resource" (J.B. Phillips).

In the next chapter we will explore the boundless resources God has given us, the full armour of God, enabling us to stand firm against the powers.

---

[13] William L. Lane, *Scripture Union Bible Study Books: Ephesians, Philippians, Colossians, 1 and 2 Thessalonians* (Grand Rapids: William B. Eerdmans, 1969), 24.

EPHESIANS 6:13-20

[13] Therefore, take up the full armor of God, so that you will be able to resist in the evil day, and having done everything, to stand firm. [14] Stand firm therefore, having girded your loins with truth, and having put on the breastplate of righteousness, [15] and having shod your feet with the preparation of the gospel of peace; [16] in addition to all, taking up the shield of faith with which you will be able to extinguish all the flaming arrows of the evil one. [17] And take the helmet of salvation, and the sword of the Spirit, which is the word of God.

[18] With all prayer and petition pray at all times in the Spirit, and with this in view, be on the alert with all perseverance and petition for all the saints, [19] and pray on my behalf, that utterance may be given to me in the opening of my mouth, to make known with boldness the mystery of the gospel, [20] for which I am an ambassador in chains; that in proclaiming it I may speak boldly, as I ought to speak.

CHAPTER 23

The Full Armour of God

EPHESIANS 6:13-20

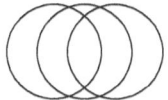

Not only does the Lord give us His strength for the struggle, He gives us the right equipment!

Because we wrestle with spiritual powers we need spiritual armour (see also 2 Corinthians 10:3-5). So take up and put on the full armour of God! Gird your loins with truth. Put on the breastplate of righteousness. Shoe your feet with the gospel of peace. Take up the shield of faith. Put on the helmet of salvation. Take up the sword of the Spirit. And pray at all times in the Spirit.

Where did Paul get this imagery? Partly from the Roman soldier guarding him in jail (6:20); Paul names off the pieces of armour in the order in which a Roman soldier would put them on.

Paul also gets the imagery from the Old Testament descriptions of God (or Messiah) the warrior. Of the coming Messiah, Isaiah says: "Righteousness will be the belt about His loins, and faithfulness the belt about His waist" (Isaiah 11:5). Of God, who comes to judge and then rescue His people, Isaiah says: "He put on righteousness like a breastplate, and a helmet of salvation on

His head" (Isaiah 59:17).

This is why Paul calls the armour "the armour of God." We are to take up and put on the very armour Isaiah says God wears! This is the armour the Gospel writers tells us Jesus wore in His wrestling with the ruler of darkness in the desert.[1]

"The full armour." *Panoplia*, is the word Paul uses. The complete suit of armour. Every piece is needed. One piece protects the head, but not the feet. Another protects the feet, but not the head.[2]

We need the whole *panoplia* in order to stand firm. And as you can see, there are both defensive and offensive pieces. Five defensive pieces: the belt of truth, the breastplate of righteousness, the boots of the gospel peace, the shield of faith, and the helmet of salvation. And two offensive weapons: the sword of the Spirit, and praying in the Spirit.

The Belt of Truth

The first defensive piece is the belt of truth. Stand firm "having girded your loins with truth" (Ephesians 6:14). Roman soldiers in Paul's day wore skirts, very much like Scottish kilts. Over these skirts they wore a cloak or tunic. When they were off duty, at home, they wore the tunic un-girded, hanging loosely on their bodies. But when they were about to enter battle, they would gather the tunic around their waist, holding it together with a belt. They would then "tuck up the tunic" under the belt, thus

---

[1] See Luke 4:1-13 and Matthew 4:1-11.
[2] David Watson, *I Believe in the Church* (Grand Rapids: William B. Eerdmans, 1978), 153.

leaving their legs free to move unimpeded.[3]

To "gird up the loins" was to prepare for action. This is why Paul begins his description of the armour here: we will not be able to stand in spiritual warfare until we have buckled around us the belt that holds everything together and frees our legs to move. That belt is truth. We gird up the loins with truth.

Now, in what sense is Paul speaking of "truth"? Does he mean that we prepare for action by grasping the truth of the gospel? Or does Paul mean that we prepare for action by living the truth? Or does Paul mean both? The belt that holds everything together and frees our legs is both the truth as doctrine and truthfulness as character?

I think it is both. We stand by being gripped by the truth that is *in* Jesus (Ephesians 4:21) and by the truth that *is* Jesus "I am the way, and the truth, and the life," He says (John 14:6). We stand by letting Jesus shape our vision of life. We stand by seeing life from His perspective: seeing as He sees. "You will know the truth," He says, "and the truth will make you free" (John 8:32).

We stand by having the truth grab us at every level of our being, especially in the loins, that place where we grapple with life. "Behold, You desire truth in the innermost being," prays King David in Psalm 51:6. We stand when we live truthful lives, sincerely, with integrity. Earlier in his letter, Paul exhorted us to be "speaking the truth in love" (Ephesians 4:15), and "laying aside falsehood, speak truth each one of you with his neighbour, for we are members of one another" (Ephesians 4:25). As John Stott warns us: "To be deceitful, to lapse into hypocrisy, to resort to

---

[3] Ray C. Stedman, *Spiritual Warfare: Winning the Daily Battle with Satan* (Portland, OR: Multnomah, 1975), 74.

intrigue and scheming, this is to play the devil's game, and we shall not be able to beat him at his own game."[4]

Jesus tells us that the enemy loves the darkness. "There is no truth in him," says Jesus, "for he is a liar and the father of lies" (John 8:44). He does all he can to keep us from "walking in the light" (1 John 1:7). We stand firm by committing ourselves to know the truth, speak the truth, and live the truth. All the more in our internet world with deception and out-right lies spreading unchecked.

The Breastplate of Righteousness

The second defensive piece of the armour is the breastplate of righteousness. The soldier's breastplate was made of metal, worn over both the front and back, and guarded the most vital parts of his body—his heart, lungs, and stomach. We stand protected when we, as individuals and as a community, put on righteousness.

Now, in what sense is Paul using this word, "righteousness"? Does he mean the righteousness that God gives us in Jesus Christ, that what protects us is the assurance that God has made us right with Himself even though we ourselves are not righteous? Or, does he mean that we protect our vital parts by actually being righteous, by living life in ways that square with God's good will? Or, does Paul mean both?

I think it is both. What guards us in the struggle and enables us to stand is both having been made right with God through

---

[4] John R.W. Stott, *God's New Society: The Message of Ephesians* [The Bible Speaks Today] (Downers Grove: InterVarsity Press, 1979), 277.

the work of Jesus Christ, and actually becoming righteous—new people with new attitudes and behaviours. We put on righteousness by saying to ourselves and to the enemy: "I have been made right with God, not on the basis of anything I have done with my life, but on the basis of what Jesus has done with His life!" There is great freedom in being able to say to the devil, the divider: "there is now no condemnation for those who are in Christ Jesus" (Romans 8:1). There is great freedom in being able to say to Satan, the accuser: "All have sinned and fall short of the glory of God, being justified [made right] as a gift by His grace…" (Romans 3:23-24).

The enemy loves to point out our sins to us, and to others! He loves to accuse our conscience. He loves to suggest that because of our sins, especially recent ones, God rejects us and no longer loves us. He then loves to get us to think that if only we work harder at being holy we can justify ourselves before God and earn the Father's favour. Put on the breastplate of righteousness: "I am accepted and acquitted by God on the basis of the finished work of Jesus Christ!"

And then, by grace, live righteousness. By grace, seek to live a life that pleases the Holy God of grace. Conscious, willful, habitual sin creates a crack in the breastplate: it gives the destroyer a foothold. The way to cover the crack is to confess the sin. For what is the promise? "If we confess our sins, He is faithful and righteous to forgive us our sins and to cleanse us from all unrighteousness" (1 John 1:9). We stand firm by seeking a righteous life: by confessing any known sin and receiving God's cleansing grace.

It is important to remember that Paul is speaking not just to individuals; he is speaking to the whole church. Unconfessed sin, though unknown to the whole church, creates a crack in the church's armour. David Watson of England was bold to say: "Personal sin in not a private matter.... my sin can make the whole church vulnerable to the devil's attacks."[5] The whole congregation of Israel suffered because of the sin of Achan (Joshua 7). The whole congregation of any community of God's people can suffer from unconfessed sin festering in an individual's life.

Sobering to contemplate, but true, especially when we gather for worship. Our unconfessed sin grieves the Holy Spirit, as Paul tells us (Ephesians 4:30); it quenches the Spirit (1 Thessalonians 5:19). This is particularly true of unconfessed bitterness, resentment, or judgmentalism. This is why we need time for confession in public worship: to bring the garbage to the cross and be cleansed again. Rats only go where there is trash; the powers can work only where there is junk. Confess anything you know to be displeasing to God. And claim again the cleansing power of grace. We stand by putting on—together—the breastplate of righteousness.

Gospel Shoes

The third piece of the armour are the gospel shoes. Stand firm "having shod your feet with the preparation of the gospel of peace" (Ephesians 6:15). Shoes were a critical piece of the Roman soldier's armour. They needed shoes so they could march quickly over the rough ground. The shoes Paul has in mind were made of leather, and were nail-studded on the bottom and tied to the

---

5 David Watson *I Believe in the Church* (Grand Rapids: William B. Eerdmans, 1978), 154-155.

ankles and shins with straps.[6] Such boots kept the soldier's feet from sliding, and gave them greater mobility. A number of historians have suggested that "the attention given to soldier's boots" accounted for Rome's ability to conquer.[7] Those of you who do a lot of hiking know how important good footwear is!

Paul calls the boots we need in order to stand firm against the powers "the preparation of the gospel of peace." Here again, the phrase can be taken in two different, but related, senses. The gospel of peace prepares us for the rough road.

And we carry the gospel of peace along the rough road.[8] That is, the gospel of peace gives us both firmness and readiness. So the New English Bible renders the text: "Let the shoes on your feet be the gospel of peace, to give you firm footing." God has made peace with us in Jesus—what Paul declares in the second chapter of his letter to the Ephesians. When we experience that peace we are standing on solid ground and cannot be moved. Hassled, buffeted, but not moved. The opposite is also true: when we are not at peace with God, we are vulnerable to the schemes of the enemy. Wrap your feet with the peace of God!

Once that peace gives us firm footing, we are ready to go forth and make peace, thus driving back the defeated powers of darkness. Satan is not threatened by soldiers with weapons of destruction. But he does tremble before soldiers who know and announce the peace won for the world on the cross. I wonder if Paul had in mind that text in Isaiah: "How lovely on the

---

[6] John R.W. Stott, *God's New Society: The Message of Ephesians* [The Bible Speaks Today] (Downers Grove: InterVarsity Press, 1979), 279.
[7] Maxie D. Dunnam, *The Communicator's Commentary: Galatians, Ephesians, Philippians, Colossians, Philemon* (Waco, TX: Word Books, 1982), 241.
[8] Ibid.

mountains are the feet of him who brings good news, who announces peace and brings good news of happiness, who announces salvation, and says to Zion, 'Your God reigns!'" (Isaiah 52:7). Stand firm, having your feet shod with the gospel of peace. Confess any lack of peace. And ask the Prince of Peace to give you His peace.

The Shield of Faith

The fourth defensive piece of armour is the shield of faith. "In addition to all, taking up the shield of faith with which you will be able to extinguish all the flaming arrows of the evil one" (Ephesians 6:16). The kind of shield Paul is referring to was made of two layers of wood, covered with linen and then leather.[9] It was long and oblong, covering a soldier's whole body, and was specially designed to defend against the most terrible weapon of that day—arrows soaked in pitch and lit on fire. The arrows might penetrate the leather and, to some degree, the wood, but the leather would extinguish the fire. Thus Paul's phrase, "the flaming arrows of the evil one," a very sobering metaphor, the reality of which we have all experienced.

Jesus' enemy is bent on destroying all that Jesus creates and redeems. He shoots fiery darts all the time. Most of us are unaware of their source. Darts of lustful, hateful, judgmental thoughts and imaginations. Darts of accusation and slander. Darts of doubt in the goodness and faithfulness of God. What

---

9 J. Armitage Robinson, *St. Paul's Epistle to the Ephesians* (London: Macmillan and Co., 1909), 215.

extinguishes these fiery missiles is the shield of faith. Faith, not just as mental assent to truth, but as trust. Mere affirmation of gospel truth is not enough. The apostle James tells us that even Satan's demons believe *that* God exists (James 2:19). It is trusting in the truth that extinguishes the missiles. It is trusting the God of truth that constitutes a shield.

We see Jesus using this piece of the armour in His hand-to-hand combat in the wilderness. He stood firm by trusting His Father in the face of evil. "Turn these stones into bread," says the tempter. "No, I will obey My Father even if it means going more days without bread." "Jump off the cliff," says the tempter, "and see if angels will catch you as promised." "No, I will trust My Father even if I see no evidence of the fulfillment of His promises." "Bow down and worship me, and I will give you the kingdoms of the world." "No, I will worship and serve My Father only, even if it means I go to the cross." No fiery missiles can penetrate such a shield.

Again, Paul is speaking to the whole church, not just to individuals. The shield of faith is something we help each other put on. We need help to trust and obey. We need each other to keep pointing to the Lord Jesus; to keep reminding one another that He is always available and fully adequate for every situation and need. I think the picture in Paul's mind is that of soldiers standing side by side, the shields forming an impenetrable wall.[10]

---

[10] David Watson, *I Believe in the Church* (Grand Rapids: William B. Eerdmans, 1978), 153-154.

The Helmet of Salvation

The fifth defensive piece of armour is the helmet of salvation (Ephesians 6:17). Paul is referring to the soldiers' helmets made of a tough metal, like iron or bronze, which were lined with felt or sponge, making the weight bearable. Says one commentator, "Nothing short of an axe or hammer could pierce a heavy helmet."[11]

What protects our heads is salvation, the salvation God accomplishes in Jesus. Salvation is in all three tenses: past, present, and future. In Jesus we have been saved, we are being saved, and we will be saved. We stand firm against the powers by declaring to ourselves and to the powers:

In Jesus I am saved! I am forgiven by God through grace. I am reconciled to God by grace. I am adopted by God by grace. I am indwelt by the Holy Spirit by grace.

In Jesus I am being saved! The Spirit is working in me, transforming me into the image of Jesus. The Spirit is cleansing me, making me a fit dwelling place for a Holy God. The Spirit is using all the circumstances of my life to mold me into a new creation.

In Jesus I will be saved! Along with the whole creation, I will be freed from sin and death. History has a goal—a new heaven and a new earth. Terrorism and greed, violence and oppression, disease and injustice will all come to an end. Jesus commands my destiny!

---

[11] Markus Barth in John R.W. Stott, *God's New Society: The Message of Ephesians* [The Bible Speaks Today] (Downers Grove: InterVarsity Press, 1979), 281.

We need to "live under the blood."[12] "Taking up the helmet of salvation" means covering our heads with the blood. The enemy hates to hear the blood-texts of Scripture quoted:

- "the blood of Jesus His Son cleanses us from all sin" (1 John 1:7).
- "you... have been brought near by the blood of Christ" (Ephesians 2:13).
- "having now been justified by His blood" (Romans 5:9).
- "In Him we have redemption through His blood" (Ephesians 1:7).
- Jesus suffered "that He might sanctify the people through His own blood" (Hebrews 13:12).
- "having made peace through the blood of His cross" (Colossians 1:20).
- "we have confidence to enter the holy place by the blood of Jesus" (Hebrews 10:19).
- Jesus "purchased with His own blood" the church (Acts 20:28).
- "how much more will the blood of Christ... cleanse your conscience" (Hebrews 9:14).

Put on the helmet of salvation: I am saved, I am being saved, and I will be saved.

I think you can already see that the full armour of God turns out to be Jesus. Be strong in the Lord Jesus. Take up and put on the Lord Jesus.

---

[12] George Mallone, *Arming for Spiritual Warfare: How Christians Can Prepare to Fight the Enemy* (Downers Grove: InterVarsity Press, 1991), 45.

The belt of truth—Jesus.

The breastplate of righteousness—Jesus.

The shoes of peace—Jesus.

The shield of faith—Jesus, faith in Jesus and the faith of Jesus.

The helmet of salvation—Jesus.

How appropriate for St. Patrick of Ireland to say in his now famous "Breastplate":

> I bind unto myself the Name, the strong name of the Trinity; by invocation of the same. The Three in One, and One in Three, of whom all nature is created, Eternal Father, Spirit, Word: Praise to the Lord of my salvation, Salvation is of Christ the Lord.

Christ be with me,
Christ within me,
Christ behind me,
Christ before me,
Christ beside me,
Christ to win me,
Christ to comfort and restore me.
Christ beneath me,
Christ above me,
Christ in quiet, Christ in danger,
Christ in hearts of all that love me,
Christ in mouth of friend and stranger.

The Sword of the Spirit

Now, let us turn our attention to the offensive pieces of the armour. There are only two. Given the true nature of the struggle, they are the two that work most effectively. And given what they are, they are the two we most need. "And take... the sword of the Spirit, which is the word of God. With all prayer and petition pray at all times in the Spirit" (Ephesians 6:17-18).

The first offensive piece of the armour is "the sword of the Spirit." Not the sword of the flesh, not the sword of any human making, but a spiritual sword, the work of the Spirit of God, the Holy Spirit. The sword imbued with the life and power of God the Spirit.

And what is this sword? "The word of God," says Paul. The word the Living God speaks. The word the Holy Spirit speaks. The word the Word-made-flesh speaks; the word Jesus of Nazareth speaks.

The apostle John brackets the last book of the Bible, the Revelation of Jesus Christ, with the images of the risen Jesus. In chapter one, Jesus is standing in the midst of His churches, and John says that "out of His mouth came a sharp two-edged sword" (Revelation 1:16). And in chapter nineteen, Jesus comes riding on a horse, and John says, "from His mouth comes a sharp sword" (Revelation 19:15). Jesus wins (that is the message of the last book of the Bible) and He wins by speaking.

Jesus' word not only informs, it performs. The Word makes things happen. Our words can hurt and heal, they can tear down and build. Our words make things happen. How much more the word of the One who made all things and holds all things together?

- "Let there be light"—and there was, lots of it!
- "Let there be animals"—and there were, lots of them!
- "Get up and walk"—and a lame man does.
- "Come out of him"—and the demons flee.
- "Hush, be still"—and the raging wind and waves die down.
- "Come out, Lazarus"—and a dead man walks out of the tomb.

The word of God not only informs, it performs. When God speaks, things happen. And when God's people speak God's speech, things happen:

> For as the rain and the snow come down from heaven,
> and do not return there without watering the earth,
> and making it bear and sprout,
> and furnishing seed to the sower and bread to the eater;
> So will My word be which goes forth from My mouth;
> it will not return to Me empty,
> without accomplishing what I desire,
> and without succeeding in the matter for which I sent it.
>
> Isaiah 55:10-11

The writer of the New Testament book we call Hebrews develops all this most fully. He makes the great claim: "For the word of God is living and active and sharper than any two-edged sword" (Hebrews 4:12). "Living." When the author quotes the Old Testament he always says, "the Holy Spirit says," never "the Holy Spirit said."

"Piercing as far as the division of soul and spirit, of both joints and marrow, and able to judge the thoughts and intentions of the heart" (Hebrews 4:12). God's word is able to penetrate any form of darkness, any form of bondage, any defenses raised against the knowledge of God. It is sufficient to break through any lies about who God is and what God is like—and any lies about who we are and what it means to be human. And God's word is able to bring us into the light and into the freedom won for us on the cross.

"Take up the Sword of the Spirit." Speak the word of God and watch what happens. Something redemptive always happens. Maybe not immediately, and maybe not visibly, but something always happens. The Word spoken in the world makes things happen in the world.

"Stand firm... take up the sword of the Spirit." Is this not what we see Jesus doing? Is He not in the Gospels regularly wielding this sword? In the wilderness, in that face-to-face confrontation with the evil one, three times He says, "It is written":

- Round one: Jesus answered: "It is written, 'Man shall not live on bread alone, but on every word that proceeds out of the mouth of God'" (Matthew 4:4).
- Round two: The tempter tries to use the sword against Jesus! "If You are the Son of God throw Yourself down [off the pinnacle of the temple], for it is written: 'He will command His angels concerning you,' and, 'On their hands they will bear You up, so that You will not strike Your foot against a stone'" (Matthew 4:6). But the tempter took the word out of context, so Jesus says, "On the other hand, it is written, 'You shall not put the Lord your God to the test'" (Matthew 4:7).

- Round three: Jesus responds: "Go, Satan! For it is written, 'You shall worship the Lord your God, and serve Him only'" (Matthew 4:10).

We see Jesus use the sword when the religious establishment begins to hassle Him. Many times He said to the stubborn and hostile Pharisees, "it is written," or, "Have you not heard?" then quoted Scripture. We see Jesus use the sword on the cross, in the great struggle with evil. Six of the seven last words are either a direct quotation or a reflection on the Old Testament.[13]

Our struggle is not against flesh and blood, but against spiritual forces and powers. So take up the sword of the Holy Spirit. Speak the word of God, and something happens to the spiritual forces and powers. To the powers? Something happens to the powers?

I hang onto the story Luke tells in the tenth chapter of his gospel. Jesus sends out seventy of His disciples on a short-term mission. He tells them to simply announce the gospel: "The kingdom of God has come near to you" (Luke 10:9). The seventy obey. In city after city they speak the word, wielding the sword of the Spirit. The seventy return with news of all kinds of kingdom-things happening: People are healed, people are reconciled, people are freed from all kinds of bondage. And Jesus says to them: "I was watching Satan fall from heaven like lightning" (Luke 10:18).

The disciples had been speaking the word to humans, and visible humans were responding. But so were the invisible rulers

---

[13] Michael Green, *I Believe in Satan's Downfall* (Grand Rapids: William B. Eerdmans, 1981), 230-231.

and authorities. Paul says in the middle of his letter: "through the church" the wisdom of God is being "made known" to "the rulers and the authorities in the heavenly places" (Ephesians 3:10).

Whenever believers announce the good news to other human beings, we are announcing the news to the principalities and powers, and things happen in the city. This happens wherever and whenever you meet for Bible study in small groups, in apartments, in houses, in offices, and in coffee shops. Wherever disciples of Jesus are opening the Book and speaking its Message, we are hearing—and so are the invisible powers at work in the parts of the city where we are meeting.

This is why the powers work so cleverly and constantly to keep us out of the Book. They work to fuel our busyness so that we do not have time to open the Book. The Bible on the shelf is no threat to the rulers and authorities. But open it, and speak its living and active word, and the rulers and authorities begin to squirm.

Pray at All Times in the Spirit

The second offensive piece of the armour is to "pray at all times in the Spirit." "In the Spirit" reminds us that prayer is not just our work, for the Spirit is at work in our praying. The Spirit moves us to pray, helps us to pray, teaches us as we pray, and empowers us to pray.

How do we address the unseen powers and principalities? We pray. "With all prayer and petition," says Paul, "pray at all times in the Spirit, and with this in view, be on the alert with all perseverance and petition for all the saints" (Ephesians 6:18). Do you see the word "all"? All the time, with all forms, for all the saints, with all perseverance.

And as we do, something always happens. Maybe not immediately, and maybe not in ways that are visible, but something always happens when we pray in the Spirit. This is powerfully portrayed in the last book of the Bible, in the Revelation of Jesus Christ. In the eighth chapter, John watches as the Lamb, Jesus Christ, breaks the last of the seven seals of the scroll of history:

> When the Lamb broke the seventh seal, there was silence in heaven for about half an hour. And I saw the seven angels who stand before God, and seven trumpets were given to them. Another angel came and stood at the altar, holding a golden censer; and much incense was given to him, so that he might *add it to the prayers of all the saints* on the golden altar which was before the throne.
>
> Revelation 8:1-3 (emphasis added)

What is going on? John is discovering that one of the ways God moves history forward is through prayer. New Testament scholar George Beasley-Murray:

> No one was more aware than John of the limitations to what individual men and women can do to change the course of history and to bring in the kingdom of heaven, particularly in [the] face of the cosmic forces against them and the transcendent character of the kingdom itself... But we can pray to him who has almighty power, and it would seem that God has willed that the prayers of his people should be part of the process by which the kingdom comes. The interaction between the sovereignty of

God and the prayers of the saints is part of the ultimate mystery of existence. Faith is called on to take both seriously.[14]

Take up the Sword of the Spirit, and pray at all times in the Spirit... and the powers and principalities begin to change. An alternative reading of reality—the true reading. Reality as it is because of Jesus Christ.

When we pray, we are saying that the way things are in the world, in the city, is not the way things are supposed to be, and not the way they one day will be. When we pray we go over the heads of the powers, and bring the inner spirituality of the powers before the One who *is* Head over all things. Jacques Ellul, when Professor of Law and Government at the University of Bordeaux, could write:

> The Christian who prays acts more effectively and more decisively on society than the person who is politically involved, with all the sincerity of his faith put into the involvement. It is not a matter of seeing them in opposition to one another, but of inverting our instinctive, cultural hierarchy of values.[15]

This is why the powers work so cleverly and constantly to keep us off our knees, to keep us from praying. They fuel our busyness so that we do not have time to pray. We jump into the day without praying. Oh, we might throw up a brief, "Help me

---

14 G.R. Beasley-Murray, *The Book of Revelation* [New Century Bible Commentary] (Grand Rapids: Wm. B. Eerdmans, 1974), 151.
15 Jacques Ellul, *Prayer and the Modern Man,* trans. C. Edward Hopkin (New York: Seabury Press, 1970), 172-173.

Jesus," which is better than nothing. But otherwise we move into all the activities in our own power leaning on our own wisdom.

Using the Armour

An alternative reading of reality: Our struggle is not with flesh and blood, not just with human beings, human institutions, and human movements. Our struggle is with the supra-man forces and powers at work in the universe. Stand firm.

Take up and put on the full armour of God. Five defensive pieces of the full armour: the belt of truth, the breastplate of righteousness, the shoes of peace, the shield of faith, and the helmet of salvation. And two offensive pieces of the full armour: the sword of the Spirit, speaking the word of God in the world, and praying in the Spirit, interceding for the world before the throne of King Jesus.

So... let us do it. I am now going to make a series of declarations. I will speak the word relative to some of the powers at work in our world. I invite you to read each of these declarations out loud, and if you agree with it, say "Yes, Lord." We will then conclude by praying the Lord's Prayer.

We declare that the powers—human and demonic, visible and invisible—behind illegal and destructive drugs are accountable to Jesus Christ. We declare that the powers are no match for Jesus Christ, that He is more powerful, and that He can set the captives free.

So Lord, we bring the powers before You, and we ask You to break the grip drugs have on people You love. Lord, we ask You to expose those who are making destructive drugs available; break the back of their empires. Lord, we ask You to free men and women, boys and girls, from this evil, and that You free drug-dealers from the deeper evil of no longer caring what happens to other people; they are also prisoners of evil. Set them free!

We declare that the powers—human and demonic, visible and invisible—at work in sex-trafficking, are accountable to Jesus Christ. We declare that the powers are no match for Jesus Christ, that He is more powerful, and can set the captives free.

So Lord, we bring those powers before You, and ask You to break their grip on people. We ask You to expose those who are doing this evil, and break the back of their empires. We ask You to come to the rescue of girls and women being used as mere objects by the forces of lust and power. And we ask You to come to the rescue of men who are buying into this evil; hell has an even greater grip on them than on the girls and women. Set them free Lord!

Now I invite you to take a few moments to declare and pray relative to issues close to your hearts. Declare that Jesus is seated far above all rule and authority and dominion and bring the powers to His feet.

Let us now together pray the way Jesus taught us to pray.

Our Father, Who art in heaven
Hallowed be Your name.
Your kingdom come,
Your will be done,
On earth as it is in heaven.
Give us this day our daily bread.

EPHESIANS

And forgive us our sins,
as we forgive those who sin against us.
And lead us not into temptation,
but deliver us from the evil-one.
For Yours is the kingdom,
and the power, and the glory. Forever.
Amen.

Afterword

"May I ask you a question?'

"Sure."

"What would you say to young, busy disciples of Jesus living in China who want to live in such a way that China is transformed?"

"I say... soak in Paul's letter to the Ephesians."

As we come to the end of our study of Paul's letter to the Ephesians, I think you can see why I answered her question that way. And as we come to the end of our study, a big part of me wants to now go back to the beginning and work it all through again. For it is so rich!

The fact is, even if we never again give direct attention to the text of Ephesians, we will never be far from the message of the text of Ephesians. For, as I trust you have come to appreciate, the letter to the Ephesians is all about reality as it is centered in and shaped by Jesus Christ. Although we may not ever fully understand this reality, we are living in it. As I trust you are coming to believe, the alternative reading of reality given to us in Ephesians is a true and accurate reading. I trust you are coming to the deep conviction that what Paul develops in his letter from a jail cell is the really real.

May you live more and more in "the really real." In the wonder and walk of being alive "in Christ."

And may you get to see how your part of the world begins to change.

Acknowledgements

As the great apostle brings his brilliant epistle to conclusion, two things he says stand out to me.

The first is his request that the disciples in Ephesus (and others in other cities of the Roman Empire in which the letter ended up being read) pray for him. As we saw in the letter, he shares what he has been praying for them – power prayers shaped by his preaching of the gospel (1:15-23 and 3:14-21). At the end of the letter he asks that they, for whom he prays, would pray for him. "And pray on my behalf, that utterance may be given to me in the opening of my mouth, to make known with boldness the mystery of the gospel" (6:19). And pray for him they did, the consequences of their act beyond human measurement in the world!

So, following Paul's lead, I want to acknowledge the fact that many disciples of Jesus have prayed for me as I have sought to understand, teach, preach, and write on Paul's letter. I have been so generously served by so many faithful intercessors. Too many to name! Though I would very much like to try to name them, I am afraid I would leave out too many names. But one person I do need to name is Betty Hightower. Since we first met in 1989 in Sacramento, California, not a week has gone by without her praying boldly for me. She knows the wonder of being "in Christ," and has prayed that I would never lose the wonder and would faithfully walk into it and preach from it. Thank you Betty!

The second thing Paul says as he concludes is that he has not written the letter all by himself. He has had help. The Lord has provided an assistant. His name is Tychicus, whom Paul calls "the beloved brother and faithful minister" (6:21). We do not know much about the man. Nor do we know just how he served Paul. But Paul knows. (Making sure Paul has food while in jail? Making sure Paul has enough ink and parchment? Taking notes as Paul dictates? Pushing Paul to clarify points he is making, suggesting other ways to make things clearer?) And Paul takes time to acknowledge his service.

So, following Paul's lead, I want to acknowledge the Tychicus-assistants the Lord has provided to help me with this book. Doug Liao served as my Executive Assistant during the time I preached Ephesians for First Baptist Church, Vancouver: typing the manuscripts from my hand-written notes, running down sources of quotes, suggesting ways to re-phrase what I said orally in written form. Chris Price of The Way Church read over the draft of the whole book at least twice, making very insightful and helpful comments. So did Craig Pagens of Tenth Church. Brandon Peterson of The Way Church and Canadian Church Leaders Network kept encouraging me to keep going during the months of Covid-19. And for Arielle Ratzlaff on her wonderful design for the book. And Oliver Hung, who as I was moving into

ACKNOWLEDGEMENTS

"retirement" mode out of full-time church service, stepped up, volunteering to serve me in anyway I needed, in particular creating a website called Preacher's Workshop, now darrelljohnson.ca, and reading over the draft many times, in particular helping me be more precise about the more challenging theological issues in the letter. It is to him and his wife Jolene Sun, who helped me obtain new glasses so I could read the new glasses shaped by Ephesians more clearly, that I dedicate "The Wonder and Walk of Being Alive 'In Christ'."

One more acknowledgement. Sharon, the faithful disciple to whom I have been married for over fifty years. No one has prayed more faithfully for me than she. And no one has done more to empower me to be who and what Jesus calls me to be than she.

Blessed be the God and Father of our Lord Jesus Christ, Who has blessed us beyond what we deserve or could imagine ever being given!

For Further Reading

The footnotes throughout the book will show you some of the many resources that I have used in my study of this wonderful letter of Paul's. For further reading, I especially commend:

Gombis, Timothy G. *The Drama of Ephesians: Participating in the Triumph of God*. Downers Grove: IVP Academic, 2010.

Hoehner, Harold W. *Ephesians: An Exegetical Commentary*. Grand Rapids: Baker Academic, 2002.

Lincoln, Andrew T. *Ephesians* [Word Biblical Commentary]. Dallas: Word Books, 1990.

Stott, John R.W. *God's New Society: The Message of Ephesians* [The Bible Speaks Today]. Downers Grove: InterVarsity Press, 1979.

Thielman, Frank. *Ephesians* [Baker Exegetical Commentary on the New Testament]. Grand Rapids: Baker Academic, 2010.

www.ingramcontent.com/pod-product-compliance
Lightning Source LLC
Chambersburg PA
CBHW021437070526
44577CB00002B/197